*There is an art of reading
as well as an art of thinking
and an art of writing*
ISAAC D'ISRAELI.

The Art of English

General Editor A. Dora Gough, B.A. (Hons.)

A Certificate Course for Secondary Schools

Keith Newson, M.A.

5

Illustrated by Tony Dyson
and Kenneth Hutchinson

SCHOFIELD AND SIMS LIMITED
HUDDERSFIELD

0 7217 0007 1

First printed 1969
Reprinted 1970
Reprinted 1971
Reprinted 1972
Reprinted 1973
Reprinted 1974
Reprinted 1975
Reprinted 1976
Revised and Reprinted 1977
Reprinted 1979
Reprinted 1981

There are ten books in **The Art of English** series:

Certificate Course		*General Course*	
C1	0 7217 0003 9	G1	0 7217 0008 X
C2	0 7217 0004 7	G2	0 7217 0009 8
C3	0 7217 0005 5	G3	0 7217 0010 1
C4	0 7217 0006 3	G4	0 7217 0011 X
C5	0 7217 0007 1	G5	0 7217 0012 8

Printed in England by
Chorley & Pickersgill Ltd, Leeds

Bound in Scotland

Contents

The passage in each chapter is followed by questions for *Appreciation and Discussion*. Where there is a poem, it is followed by a section *Discussing the Poem*. The *Techniques* exercises and composition subjects in *Topics for Written Work* are listed below. Each chapter also contains further sections of *Oral Work*, *Activities and Research*, and *Further Reading*.

Exercises marked * here, and in the text, can be omitted by pupils who are not studying clause analysis.

iv

v

ACKNOWLEDGMENTS

The author and publishers wish to thank the following for permission to include the copyright material listed below:

Chatto & Windus Ltd., for extracts from *A High Wind in Jamaica* by Richard Hughes, and *The Uses of Literacy* by Richard Hoggart.

Faber & Faber Ltd., for the poem *Wind* from *The Hawk in the Rain* by Ted Hughes, and for an extract from *Lord of the Flies* by William Golding.

New Scientist for the article *An Aerial Watch on Hurricanes.*

Jonathan Cape Ltd. and The Executors of the James Joyce Estate, for an extract from *A Painful Case* from *Dubliners* by James Joyce.

Jonathan Cape Ltd., for an extract from *Roots* by Arnold Wesker.

Penguin Books Ltd., for extracts from *Sense and Nonsense in Psychology* by H. J. Eysenck, *The Contemporary Cinema* by Penelope Houston, and *Coming of Age in Samoa* by Margaret Mead.

Mrs. Myfanwy Thomas for the poem *May the Twenty-third* by Edward Thomas from *Collected Poems.*

Addison-Wesley Publishing Co. Inc., for an extract from *The Nature of Prejudice* by Gordon W. Allport (1954).

Routledge & Kegan Paul Ltd., for an extract from the poem *This Landscape, These People* from *The Loss of India* by Zulfikar Ghose.

J. Garnet Miller Ltd., for an extract from *Incident* by David Campton.

Michael Joseph Ltd., for an extract from *The Horse's Mouth* by Joyce Cary.

The Listener, for extracts from articles by Edmund Leach, entitled *Ourselves and Others (3rd Reith Lecture),* and *Men and Learning (5th Reith Lecture),* © Edmund Leach 1967, from *A Runaway World?* published by BBC Publications and Oxford University Press, and Robin Clarke, entitled *Chemical and Biological Warfare.*

Mad magazine, for *The Ides of Mad,* copyright © 1968 by E. C. Publications Inc.

Mrs. G. M. Mathews, for the poem *Bad Taste* by Raymond Richardson.

The Daily Mirror, for an extract from an article by Audrey Whiting, reproduced by permission.

The Public Trustee and The Society of Authors for extracts from *The Preface to St. Joan* and *Pygmalion* by George Bernard Shaw.

William Heinemann Ltd., for extracts from *The Destructors* from *Twenty-one Stories* by Graham Greene, and *Children of the Ashes* by Robert Jungk, translated by Constantine FitzGibbon.

Vernon Scannell for his poem *Incendiary* from *A Sense of Danger.*

Hamish Hamilton Ltd., for an extract from *Silent Spring* by Rachel Carson, reproduced by permission of Marie Rodell, the Literary Trustee.

Michael Baldwin and Secker & Warburg Ltd., for the poem *Hunting with a Stick* by Michael Baldwin.

H.M. Stationery Office, for an extract from the *Report of the Committee on Broadcasting 1960 Cmnd. 1753 (The Pilkington Report).*

BBC Publications Ltd., for an extract from *The Conscience of the Programme Director,* an address made by Sir Hugh Greene, Director-General of the BBC, to the International Catholic Association for Radio and Television in Rome, February 1965.

John Murray Ltd., for an extract from *A Pattern of Islands* by Sir Arthur Grimble.

The Guardian, for extracts from articles by Ronald Lloyd entitled *Festival at Epidaurus,* and Gillian Tindall entitled *Gillian Tindall on an Unpopular Subject.*

Mrs. George Bambridge and Macmillan & Co. Ltd., for extracts from *On the Great Wall* from *Puck of Pook's Hill* by Rudyard Kipling.

Robert Graves and Cassell & Co. Ltd., for extracts from *Goodbye to all That* by Robert Graves.

Harmony Music Ltd., for the poem *Where have all the Flowers gone?* by Pete Seeger.

Peter Appleton for his poem *The Responsibility* from *Rhyme and Reason.*

Methuen & Co. Ltd., for an extract from *Prater Violet* by Christopher Isherwood.

Thames & Hudson Ltd., for an extract from *Roaring Boys* by Edward Blishen.

Laurence Pollinger Ltd., William Heinemann Ltd., and the Estate of the late Mrs. Frieda Lawrence for the poem *Last Lesson of the Afternoon* from *The Complete Poems of D. H. Lawrence.*

Macmillan & Co. Ltd., The Macmillan Co. of Canada Ltd., and the Trustees of the Hardy Estate, for an extract from *Far from the Madding Crowd* by Thomas Hardy.

Leo Aylen for his poem *If You'll give me a Kiss and be My Girl.*

Houghton Mifflin Co., for the poem *A Decade* from *The Complete Poetical Works of Amy Lowell.*

And the following for permission to use copyright photographs:

Her Majesty's Stationery Office (Crown copyright) p. 17. Keystone Press Agency Ltd, pp. 40, 192, 258. Paul Popper Ltd, p. 162. The Imperial War Museum pp. 170, 178. Still photograph from film "Lord of the Flies" by courtesy of British Lion Films Ltd, p. 209.

The cartoons on p. 83 are reproduced by kind permission of Saul Steinberg and *The Daily Mirror.*

AUTHOR'S NOTE

THE ART OF ENGLISH is a five-year English series for secondary schools, comprising two complete but closely integrated courses. *The Certificate Course* is suitable for those pupils in grammar, comprehensive and modern schools who aim at an Ordinary Level Certificate in English Language. *The General Course* is designed for the less academic pupils in comprehensive and modern schools. The two courses are planned on a common basis, with obvious similarities in topics and layout. Both courses cover work for the Certificate of Secondary Education, though the approaches naturally differ.

Although *The Certificate Course* meets the demands of the most rigorous Ordinary Level Certificate syllabuses, it was devised in the belief that examination success should be the natural outcome of a wide and stimulating range of experience; it is therefore more than an English language textbook. The choice of poems and extracts is intended to develop pupils' reading, their critical awareness of literature and their interest in drama and film. The topics chosen lead to much discussion and further activities, and are particularly chosen as a stimulus to composition of all kinds.

Together, *The Certificate* and *General Courses* form the basis for a complete English syllabus for secondary schools.

Book Five of *The Certificate Course* follows the pattern of *Book Four*, and includes further material for discussion of contemporary social and political problems: the challenges to our attitudes and values that are repeatedly reflected in literature. The self-contained extracts from good, suitable books (many of them now set texts at Ordinary Level), and the poems, should arouse interest and discussion; they offer ample comprehension and appreciation work, and are also the basis for work on techniques, which includes making notes and summaries and practice in clear thinking and appropriate English usage. Each chapter topic leads on to at least two different kinds of composition, and oral work and further activities, which include film-work as well as drama, debate and various research projects. Each chapter ends with some recommended reading: books either by the authors of the extracts or pursuing that chapter's interests.

The more formal analytical grammar work, still demanded by some Ordinary Level syllabuses, is developed in sections marked with an asterisk, both in the chapters and in the Supplementary Exercises. These also include other revision work.

*   *   *

Finally, I should like to thank the many colleagues and pupils at Wandsworth School who have contributed ideas and material to these five books, and my wife and family for their help and tolerance while I have been absorbed in compiling them.

KEITH NEWSON

CHAPTER ONE

Wind and Weather

The Thorntons were an English family, living in what was once an overseer's house on a disused sugar plantation in nineteenth-century Jamaica. Emily experienced her first minor earthquake the day after her tenth birthday. The next day brought a hurricane.

The earthquake had done little to clear the air. It was as hot as ever. In the animal world there seemed some strange commotion, as if they had wind of something. The usual lizards and mosquitoes were still absent: but in their place the earth's most horrid progeny, creatures of darkness, sought the open: land-crabs wandered about aimlessly, angrily twiddling their claws: and the ground seemed almost alive with red ants and cockroaches. Up on the roof the pigeons were gathered, talking to each other fearfully. . . .

It was the custom that, whenever Mr. Thornton had been to St. Anne's, John and Emily should run out to meet him, and ride back with him, one perched on each of his stirrups.

That Sunday evening they ran out as soon as they saw him coming, in spite of the thunderstorm that by now was clattering over their very heads—and not only over their heads either, for in the Tropics a thunderstorm is not a remote affair up in the sky, as it is in England, but is all round you: lightning plays ducks and drakes across the water, bounds from tree to tree, bounces about the ground, while the thunder seems to proceed from violent explosions in your own very core.

"Go back! Go back, you damned little fools!" he yelled furiously: "Get into the house!"

They stopped, aghast: and began to realize that after all it was a storm of more than ordinary violence. They discovered that they were drenched to the skin—must have been the moment they left the house. The lightning kept up a continuous blaze: it was playing about their father's very stirrup-irons; and all of a sudden they realized that he was afraid. They fled to the house, shocked to the heart: and he was in the house almost as soon as they were. Mrs. Thornton rushed out:

"My dear, I'm so glad . . ."

"I've never seen such a storm! Why on earth did you let the children come out?"

"I never dreamt they would be so silly! And all the time I was thinking—but thank Heaven you're back!"

"I think the worst is over now."

Perhaps it was; but all through supper the lightning shone almost without flickering. And John and Emily could hardly eat: the memory of that momentary look on their father's face haunted them. . . .

(During supper, Emily and John were alarmed to see wild cats chasing their own pet tomcat, Tabby, to his death in the jungle.)

After supper Mrs. Thornton sat heroically in a chair, her brood all grouped round her, saying the Psalms, and the poems of Sir Walter Scott, over by heart: while Emily tried to keep her mind off Tabby by going over in her head all the details of her Earthquake. At times the din, the rocketing of the thunder and torrential shriek of the wind, became so loud as almost to impinge on her inner world: she wished this wretched thunderstorm would hurry up and get over. First she held an actual performance of the earthquake, went over it direct, as if it was again happening. Then she put it into Oratio Recta, told it as a story, beginning with that magic phrase, "Once I was in an Earthquake". But before long the dramatic element reappeared —this time, the awed comments of her imaginary English audience. When that was done, she put it into the Historical—a Voice, declaring that a girl called Emily was once in an Earthquake. And so on, right through the whole thing a third time.

The horrid fate of poor Tabby appeared suddenly before her eyes, caught her unawares: and she was all but sick again. Even her earthquake had failed her. Caught by the incubus, her mind struggled frantically to clutch at even the outside world, as an only remaining straw. She tried to fix her interest on every least detail of the scene around her—to count the slats in the shutters, any least detail that was *outward*. So it was that for the first time she really began to notice the weather.

The wind by now was more than redoubled. The shutters were bulging as if tired elephants were leaning against them, and Father was trying to tie the fastening with his handkerchief. But to push against this wind was like pushing against rock. The handkerchief, shutters, everything burst: the rain poured in like the sea into a sinking ship, the wind occupied the room, snatching pictures from the wall, sweeping the table bare. Through the gaping frames the lightning-lit scene without was visible. The creepers, which before had looked like cobwebs, now streamed up into the sky like new-combed hair. Bushes were lying flat, laid back on the ground as close as a rabbit lays back his ears. Branches were leaping about loose in the sky. The Negro huts were clean gone, and the Negroes crawling on their stomachs across the compound to gain the shelter of the house. The bouncing rain seemed to cover the ground with a white smoke, a sort of sea in which the Negroes wallowed like porpoises. One boy began to roll away: his mother, forgetting caution, rose to her feet: and immediately the fat old beldam was blown clean away, bowling along across fields and hedgerows like someone in a funny fairy-story, till she fetched up against a wall and was pinned there, unable to move. But the others managed to reach the house, and soon could be heard in the cellar underneath.

Moreover the very floor began to ripple, as a loose carpet will ripple on a gusty day: in opening the cellar door the Negroes had let the wind in, and now for some time they could not shut it again. The wind, to push against, was more like a solid block than a current of air.

Mr. Thornton went round the house—to see what could be done, he said. He soon realized that the next thing to go would be the roof. So he returned to the group in the dining-room. Mrs. Thornton was half-way through *The Lady of the Lake*, the smaller children listening with rapt attention. Exasperated, he told them that they would probably not be alive in half an hour. No one seemed particularly interested in his news: Mrs. Thornton continued her recitation with faultless memory.

After another couple of cantos the threatened roof went. Fortunately, the wind taking it from inside, most of it was blown clear of the house: but one of the coupled beams collapsed skew-eyed, and was hung up on what was left of the dining-room door—within an ace of hitting John. Emily, to her intense resentment, suddenly felt cold. All at once, she found she had had enough of the storm: it had become intolerable, instead of a welcome distraction.

Mr. Thornton began to look for something to break through the floor. If only he could make a hole in it, he might get his wife and children down into the cellar. Fortunately he did not have to look far: one arm of the fallen couple had already done

11

the work for him. Laura, Rachel, Emily, Edward and John, Mrs. Thornton, and finally Mr. Thornton himself, were passed down into the darkness already thronged with Negroes and goats.

With great good sense, Mr. Thornton brought with him from the room above a couple of decanters of madeira, and everyone had a swig, from Laura to the oldest Negro. All the children made the most of this unholy chance, but somehow to Emily the bottle got passed twice, and each time she took a good pull. It was enough, at their age; and while what was left of the house was blown away over their heads, through the lull and the ensuing aerial return match, John, Emily, Edward, Rachel, and Laura, blind drunk, slept in a heap on the cellar floor: a sleep over which the appalling fate of Tabby, torn to pieces by those fiends almost under their very eyes, dominated with the easy empire of nightmare.

(from *A High Wind in Jamaica* by Richard Hughes)

Appreciation and Discussion

1. What was unusual about the behaviour of the animals before the storm?
2. (a) Why was Mr. Thornton so furious with John and Emily?
   (b) What emotion was he really feeling, and what effect did this have on the children?
3. What is the effect of the word "heroically" when applied to Mrs. Thornton's recitation?

4. What words and phrases suggest that Tabby's death disturbed Emily more than the storm itself?
5. What brought Emily's thoughts back to the storm?
6. "The Lady of the Lake" is a poem divided into cantos: who wrote it? Why did Mrs. Thornton keep on reciting it? Did she have the book?
7. In what ways had the storm been a welcome distraction to Emily until the roof went?
8. Why was it "good sense" to take down the decanters of madeira into the cellar?
9. Remembering that this was a hurricane, can you explain the reference to the "lull and the ensuing aerial return match"?
10. (a) How does this passage illustrate the difference between a tropical storm and an English thunderstorm?
    (b) In what ways is this storm made to appear terrible even by tropical standards?
11. Why does Emily refer to the earthquake as "her Earthquake"? What difference would there be in her three ways of recalling it? ("Oratio Recta" is "direct speech".)
12. What is an "incubus", and what does it refer to in the context of Emily's thoughts?
13. Explain the remark: "Even her Earthquake had failed her".
14. At what points during this incident were the children in danger, and how were they threatened?
15. Discuss and explain the meaning of the following words and phrases:
    the earth's most horrid progeny; lightning plays ducks and drakes; the dramatic element reappeared; one of the coupled beams collapsed skew-eyed; dominated with the easy empire of nightmare.
16. How effective were Mr. Thornton's efforts to save his family? Why was he "exasperated" when he told them they would soon be dead?
17. Examine and discuss the paragraphs beginning: "The wind by now was more than redoubled", and "Moreover the floor began to ripple". Refer particularly to the similes and metaphors used to make us vividly aware of the storm.
18. Illustrate the differences between the children's and the adults' attitudes to the storm. Do you find the description of Emily's reactions and thoughts credible?

Wind

This house has been far out at sea all night,
The woods crashing through darkness, the booming hills,
Wind stampeding the fields under the windows
Floundering black astride and blinding wet

Till day rose. Then, under an orange sky,
The hills had new places, and wind wielded
Blade-light, luminous black and emerald
Flexing like the lens of a mad eye.

At noon I scaled along the house-side as far as
The coal-house door. I dared once to look up:
Through the brunt wind that dented the balls of my eyes
The tent of the hills drummed and strained its guy-rope,

The fields quivering, the skyline a grimace,
At any second to bang and vanish with a flap:
The wind flung a magpie away, and a black
Back gull bent like an iron bar slowly. The house

Rang like some fine green goblet in the note
That any second would shatter it. Now deep
In chairs, in front of the great fire, we grip
Our hearts and cannot entertain book, thought,

Or each other. We watch the fire blazing,
And feel the roots of the house move, but sit on,
Seeing the window tremble to come in,
Hearing the stones cry out under the horizons.

TED HUGHES

Discussing the Poem

1. This poem describes a gale experienced in a house on a hill-top in the Pennines. What details in the poem seem to suggest the stony hill landscape? How do the inhabitants of the house feel about the wind?
2. Discuss the "imagery" of this poem: the comparisons of the wind to a rider on the backs of fields that are like stampeding horses, or of the hills to a vast marquee about to be blown away, and so on.

3. The poet's choice of words is also original; discuss the effect of describing hills as "booming", or using nouns like "brunt" as adjectives, or phrases such as "seeing the window tremble to come in", etc.
4. Many of the line-endings interrupt the normal flow of sentences. Does this seem appropriate in a poem about a wind whose gusts shake up the normal world? Consider the effect of breaking up: "and a blackback gull bent like an iron bar slowly", as an example of this.

Techniques

Exercise 1. Revise the eight "précis rules" given in Book Four: Redundancy and Repetition, Recasting Sentences, Illustrations, Figurative Language, Generalising, Planning, Your Own Words, and Reported Speech.

Usually, summaries are about one-third of the length of the original passage. If one follows the original *paragraphing*, this very often leaves the summary with paragraphs only one or two sentences long, and the result is a very disjointed piece of English, rather like short notes. Since passages chosen for précis are usually on one central theme, or one is asked to summarise one particular kind of information or argument, it is reasonable to reduce the summary to *one* paragraph.

The following passage contains about 280 words but can be reduced to less than one-third its length, making one paragraph of not more than 90 of your own words. Apply any of Précis Rules 1 to 8. In summarising a factual passage like this, it will be necessary to keep some of the technical vocabulary, such as "dropsonde".

AERIAL WATCH ON HURRICANES

Keeping watch on hurricanes, as they build up and move over the ocean, is still the responsibility of weather aircraft but the technique has changed with the years and there is rarely any need today for these modified bombers to fly into the rotating storm. Observation is now divided between the weather satellites, which reveal the hurricanes, and a sort of aerial sonobuoy which records and transmits their vital statistics.

When one of these tropical disturbances is located, the weather aircraft keep it in sight and note its course. They also fly over the top of it, often at a height of about 30,000 ft, and drop into it a "dropsonde". This instrument descends on its parachute at a regular speed, noting pressure, humidity, temperature and wind speed together with its time scale and transmits these data back to the aeroplane.

From the mothership the details are sent to the tracking centre of the US Weather Bureau where the necessary deductions are made as to the probable course and the degree of violence. On occasions penetrations by aircraft are still desirable but most often the essential facts can now be obtained "from the wings" with the help of modern apparatus.

In 1966, 11 tropical storms were spotted, of which 7 reached hurricane velocity. Two of the hurricanes howled through the Caribbean islands and Central America, and struck the US mainland, claiming 54 lives and causing an estimated $15,500,000 damage there.

With the aid of a network of 16 ground-based radar stations along the Atlantic and Gulf coasts, better statistical techniques for forecasting hurricane movements, plus these aerial observations, forecasters now expect to predict where a hurricane will hit to within 75 miles, 24 hours ahead. (From *New Scientist*)

Précis Rule 9. PARAGRAPHING:

A précis should never contain more paragraphs than the original passage. Two or more paragraphs in the original should become one in the summary, unless there is a very clear break in the sense. Do not use many short paragraphs.

Exercise 2. As punctuation revision, rewrite six paragraphs from the extract from *A High Wind in Jamaica*. The capital letters have been carefully printed here, but all other punctuation and the setting out in paragraphs has to be worked out. Turn back to the punctuation on pages 9–10 only when you have completed your own version. If you find your version different from that of Richard Hughes, discuss whether your changes are equally correct.

Go back Go back you damned little fools he yelled furiously Get into the house They stopped aghast and began to realise that after all it was a storm of more than ordinary violence They discovered that they were drenched to the skin must have been the moment they left the house The lightning kept up a continuous blaze it was playing about their fathers very stirrup-irons and all of a sudden they realised that he was afraid They fled to the house shocked to the heart and he was in the house almost as soon as they were Mrs Thornton rushed out My dear Im so glad . . . Ive never seen such a storm Why on earth did you let the children come out I never dreamt they would be so silly And all the time I was thinking but thank Heaven youre back

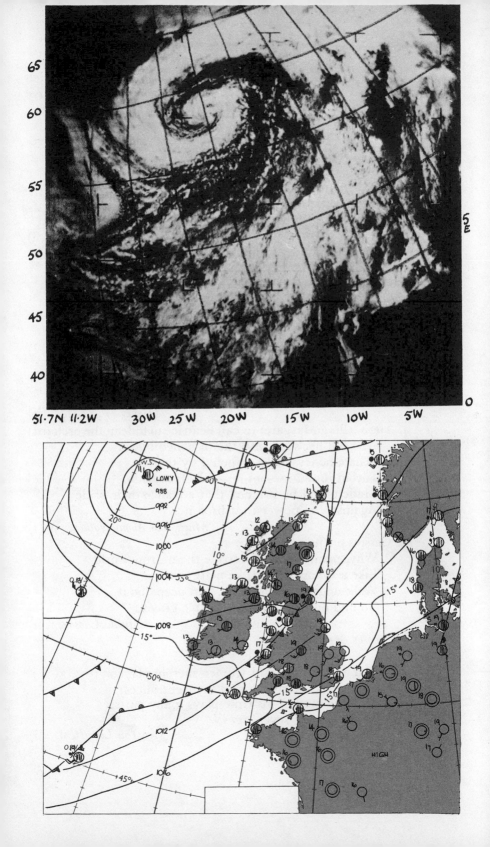

Exercise 3. (a) Both the passage and the poem, *"Wind"*, are rich in comparisons, both similes and metaphors. The most effective are those with several points of comparison. Discuss what is compared to what in examples from the passage or poem.

(i) Discuss each of the following famous examples of images from Shakespeare's plays:

1. Juliet to Romeo:
   My bounty is as boundless as the sea,
   My love as deep; the more I give to thee,
   The more I have, for both are infinite.
   (Romeo & Juliet, ii, i)

2. John of Gaunt describing England:
   This other Eden, demi-Paradise;
   This fortress built by Nature for herself
   Against infection and the hand of war,
   This happy breed of men, this little world;
   This precious stone set in the silver sea,
   (Richard II, ii, i)

3. Prince Henry about the fat knight, Falstaff:
   Falstaff sweats to death,
   And lards the lean earth as he walks along.
   (Henry IV, pt. 1, ii, ii)

4. Hero telling Margaret to call Beatrice to hide in the orchard:
   And bid her steal into the pleached bower
   Where honeysuckles, ripen'd by the sun,
   Forbid the sun to enter;—like favourites,
   Made proud by princes, that advance their pride
   Against that power that bred it:
   (Much Ado About Nothing, iii, i)

5. Cassius on Julius Caesar:
   Why, man, he doth bestride the narrow world
   Like a Colossus; and we petty men
   Walk under his huge legs, and peep about
   To find ourselves dishonourable graves.
   (Julius Caesar, i, ii)

6. Jaques describes life:
   All the world's a stage,
   And all the men and women merely players:
   They have their exits and their entrances;
   And one man in his time plays many parts,
   His acts being seven ages.
   (As You Like It, ii, vii)

7. Hamlet, sickened by his mother's hasty marriage to his father's brother, despairing:

> O God! God!
> How weary, stale, flat, and unprofitable
> Seem to me all the uses of this world!
> Fie on't! O, fie! 'tis an unweeded garden,
> That grows to seed; things rank and gross in nature
> Possess it merely.
>
> *(Hamlet,* I, ii)

8. Lady Macbeth, taunting Macbeth because he is going back on his determination to kill King Duncan in order to become king himself:

> Was the hope drunk
> Wherein you dress'd yourself? hath it slept since?
> And wakes it now to look so green and pale
> At what it did so freely?
>
> *(Macbeth,* I, vii)

(ii) Work out a number of extended comparisons, suggesting several points of comparison in one basic image, e.g.

> willow trees—girls' hair
> The willows stand by the water's edge, their fine green branches dripping down, like girls who have thrown their long hair forward over their heads to dry in the sun.

Here are some suggestions:
1. a mountain track—a snake
2. a storm—a battle
3. a crowd—a flock of birds
4. history—a long voyage
5. chimney-stacks—fingers
6. a stained glass window—a piece of music
7. starlings—spray from a fountain
8. dew on cobwebs—stars
9. a government—an orchestra
10. a log—a crocodile

(b) The poem *"Wind"* contains examples of *onomatopoeia* and *alliteration.* The following are examples of onomatopoeia:

> The woods *crashing* through darkness, the *booming* hills.

Find others and discuss them. The sounds of "crashing" and "booming" suggest a violent, destructive force; what other onomatopoeic words can you think of to suggest this kind of destructive power?

Now jot down words of your own that suggest by their sound a gentle, cooling breeze. You may invent some of the words if you wish.

Consider this example of alliteration from the poem.

"... and a black
Back gull bent like an iron bar ..."

What other examples of alliteration can you find in the poem and in the passage?

Make up vivid alliterative sentences to describe different kinds of weather.

e.g. Barbed, bashing wind boomeranged back and forth.

Soft, sleepy snow slid from the sky.

Topics for Written Work

1. Write a *description* of any kind of exceptional weather conditions or natural phenomenon. Avoid exaggeration: the art of vivid description is largely to capture detail as realistically as possible, and to reduce vast events to a human scale, that is, what one person can experience and comprehend. Use simile and metaphor to make strange sights seem comparable with more familiar things. Write personally, adapting your own experience and imagination, *without* allowing your description to become a narrative—a story of what you did.

Here are some suggested topics:

A storm at sea or on shore.

A thunderstorm and cloudburst over a dry, dusty city.

Heavy, soaking rain on the hills or mountains.

A blizzard.

Prolonged drought.

A gale among trees.

Exceptionally hot, calm weather.

An earthquake.

A flood.

Thunder and lightning at night.

Your description could take the form of a poem, or you could attempt the same subject, first as a poem, then as a prose description. Here are two examples by fifth formers:

20

Rain

Then it came, twisting in the wind,
Rain, lashing, clubbing my bag,
Drenching my hat, the dye trickling
In streams into my mouth,
Wrinkling, torturing, freezing on the road
Lashing, splattering, cascading and dropping,
In effervescent globules down my neck.
When suddenly after three hours,
It stopped. I could see that, but I still
Heard it silently tapping, tap, tap, tap,
And then suddenly silence.
Just silence.

RICHARD

Skywater

I'd been out of the building two minutes when the clouds, looming unseen in the dark vaults of the night sky, burst open and cascaded water all over the city. It came down, the wind catching it and whipping it into neat parallel lines that shimmered silver in the moonlight. It accumulated in my hair, plastered it into straggly streaks and dripped in teardrops down my face. Little rivulets met at the tip of my nose and discharged, one at a time, in driplets of rain that vanished towards my squeaking shoes.

As I ran, the sound of my own breathing was drowned by the splatter, clatter and batter of hard little raindrops on tin roofs of sheds, tile roofs of houses and paned roofs of greenhouses. The water gurgled eagerly into drains, found them already full and swirled back in currents of overflow along the gutters.

I ran, crouched over and whipped by the celestial debris (there's a term to conjure with!) into the main street, alive with brassy windows and panicked traffic. The streets swam with reflections of tail-lights, as if the cars were churning through the night thorough-fares of Venice.

People were clustered in shop doorways, each valiantly ignoring the stench of the other's damp garments, as I pelted through the rain. The swish and hum of windscreen wipers was inaudible above the snarl of car engines, desperate to avoid the taint of rust on their chassis; and the shop awnings defied physics. Roofs before walls, the latter being added later as the rain poured off three sides in solid sheets of water.

My hands were fumbling together, nursing each other for warmth, red and raw in the cold wind and patterned by shaky trails of liquidity. I shivered.

A key in the lock—a twist with a little resistance—an open door. I splashed in, wiping my glistening shoes on the mat and reaching

21

for the light switch. Outside, the rain continued unabated. A flow that would have reduced a drought-plagued farmer to tears, but here it only evoked curses and made trouserleg-bottoms soggy and uncomfortable. It gurgled and splashed and distorted.

MICHAEL

2. Study the following table of basic meteorological figures for six holiday resorts.
(a) Write a general account comparing all six, showing the advantages and disadvantages of selecting each of these for an Easter, June or Summer holiday in an average year. Avoid too much repetition of figures—assume that you are writing comment to accompany the table.
(b) Write a paragraph publicising any *one* of these resorts on the basis of the weather records given here.

AVERAGE MONTHLY SUNSHINE, TEMPERATURE AND RAINFALL

| | APRIL | | | JUNE | | | AUGUST | | |
	Sun	Temp	Rain	Sun	Temp	Rain	Sun	Temp	Rain
	hrs	°C	mm	hrs	°C	mm	hrs	°C	mm
Blackpool	5·5	8·6	48·5	7·1	14·3	55·5	5·5	16·0	94·0
Brighton	5·6	9·1	46·0	7·7	15·4	38·0	6·8	17·7	58·0
Margate	6·0	9·1	35·5	7·9	15·4	30·5	7·0	18·3	48·5
Scilly Isles	6·2	9·7	53·0	7·6	14·3	43·5	6·5	16·6	63·5
Skegness	5·3	8·0	40·5	6·9	14·3	38·0	5·8	16·6	53·0
Torquay	6·0	9·7	58·0	7·8	15·4	46·0	6·7	17·1	66·0

Oral Work

1. Human beings, and particularly writers and other artists, are often guilty of what Ruskin called "the pathetic fallacy" —the conviction that the weather and the seasons alter in sympathy with our feelings, or vice versa. Different kinds of weather symbolize different moods, and writers and film directors often use storms, droughts, gales, gentle rain or fog to reinforce what is happening to their human characters. Is there some suggestion of this in the raging hurricane in the extract, used as a background to the turmoil in Emily's mind?

Rain can represent a number of ideas. It is often used to symbolize release of some kind. At the end of the film—after the hero and heroine have solved the difficulties which confronted them, after they have escaped from all the dangers, after the tension has broken—a gentle fall of rain will signify their relief and their new-found peace.

22

What other ideas and emotions do you associate with rain?
Think of scenes, from books and films, in which rain occurs and
say what connection there is between the rain and the atmosphere of each scene.

Now say what associations the following kinds of weather
have for you. What pictures do they conjure up? What ideas
and feelings could they symbolize? Can you remember any of
them occurring in a film or a book? Suggest scenes for which
they would form a suitable background. Say what qualities
they would emphasize in these scenes:

(a) the lull before a storm—black, threatening clouds etc.;
(b) softly falling snow;
(c) a relentless, scorching sun;
(d) steady, drenching rain;
(e) frost and icicles.

Find extracts and short poems that can be read to the class
to illustrate the uses of different kinds of weather or seasons in
this way; for instance, the storm in *King Lear*, the fog in *Hard
Times*, the rain in Edith Sitwell's poem, the drought in *The
Ancient Mariner*, frost in poems by Coleridge or Wordsworth,
Keats' *Ode to Autumn*, Robert Frost's poems, and so on.
2. Attempt to match words with music that suggests particular
kinds of weather (for instance in Beethoven's *Pastoral Symphony*).
Take poems collected by members of the class and record them
against an appropriate background. With a few basic instruments, such as guitar, drums and a wind instrument or piano,
it is not difficult to improvise a suitable background to poems
written by the class. The record *Red Bird*, with poems by Christopher Logue and music by Tony Kinsey, illustrates very well
how interestingly modern poetry can be matched with modern
music.

Activities and Research

1. Find out how weather forecasts are prepared, what factors
influence the weather in this part of the world, and how much
information can be deduced from a weather map. Prepare a
clear explanation of the satellite photograph and the accom-
panying weather map on page 17. Where are the permanent
weather stations and weather ships? What information do they
record, and how? What use is now being made of weather
satellites and aerial photography?

2. Compile a class anthology of poems and short extracts about weather. Copy out neatly the pieces that you select. See if you can find, in newspapers and magazines, photographs and drawings to illustrate the written material. Part of the anthology could consist of poems and descriptions written by members of the class.

Further Reading

A High Wind in Jamaica by RICHARD HUGHES (Chatto & Windus; Penguin).
The earthquake and the hurricane mark the beginning of a series of unusual and exciting adventures for the children. As you can tell from this chapter's extract, the descriptive passages are most effective; and there are some fascinating insights into the minds of children. The lack of emotion in the writing makes disasters seem all the more shocking.

In Hazard by RICHARD HUGHES (Chatto & Windus; Penguin).
A hurricane is again featured in this novel, which is also set in the Caribbean. A British cargo vessel, the *Archimedes*, encounters a violent storm; there are interesting studies of the crew's reaction to the danger which threatens to overwhelm them. It is an exciting and simply told story.

Typhoon by JOSEPH CONRAD (Longmans; Heinemann).
In its plot this long short story is very similar to *In Hazard*. It tells what happens to a steamer, her crew and her extremely lively cargo during a 36-hour battering by a tropical storm. Captain McWhirr is a simple, unimaginative man who carries on triumphantly through the chaotic turmoil of the typhoon.

CHAPTER TWO

People

1. A BOY PICKPOCKET

Henry Mayhew collected information about the poor in Victorian London by interviewing them.

To show the class of characters usually frequenting these lodging-houses, I will now give the statement of a boy—a young pickpocket—without shoes or stockings. He wore a ragged, dirty, and very thin great coat, of some dark jean or linen, under which was another thin coat, so arranged that what appeared rents—and, indeed, were rents, but designedly made—in the outer garment, were slits through which the hand readily reached the pockets of the inner garment, and could here deposit any booty. He was a slim, agile lad, with a sharp but not vulgar expression, and small features. His hands were of singular delicacy and beauty. . . .

I asked him what he, as a sharp lad, thought was the cause of so many boys becoming vagrant pickpockets? He answered, "Why sir, if boys runs away, and has to shelter in low lodging-houses—and many runs away from cruel treatment at home—they meet there with boys such as me, or as bad, and the devil soon lays his hands on them. If there wasn't so many lodging-houses there wouldn't be so many bad boys—there couldn't. . . ."

He answered readily to my inquiry, as to what he thought would become of him?—"Transportation. If a boy has great luck he may carry on for eight years. Three or four years is the common run, but transportation is what he's sure to come to in the end." This lad picked my pocket at my request, and so dexterously did he do his "work", that though I was alive to what he was trying to do, it was impossible for me to detect the least movement of my coat. To see him pick the pockets, as he did, of some of the gentlemen who were present on the occasion, was a curious sight. He crept behind much like a cat with his claws out, and while in the act held his breath with suspense: but immediately the handkerchief was safe in his hand, the change in the expression of his countenance was most marked. He then seemed almost to be convulsed with delight at the success of his perilous adventure, and, turning his back, held up the handkerchief to discover the value of his prize with intense glee evident in every feature.

(from *London Labour and the London Poor*, 1851)

Appreciation and Discussion

1. What did Mayhew find remarkable about the boy's hands and how might this be connected with his "work"?
2. What other aspects of the boy's appearance were particularly connected with his activities?
3. How and why, according to this lad, did boys become pick-pockets in nineteenth-century London?
4. This boy had already been in prison thirteen times when Mayhew talked to him. What punishment did he expect in the end, and what form would this take?
5. What more did Mayhew learn about the boy from watching him at "work"?
6. Was this boy making a good living from picking pockets, as far as one can tell from this passage? What is his own attitude to his own way of life—does he justify himself?
7. Find more modern or more common words or phrases for these in this passage: rents; designedly made; of singular delicacy; vagrant; I was alive to; most marked; intense glee evident in every feature.

2. A BANK CASHIER
James Joyce describes a meticulous, middle-aged resident of Edwardian Dublin.

Mr. James Duffy lived in Chapelizod because he wished to live as far as possible from the city of which he was a citizen and because he found all the other suburbs of Dublin mean, modern, and pretentious. He lived in an old sombre house, and from his windows he could look into the disused distillery or upwards along the shallow river on which Dublin is built. The lofty walls of his uncarpeted room were free from pictures. He had himself bought every article of furniture in the room: a black iron bedstead, an iron wash-stand, four cane chairs, a clothes-rack, a coal-scuttle, a fender and irons, and a square table on which lay a double desk. A bookcase had been made in an alcove by means of shelves of white wood. The bed was clothed with white bedclothes and a black and scarlet rug covered the foot. A little hand-mirror hung above the wash-stand and during the day a white-shaded lamp stood as the sole ornament of the mantelpiece. The books on the white wooden shelves were arranged from below upwards according to bulk. . . .

Mr. Duffy abhorred anything which betokened physical or mental disorder. A medieval doctor would have called him saturnine. His face, which carried the entire tale of his years, was of the brown tint of Dublin streets. On his long and rather large head grew dry black hair, and a tawny moustache did not quite cover an unamiable mouth. His cheekbones also gave his face a harsh character; but there was no harshness in the eyes which, looking at the world from under their tawny eyebrows, gave the impression of a man ever alert to greet a redeeming instinct in others but often disappointed. He lived at a little distance from his body, regarding his own acts with doubtful side-glances. He had an odd autobiographical habit which led him to compose in his mind from time to time a short sentence about himself containing a subject in the third person and a predicate in the past tense. He never gave alms to beggars, and walked firmly, carrying a stout hazel.

He had been for many years cashier of a private bank in Baggot Street. Every morning he came in from Chapelizod by tram. At midday he went to Dan Burke's and took his lunch — a bottle of lager beer and a small trayful of arrowroot biscuits. At four o'clock he was set free. He dined in an eating-house in George's Street where he felt himself safe from the society of Dublin's gilded youth and where there was a certain plain honesty in the bill of fare. His evenings were spent either before his landlady's piano or roaming about the outskirts of the city. His liking for Mozart's music brought him sometimes to an opera or a concert: these were the only dissipations of his life.

(from the short story *A Painful Case* from *Dubliners*)

Appreciation and Discussion

1. Examine the colours of the furniture and furnishings in Mr. Duffy's room. What overall effect would you expect the colour scheme to have?
2. What features of Mr. Duffy's room and of his daily routine suggest a man who "abhorred physical or mental disorder"?
3. What aspects of the main city of Dublin, and its inhabitants, does he seem to dislike?
4. What evidence is there that Mr. Duffy did not really enjoy his work?
5. Which features of Mr. Duffy's face were pleasant or sympathetic and which unpleasant?
6. What was Mr. Duffy's attitude to himself and to others?
7. Make up an example of the kind of "sentence about himself" that you think James Joyce refers to in the second paragraph?
8. Explain the following words or phrases as used here: pretentious; saturnine; tawny; unamiable; a redeeming instinct; gilded youth; bill of fare; dissipations.

3. A Warrior Saint

George Bernard Shaw reconsiders the most remarkable peasant girl of the fifteenth century.

Joan of Arc, a village girl from the Vosges, was born about 1412; burnt for heresy, witchcraft, and sorcery in 1431; rehabilitated after a fashion in 1456; designated Venerable in 1904; declared Blessed in 1908; and finally canonized in 1920. She is the most notable Warrior Saint in the Christian calender, and the queerest fish among the eccentric worthies of the Middle Ages. Though a professed and most pious Catholic, and the projector of a Crusade against the Hussites, she was in fact one of the first Protestant martyrs. She was also one of the apostles of Nationalism, and the first French practitioner of Napoleonic realism in warfare as distinguished from the sporting ransom-gambling chivalry of her time. She was the pioneer of rational dressing for women, and, like Queen Christina of Sweden two centuries later, to say nothing of Catalina de Erauso and innumerable obscure heroines who have disguised themselves as men to serve as soldiers and sailors, she refused to accept the specific woman's lot, and dressed and fought and lived as men did. . . .

We may accept and admire Joan, then, as a sane and shrewd country girl of extraordinary strength of mind and hardihood of body. Everything she did was thoroughly calculated; and though the process was so rapid that she was hardly conscious of it, and ascribed it all to her voices, she was a woman of policy and not of blind impulse. In war she was as much a realist as Napoleon: she had his eye for artillery and his knowledge of what it could do. She did not expect beseiged cities to fall Jerichowise at the sound of her trumpet, but, like Wellington, adapted her methods of attack to the pecularities of the defence; and she anticipated the Napoleonic calculation that if you only hold on long enough the other fellow will give in: for example, her final triumph at Orleans was achieved after her commander Dunois had sounded the retreat at the end of a day's fighting without a decision. She was never for a moment what so many romancers and playwrights have pretended: a romantic young lady. She was a thorough daughter of the soil in her peasantlike matter-of-factness and doggedness, and her acceptance of great lords and kings and prelates as such without idolatry or snobbery, seeing at a glance how much they were individually good for. She had the respectable countrywoman's sense of the value of public decency, and would not tolerate foul language and neglect of religious observance, nor allow disreputable women to hang about her soldiers. She had one pious ejaculation "En nom Dé!" and one meaningless oath "Par mon martin"; and this much swearing she allowed to the incorrigibly blasphemous La Hire equally with herself. The value of this prudery was so great in restoring the self-respect of the badly demoralized army that, like most of her policy, it justified itself as soundly calculated. She talked to and dealt with people of all classes, from labourers to kings, without embarrassment or affectation, and got them to do what she wanted when they were not afraid or corrupt. She could coax and she could hustle, her tongue having a soft side and sharp edge. She was very capable: a born boss.

(from the Preface to the play *Saint Joan*)

Appreciation and Discussion

1. In what different ways was Joan a "pioneer", according to the author? (There are at least four.)

2. He calls Joan a "woman of policy". What does he mean by this, and what examples of it does he give?

3. What contrast is being drawn here between the fall of Jericho and the fall of Orleans?

4. In what ways, according to the evidence in this passage, was Joan (a) an early Protestant; (b) one of the first apostles of Nationalism; and (c) a Napoleonic realist in battle?

5. The author refers to Joan as a "village girl" a "country girl" and a "daughter of the soil". What qualities did her farm background give Joan, according to the author? List at least five qualities.

6. How did Joan treat other people?

7. Did the author regard Joan as a "feminist"?

8. What is Bernard Shaw's attitude to Joan? Is he admiring or mocking her? Does he emphasise her saintliness or purity? Does he seem to share her Catholic faith or believe in her "voices" which she said inspired her?

9. Bernard Shaw's style of writing is polemical without being abstract. He reduces arguments to very definite and concrete language or examples. Demonstrate this by studying this passage.

10. What contrasts are there between this passage and the other two descriptions in this chapter?

Old Jack Noman

At mid-day then along the lane
Old Jack Noman appeared again,
Jaunty and old, crooked and tall,
And stopped and grinned at me over the wall,
With a cowslip bunch in his button-hole
And one in his cap. Who could say if his roll
Came from flints in the road, the weather, or ale?
He was welcome as the nightingale.
Not an hour of the sun had been wasted on Jack.
"I've got my Indian complexion back,"
Said he. He was tanned like a harvester,
Like his short clay pipe, like the leaf and burr
That clung to his coat from last night's bed,
Like the ploughland crumbling red.
Fairer flowers were none on the earth
Than his cowslips wet with the dew of their birth,
Or fresher leaves than the cress in his basket.
"Where did they come from, Jack?" "Don't ask it.
And you'll be told no lies." "Very well:
Then I can't buy." "I don't want to sell.
Take them and these flowers, too, free.
Perhaps you have something to give me?
Wait till next time. The better the day . . .
The Lord couldn't make a better, I say;
If he could, he never has done."
So off went Jack with his roll-walk-run,
Leaving his cresses from Oakshott rill
And his cowslips from Wheatham hill.

from *May the Twenty-Third* by EDWARD THOMAS

Discussing the Poem

1. What details suggest the poet's affection for Old Jack Noman? What likeable qualities does Jack show?
2. In various ways, Old Jack Noman is closely associated with the countryside of which he is an integral part. Pick out some of the details and comparisons that suggest this association.
3. Are there some elements of *paradox* about Jack or the words used to describe him?
4. Attempt a prose description of Old Jack Noman, as you

31

imagine him after reading this poem, and using all the evidence it gives or suggests.

Techniques

Exercise 1. Read and discuss the following passage, and then make a summary of it in not more than 145 of your own words. The passage contains about 412 words. Put the exact number of words you use in brackets at the end.

What is a normal person? This is a difficult question to answer because this word "normal" has several meanings and at least two distinct definitions. When we are dealing with figures, such as population statistics, we assume that the normal is the average, or something close to it. From such figures, we can form a picture of a normal person who is likely to have a particular height, and we can say that the average person of that height has a certain normal weight. By averaging from the mental capabilities of people who are very clever or very slow at reasoning, we arrive at an average intelligence. By considering everyone's salary or wages, we can work out an average income; and similarly we know the size of the average family at any particular time. This "normal" person would, of course, not be very fit—he would have to suffer an average number of illnesses; nor could he be very contented, since he would have to suffer a number of misfortunes. If he were noticeably successful in life, or particularly handsome or charming, he would cease to be "normal". Even his opinions would have to be rather restrained, because we should work out the way he votes, the church he belongs to, his ideas of what is right and what is wrong, and his choice of clothes, furniture, entertainment and everything else by averaging out the views of the total population from one extreme to the other in each case.

On the other hand, the same word "normal" also suggests to us a particularly satisfactory state of affairs. When the doctor assures us we are in normal health, he means that our minds and bodies are free from illness and functioning well. If we were "abnormal", we should be worried. In this sense, we use the word normal to sum up a rather admirable set of conditions: it is "normal" to be above average in health, to have sound common sense and reliable opinions. We would expect the normal person to act with careful thought and consideration, and not to make silly mistakes. We are now generalizing from our own limited experience and ideas to form a picture of what is the right and proper behaviour in our particular part of the world. For instance, we may think it natural and normal for a man to be aggressive and dominating, or for adolescents to be rebellious, without any statistical or biological evidence to support us.

Exercise 2. Of the various ways of classifying human beings, and describing their basic temperaments or personalities, the oldest in western civilisation is that of the four "humours", classified by Hippocrates, the ancient Greek physician, as blood, black bile, yellow bile and phlegm. The combination of these fluids in the body was supposed to determine both physical and mental characteristics; a perfect balance of all four would create an ideal person, but in most people one or other tended to be dominant:

sanguine—predominance of blood (hot and wet): a heavy, red-faced, jolly, generous, self-indulgent sort of person.

melancholy—predominance of black bile (cold and dry): a gloomy, pessimistic, quiet and brooding person.

choleric—predominance of yellow bile (hot and dry): a quick-tempered, excitable, aggressive and energetic person, usually thin and wiry.

phlegmatic—predominance of phlegm (cold and wet): a slow, lethargic, apathetic, dull kind of person.

Although this medical theory was superseded hundreds of years ago, its vocabulary is still in use. We still talk of "good humoured" people; and the word "complexion", which originally meant the basic combination of humours in an individual, has come to mean his outward appearance, especially the skin of his face.

(a) Here are fifty words describing people or their characteristics. Check that you know the meaning of them all, and could use them in suitable contexts.

Group them (i) as favourable, critical or neutral adjectives—i.e. whether they are complimentary or not; (ii) by similarity of meaning, so that you have a number of lists of loosely synonymous or related adjectives.

acrimonious	facetious	malicious	spry
avaricious	fanatical	mercenary	staid
benign	fastidious	meretricious	stoical
cadaverous	fulsome	nonchalant	supercilious
candid	gregarious	nubile	sycophantic
cantankerous	impetuous	obsequious	uncouth
cordial	improvident	penurious	unctuous
debonair	intrepid	precocious	unkempt
demure	irascible	prepossessing	urbane
diffident	lachrymose	pretentious	vehement
dissipated	licentious	punctilious	wanton
ebullient	lugubrious	querulous	witty
execrable	magnanimous		

33

(b) Explain what you understand by each of the following nouns as applied to the qualities of people, and discuss which are the qualities you would admire in someone:

1. vigour, toughness, stamina, virility, mettle.
2. elegance, refinement, grace, delicacy, charm.
3. generosity, munificence, liberality, altruism, tolerance.
4. wit, genius, percipience, intuition, sagacity.
5. ambition, diligence, initiative, drive, ruthlessness.
6. sensitivity, imagination, talent, squeamishness.
7. innocence, naïvety, integrity, modesty, temperance.
8. heroism, daring, foolhardiness, courage, audacity.
9. petulance, pugnacity, resentment, irritation, perversity.
10. affection, tenderness, courtesy, humility, deference.

Exercise 3. Six of the most common functions of a noun in English are illustrated by the word "pickpocket" in the following sentences.

Discuss the function in each case:
1. Pickpockets were common in Victorian London.
2. Mayhew met many pickpockets.
3. This boy was a young pickpocket.
4. This boy, a young pickpocket, demonstrated his skill.
5. The judges were very severe upon pickpockets.
6. In the end they would take steps to transport pickpockets for life.

Noun phrases and noun clauses can perform the same functions in a sentence. Identify the noun clauses in the following examples (adapted from the extracts) and show how each corresponds to the noun "pickpocket" in its functions above.
   (i)   What appeared rents in the outer garments were slits.
   (ii) I asked him what was the cause of boys becoming pickpockets.
   (iii) Transportation is what he is sure to come to.
   (iv) She anticipated the Napoleonic calculation that the other fellow will give in.
   (v)   She had his knowledge of what artillery could do.
   (vi) She got them to do what she wanted.
   Three of these are types of noun clauses that we have not dealt with before: the noun clause in apposition to a noun (itself usually subject, object or complement), the noun clause object of a preposition, and the noun clause object of an infinitive (rather than object of a finite verb).
   Make up suitable noun clauses (or parts of them) to complete the following sentences, and then write out the noun clause in each case, stating the exact function of the subordinate clause in relation to the main clause.

34

e.g. She got them to do...........
      She got them to do what was wanted.
      What was wanted—subordinate noun clause, object of
      infinitive "to do" in main clause.
(a) Joan of Arc was never what..............
(b) What...............was almost a miracle.
(c) She was determined to say what...............
(d) He means what...............
(e) One can form a picture of what...............
(f) The theme of his sermon, that...............was a call to vigorous
     action.
(g) I challenged his assertion...............
(h) He was arguing...............
(i) I could not believe...............
(j) I could not believe in...............
(k) To do what...............is not always easy.
(l) I begged him to try to see how...............

Topics for Written Work

1. Write a description of a person. The extracts at the beginning of this chapter suggest different approaches, or different
elements that could be made part of one description. The
account of the pickpocket uses his own words and actions to
indicate his individual personality and enlist the readers'
sympathy. The description of Mr. Duffy is greatly enriched by
the background of his room and his daily routine, which tell us
a great deal about him. Bernard Shaw's view of Joan of Arc is
more analytical and makes fuller use of bold statements,
summarizing her character and her place in history as Shaw
sees it.

A well-written description should convey the subject's
personality so that the reader feels that he has met the person or
would recognize him or her if he did meet them. It should also
endeavour to add depth, so that we see the subject in a typical
context or in action or in speech. Be selective in physical
description, concentrating on the features that one notices or
picks out as striking or characteristic.

Here are some suggested subjects:

A favourite relative.
Your best friend.
The oddest person you know.
A typical teacher, clergyman or youth leader.
The historical person you most admire.
The fictional character you would most like to meet.
A child or an old age pensioner.
A tramp.
The mother or father of a large family.
A gossip or a "henpecked" husband.

2. You may remember from Book Three the list of headings used by the police in compiling a description of "wanted" or missing persons. Imagine that you have seen (or lost) such a person and are asked to write a description of him for the authorities. This will be a short piece, concentrating on physical characteristics of all kinds, such as would lead to rapid and reliable recognition of the missing or wanted person.

Oral Work

If you can borrow a tape-recorder, preferably a battery-operated one, collect a series of contrasting views from people of different occupations, ages, sex and social class on some controversial topic. As interviewers, you need to give considerable thought and preparation to your choice of questions. Local or topical issues, such as a plan to rebuild some part of the town or demolish a landmark, or views expressed recently by someone well-known, are usually most interesting, but there are a number of perennial topics, such as:

Are you influenced by advertising?
Do we make too much fuss of animals?
Should more be spent on young people, or old-age
    pensioners?
What makes an ideal husband/wife?
Are we a nation of gamblers?
Should religion be taught in schools?
What would you do about crime?

Interviewers should have a whole series of questions or variations on the same basic questions, and to ensure that the

interviews are interesting, it is necessary to think of different ways of putting the same questions and to be prepared to follow up the first question with others in response to the particular replies. Interviewers should always be polite and good listeners.

Collected interviews may need some editing and should then be presented with comment to the class by the group who made them.

Alternatively, it can be interesting to record an extended interview with just one person who has had long or interesting experience—an old person, perhaps, or someone who has particularly fascinating work or hobbies.

Activities and Research

1. What kind of people are the following advertisements aimed at?

"£34,000 Regent's Park Terrace (off). Admirable, fairly low-built house . . . with revolting Victorian exterior of the type that is next due to become fashionable. 5 bedrooms, etc. Garden. Interesting neighbours."

"£27,500 Wimbledon. Desirable semi. 3 bedrooms. Half-tiled bathroom. Well-planned kitchen-diner. Lovely through-lounge. Good decorative order. 13-amp wiring. Nice little garden."

"Attractive and insatiable VAUXHALL VIVA DL seeks dominant driver to share mutual pleasures, curvaceous, shapely figure, impeccably kept, will prove trustworthy and loyal, but will turn other men's heads—£1450."

"1976 VAUXHALL VIVA de luxe, green, one owner, excellent condition—£1450."

Collect examples of unusual or contrasting advertisements and mount these, together with comments on the style, and on the kind of people (age, social class, sex, employment, interests) that each is aimed at.

Further Reading

Mayhew's Characters by PETER QUENNELL (ed.) (Spring Books)
(331.8)
The young pickpocket is only one of many fascinating characters from the poor and the underworld of Victorian London interviewed by Henry Mayhew. His encounters with them are recorded with little comment—yet we are made vividly aware of the social evils of the time and the humanity and sympathy of the interviewer.

Dubliners by JAMES JOYCE (Chatto; Cape; Penguin)
These early stories by a remarkable Irish writer are essentially studies of characters in action. His writing is objective but sympathetic as he looks at a variety of Dublin characters and their lives in the early years of this century. The style, unlike much of Joyce's later work, is clear and straightforward.

Saint Joan by GEORGE BERNARD SHAW (Longmans; Penguin)
(822.91)
Even more than his prefaces, Shaw's plays are all excellent examples of polemical writing, in which characters argue out all kinds of social, political and religious issues vigorously and lucidly. But Shaw's characters, and especially his Joan of Arc, are very much alive, so that we become involved in their stories. The dialogue is always fluent and full of wit and individuality, so that the plays read just as well as they act. Here is an introductory selection:

Androcles and the Lion (822.91)—an old fable which, in a light-hearted way, considers the early Christians and their motives for martyrdom.
Pygmalion (822.91)—what happens when a professor of phonetics transforms a cockney flower-seller into a debutante.
Caesar and Cleopatra (822.91)—Shaw's own view of the relations between the Roman general and the young queen he conquered.
Arms and the Man (822.91)—a comedy suggesting that discretion is rather more important to a soldier than valour.

CHAPTER THREE

Prejudice - I

THE NATURE OF PREJUDICE

Scorn felt by one group of people for another has been common for centuries and in all parts of the world. This study suggests that it frequently has no reasonable foundation and may lead to serious conflict.

We have said that an adequate definition of prejudice contains two essential ingredients. There must be an *attitude* of favor or disfavor, and it must be related to an overgeneralized, (and therefore erroneous) *belief*. Prejudiced statements sometimes express the attitudinal factor, sometimes the belief factor. In the following series the first item expresses attitude, the second, belief.

> I can't abide Negroes.
> Negroes are smelly.
>
> I wouldn't live in an apartment house with Jews.
> There are a few exceptions, but in general all Jews are pretty much alike.
>
> I don't want Japanese-Americans in my town.
> Japanese-Americans are sly and tricky.

Is it important to distinguish between the attitudinal and belief aspects of prejudices? For some purposes, no. When we find one we usually find the other. Without some generalized beliefs concerning a group as a whole, a hostile attitude could not long be sustained. In modern researches it turns out that people who express a high degree of antagonistic attitudes on a test for prejudice, also show that they believe to a high degree that the groups they are prejudiced against have a large number of objectionable qualities.

But for some purposes it is useful to distinguish attitude from belief. For example, we shall see in Chapter 30 that certain programs designed to reduce prejudice succeed in altering beliefs but not in changing attitudes. Beliefs, to some extent, can be rationally attacked and altered. Usually, however, they have the slippery propensity of accommodating themselves some-how to the negative attitude which is much harder to change. The following dialogue illustrates the point:

Mr. X: The trouble with the Jews is that they only take care of their own group.

Mr. Y: But the record of the Community Chest campaign shows that they give more generously, in proportion to their numbers, to the general charities of the community, than do non-Jews.

Mr. X: That shows they are always trying to buy favor and in-trude into Christian affairs. They think of nothing but money; that is why there are so many Jewish bankers.

Mr. Y: But a recent study shows that the percentage of Jews in the banking business is negligible, far smaller than the percentage of non-Jews.

Mr. X: That's just it, they don't go in for respectable business; they are only in the movie business or run night clubs.

Thus the belief system has a way of slithering around to justify the more permanent attitude. The process is one of *rational-ization*—of the accommodation of beliefs to attitudes.

It is well to keep these two aspects of prejudice in mind, for in our subsequent discussions we shall have occasion to make use of the distinction. But wherever the term *prejudice* is used without specifying these aspects, the reader may assume that both attitude and belief are intended.

ACTING OUT PREJUDICE

What people actually do in relation to groups they dislike is not always directly related to what they think or feel about them. Two employers, for example, may dislike Jews to an equal degree. One may keep his feelings to himself and may hire Jews on the same basis as any workers—perhaps because he wants to gain goodwill for his factory or store in the Jewish community. The other may translate his dislike into his employment policy, and refuse to hire Jews. Both men are prejudiced, but only one of them practices *discrimination*.

It is true that any negative attitude tends somehow, some-where, to express itself in action. Few people keep their anti-pathies entirely to themselves. The more intense the attitude the more likely it is to result in vigorously hostile action.

We may venture to distinguish certain degrees of negative action from the least energetic to the most.

1. *Antilocution*. Most people who have prejudices talk about them. With like-minded friends, occasionally with strangers,

they may express their antagonism freely. But many people never go beyond this mild degree of antipathetic action.

2. *Avoidance.* If the prejudice is more intense, it leads the individual to avoid members of the disliked group, even perhaps at the cost of considerable inconvenience. In this case, the bearer of prejudice does not directly inflict harm upon the group he dislikes. He takes the burden of accommodation and withdrawal entirely upon himself.

3. *Discrimination.* Here the prejudiced person makes detrimental distinctions of an active sort. He undertakes to exclude all members of the group in question from certain types of employment, from residential housing, political rights, educational or recreational opportunities, churches, hospitals, or from some other social privileges. Segregation is an institutionalized form of discrimination enforced legally or by common custom.

4. *Physical attack.* Under conditions of heightened emotion prejudice may lead to acts of violence or semi-violence. An unwanted Negro family may be forcibly ejected from a neighborhood, or so severely threatened that it leaves in fear. Gravestones in Jewish cemeteries may be desecrated. The Northside's Italian gang may lie in wait for the Southside's Irish gang.

5. *Extermination.* Lynchings, pogroms, massacres, and the Hitlerian program of genocide mark the ultimate degree of violent expression of prejudice.

This five-point scale is not mathematically constructed, but it serves to call attention to the enormous range of activities that may issue from prejudiced attitudes and beliefs. While many people would never move from antilocution to avoidance, or from avoidance to active discrimination, or higher on the scale, still it is true that activity on one level makes transition to a more intense level easier. It was Hitler's antilocution that led Germans to avoid Jewish neighbors and erstwhile friends. This preparation made it easier to enact the Nürnberg Laws of discrimination which, in turn, made the subsequent burning of synagogues and street attacks upon Jews seem natural. The final step in the macabre progression was the ovens at Auschwitz.

From the point of view of social consequences much "polite prejudice" is harmless enough—being confined to idle chatter. But unfortunately, the fateful progression is, in this century,

43

growing in frequency. And as the people of the earth grow ever more interdependent, they can tolerate less well the mounting friction.

(from *The Nature of Prejudice* by Gordon W. Allport)

Appreciation and Discussion

1. What do you understand to be the difference between an attitude and a belief?
2. (a) Which is easier to change, and why, an attitude or a belief? (b) Are beliefs necessary to sustain attitudes?
3. Why does the author say that beliefs can be rationally altered *only* "to some extent"?
4. What do modern researches show about the connections between prejudiced attitudes and beliefs?
5. What, if anything, is harmful about a prejudiced attitude that goes no further than "antilocution"?
6. Explain what the author means by "the fateful progression". If it is "growing in frequency", can you give other examples of it, from recent history or current affairs?
7. In the fifth line of the first paragraph, the author uses the adjective "attitudinal", derived from the noun "attitude". Find the adjectives (they appear in this order in the passage) that he uses, derived from: antagonize; objection; neglect; antipathy; detriment; residence; Hitler; fate.
8. Discuss or write down a brief phrase or single word to mean the same as each of the following words as used in this passage: rationally; propensity; accommodating; antagonism; social privileges; desecrated; lynching; pogroms; genocide; enact; macabre.
9. Discuss the three examples of beliefs given in the first paragraph, showing that they are "overgeneralized (and therefore erroneous)". How could people come to accept such wrong beliefs?
10. Make up a similar example of "rationalization" to the conversation between X and Y, this time showing prejudice against West Indians, the Irish, Pakistanis, Poles, Catholics or any other minority group.
11. Give an example of a country or area where segregation is (or was) practised "legally or by common custom". Can the segregation of one community from another in the same area *ever* be fair or morally justified?

12. What is the difference between genuine dislike of a certain kind of person and a prejudice against such people?
13. Where did Hitler's anti-Jewish campaign end?
14. Many people in the past have had an unfounded dislike of "foreigners". Why then is racial prejudice a more serious problem in the modern world than ever before? Would you rank it as one of the most serious problems facing your generation?
15. Make up *definitions* of each of the following: (a) attitude; (b) belief; (c) rationalization; (d) discrimination; (e) genocide.
16. Discuss the following definition of racial prejudice as given by the author of this passage a little earlier in the book; "Ethnic prejudice is an antipathy based upon a faulty and inflexible generalization. It may be felt or expressed. It may be directed toward a group as a whole, or toward an individual because he is a member of that group."

Look up the definition of prejudice given in the *Shorter Oxford Dictionary* for comparison. Does racial prejudice always include an element of generalization and misconception?

From *This Landscape — These People*

My eighth spring in England I walk among
  The silver birches of Putney Heath,
  Stepping over twigs and stones: being stranger,
  I see but do not touch; only the earth
  Permits an attachment. I do not wish
To be seen, and move, eyes at my sides, like a fish.

And do they notice me, I wonder, these
  Englishmen, strolling with stiff country strides?
  I lean against a tree, my eyes are knots
  In its bark, my skin the wrinkles in its sides.
  I leap hedges, duck under chestnut boughs,
And through the black clay let my swift heels trail like ploughs.

A child at a museum, England for me
  Is an exhibit within a glass case.
  The country, like an antique chair, has a rope
  Across it. I may not sit, only pace
  Its frontiers. I slip through ponds, jump ditches,
Through galleries of ferns see England in pictures.

ZULFIKAR GHOSE

Discussing the Poem

1. Zulfikar Ghose is a poet and writer from Pakistan who writes in English. How long had he been in England when he wrote this poem? What, apparently, makes him still feel a stranger here?
2. Notice the way he walks, moves and stands. What feeling does he seem to have about the English landscape? Is he really coming to know and understand England and its inhabitants? Who makes it difficult for him to do so — the poet himself or "these Englishmen"?
3. Discuss the use of rhyme and half-rhyme in the poem, and its regular structure. Give examples of the poet's bold use of metaphor and discuss its effectiveness.
4. Is the poem bitter or critical about the English? If you are English yourself, are you ashamed of the fact that England made this impression upon a foreigner? If you are from elsewhere in Britain or from some other English-speaking country, comment on *your* feelings about the English. Is it wrong to generalize about Englishmen anyway?

Techniques

Exercise 1. Read the following passage carefully, and answer the questions below:

Race problems, race conflicts, race riots, racial prejudice and racial disturbances are common enough today. There is trouble about "apartheid" in South Africa, about Negroes going to white schools in parts of the United States and about coloured
5   immigration to Britain. But when scientists try to define for us what a "race" is, they can find very little proof of any measurable difference between the members of one "race" and those of another.

Most of us think in terms of skin colour. When we read about
10   race riots in our newspapers, we visualize violent clashes between white-skinned and dark-skinned youths. But the difficulty is where to draw the line. If a human being is born with a predominance of one pigment in the skin, he looks yellow; with a predominance of another he looks brown or black; and with a
15   little of each, and the blood showing through, he looks pink or "white". Everyone has *some* of each pigment, and there is an infinite variety of shades between the extremes. When, then, is a "coloured" man pale enough to be called "white"? It is the same with all the other popular ways of distinguishing races.

20 Some say races are either "Long-headed" or "Broad-headed",
or either narrow-eyed or round-eyed; or they discriminate between woolly-haired, straight-haired and wavy-haired peoples.
Others judge by the shape of the nose or the build of the body.
But not one of these criteria is easily measured; and all over the
25 world one finds awkward exceptions, such as African tribes that
are "negroid" by one definition and "Caucasian" or "European" in appearance by another.

The fact is that biologically there is only one "race" and that
is the whole human species. They have much more in common
30 than they have to divide them. What we call "race" is, like
beauty, largely skin-deep. In our veins run the same blood-
groups, and generally we suffer the same ills and need the same
nourishment. Contrary to general belief, there is absolutely no
reason why a "white" person's blood should not be transfused
35 to a coloured person of the same blood group, or vice versa;
and there is no reason why children born of mixed marriages
should not be as healthy and intelligent as the children of any
other marriage.

It would, however, be foolish to pretend that there are there-
40 fore no divisions between peoples. But we must realize that these
divisions are social, and not biological. In one part of the world
we find people who look similar, share a common culture and
history, and pass on to their children a particular set of attitudes. A group of strangers coming amongst them will often
45 have a very different way of life and therefore be viewed with
suspicion. If these strangers remain conspicuous by their looks,
it will be easy to go on thinking of them as "different" or "inferior". Here we have the seeds of racial prejudice.

(a) "Skin colour" is one of several ways of distinguishing races.
List the others mentioned, generalizing from any examples
given.
(b) Show the various reasons why these ways of distinguishing
races are in fact unreliable.
(c) Why is it appropriate and fair to call the idea of race "skin
deep"?
(d) What are the two popular prejudices that the author
refutes in the third paragraph?
(e) Comment on the various different ways in which inverted
commas are used in this passage.
(f) Explain the following words or phrases as used here:
apartheid (line 3); immigration (line 5); visualize (line 10);
predominance (lines 12–13); an infinite variety (lines
16–17); discriminate (line 21); criteria (line 24); transfused

47

(line 34); with suspicion (lines 45–46); conspicuous (line 46).
(g) Write a summary of this passage, which contains about 480 words. Use between 150 and 170 words, avoiding the original language as far as possible, and stating at the end the exact number of words that you have used.

Exercise 2. The extract from *The Nature of Prejudice* and the passage for précis are rich in *abstract nouns*, or nouns used in an abstract sense.
(a) Fifteen of these have been used to form the table below, where the corresponding adjective, adverbs and verbs are also given. In each case there are two gaps: rewrite the table filling in the gaps to complete it.

	NOUN	ADJECTIVE	ADVERB	VERB
e.g.	nature	natural	naturally	naturalize
1.	prejudice	prejudicial	—	—
2.	scorn	—	—	scorn
3.	—	—	definitely	define
4.	—	favourable	favourably	—
5.	belief	believable	—	—
6.	rationalization	—	—	rationalize
7.	avoidance	—	—	avoid
8.	—	—	inconveniently	inconvenience
9.	—	distinct	distinctly	—
10.	expression	expressive	—	—
11.	—	—	progressively	progress
12.	—	frequent	frequently	—
13.	difference	different	—	—
14.	predominance	—	—	predominate
15.	—	suspicious	suspiciously	—

(b) Form an abstract noun from each of the following verbs, and compose a sentence to illustrate its correct use.
e.g. resume—resumption: The strike was settled when the men agreed to an immediate resumption of work while their leaders negotiated for better pay and conditions.

1. absorb 3. defy 5. dissolve 7. propel 9. reduce
2. abstain 4. dispose 6. expand 8. recur 10. transfer

Exercise 3. (a) The extract from *The Nature of Prejudice* is from an American book, and includes several examples of American spelling:

programs favor neighbor practices (verb).

What would the normal English spelling be for these and for the
following?

anesthetic; vigor; mold; canceled; traveling; fulfillment;
skillful; worshiped; center; defense.

Each of these is representative of a group of words where the
American spelling differs from the English in one particular
way; the word "maneuver" represents two of these "rules" at
once. Deduce the rule in each case, and find at least one other
example of it.

(b) American English also differs from British English in
pronunciation. We saw in Book Four that English spelling is no
real guide to pronunciation:

"rough" is pronounced quite differently from "dough";
"few" is not at all like "sew";
"low" is quite unlike "sow" when the latter is a pig.

Many dictionaries therefore use a *phonetic alphabet*, and attempt
to create a distinct symbol for every sound. Even within the
British Isles, this may lead to difficulties since "brass", for
instance, has a long ā sound (â) in the south, but a short a (a)
in the north. However, an English dictionary gives the following
phonetic versions of twenty words taken (in this order) from the
passage in Exercise 1. The first is "race". Can you identify the
others?

rās	nūz-pā′pər	spē′shez
kon′flikt	thrōō	kon′trə-ri
prej′oo-dis	in′fin-it	pər′sn
i-nuf′	dis-krim′i-nāt	mar′ij
a-pärt′hāt	ik-sept-shən	sō′shl
dif′ər-əns	ni′groid	səs-pish′ən
rēd	di-fīni′shən	kən-spik′ū-əs

(c) Now see if you can pronounce the following words in both
the Standard English and the American English pronunciations
as given in phonetic form:

klärk—klərk	pē′ə-nist—pi-an′ist
dō′sīl—dos′il	prō′ses—pros′es
lezh′ər—lē′zhər	shed′ūl—sked′ūl
lef-ten′ənt—lūten′ənt	sut′l—sub′til
mis′īl—mis′l	tə-mä′tō—tō-mā′tō

Topics for Written Work

1. The existence of national, racial, religious and political prejudice and misunderstanding underlies most of the world's problems today. The subject is a vast one; choose *one* aspect of it for a discussion essay. Try to write factually and objectively, keeping opinion distinct from evidence. Prepare thoroughly by using reference books, newspaper articles, etc. Below are a number of possible subjects:

(a) The history of prejudice: religious persecutions in the past. The treatment of Jews in Europe, native tribes in Africa, slaves in America, etc. The ideal of the British Commonwealth and the problems resulting from free travel to Britain.

(b) Migrations of peoples: the growth of the United States and the British Dominions. Do any "pure" races exist? What prevents completely free movement from one part of the world to another? Why has Britain attracted people born in other parts of the world? List the main places they come from.

(c) Theories of segregation: The cases for and against the doctrine of "apartheid". Is integration possible? Examples of multi-racial societies.

(d) Race problems in Britain: discrimination in housing, employment and elsewhere. The growing number of coloured people born and bred in Britain. How far can legislation help? Can we alter attitudes? (See passage on pp. 262–3, Précis Ex. 1.)

(e) Conflict and violence: why has tension led to violence? Can Britain avoid the racial violence the United States has seen? Could the whole world split on racial lines? What should we do?

2. Imagine that you have fallen in love with a person of a different skin colour, religion or social background from yourself and know you will meet objections from your family if you marry him or her. Write a letter to a relative who is prejudiced against your marriage, trying to allay his fears and convince him that you must marry the person you love.

COMMONWEALTH MIGRATION TO AND FROM U.K.

(in thousands)	By Sea only				By Sea & Air			
	1960	1962	1964	1966	1968	1970	1972	1974
From: Canada, Australia New Zealand	28·5	23·6	31·9	36·5	49·0	53·4	48·7	39·4
From: Rest of Commonwealth	45·8	35·2	87·4	77·6	87·7	69·4	81·8	50·7
Total Immigration	74·3	58·8	119·3	114·1	136·7	122·8	130·5	90·1
Total Emigration	88·7	91·2	166·8	203·1	169·3	169·8	133·1	155·8

Oral Work

1. Hold a discussion on the racial problem in this country. What can and should be done to help people of different races live happily together in Britain?

What, in your opinion, are the main reasons for racial tension and prejudice? Does more prejudice exist against coloured immigrants than against white immigrants? Is there any foundation for such prejudice? (Do not rely on hearsay and limited personal experience; try to obtain statistics and objective facts.) List the countries from which immigrants to Britain come. What proportion of these immigrants are coloured? Should the entry of all immigrants be controlled? Is there any justification for controlling only the immigration of coloured people? Once immigrants have been accepted into this country, what can be done to ensure that they are treated on an equal basis with other citizens? Should the authorities try to prevent certain areas being heavily populated by certain racial groups, or should these people be allowed to live wherever they choose? What can be done to dispel racial prejudice and distrust?

2. The subject of civil rights and equality for coloured peoples has inspired a whole protest movement with its own poetry and music. Collect together an anthology of words and songs, printed and recorded and from this select a programme to illustrate the theme of protest and the history of folk-songs on this theme, particularly in the United States and from the original Negro traditions. Link your programme with an explanatory narrative summing up the history of this struggle for freedom and true equality.

Activities and Research

1. Investigate the world's race problems from both background books and current newspaper reports. Find out about:

Apartheid in South Africa, the pass laws and Sharpeville.

The Ku-Klux Klan, the Civil Rights movement and Black Power in the U.S.A., the freedom marchers.

Dr. Martin Luther King, Mahatma Ghandi, Pastor Niemuller, Alan Paton, Chief Albert Lutuli, Father Trevor Huddleston.

The history of the Abolition of Slavery, including the work of Wilberforce in Britain and Lincoln and others in the American Civil War.

51

Further Reading

The Nature of Prejudice by GORDON W. ALLPORT (Addison-Wesley) (301.15)
This is a comprehensive study of all aspects of prejudice as seen by an eminent American professor of psychology. It is packed with examples and facts, and is an excellent source-book for anyone who wishes to think straight on this highly emotional subject.

Uses and Abuses of Psychology by H. J. EYSENCK (Penguin) (159.9)
This contains a shorter but very thought-provoking section on "Social Attitudes", including our tendency to generalize by national "stereotypes" and the psychology of anti-semitism.

To Sir, With Love by E. R. BRAITHWAITE (Blackie; Bodley Head; Heinemann)
This is the story of a West Indian teacher in a tough school in London's East End, and of how he gradually wins not only his pupil's respect but also their affection.

Paid Servant by E. R. BRAITHWAITE (Bodley Head; Four Square)
The search for foster-parents for a four-and-a-half-year-old coloured boy is described with "unsentimental warmth".

A Dance in the Sun by DAN JACOBSON (Penguin)
At one level this can be enjoyed simply as a novel of suspense; but the real subject of the book is race relationships in South Africa.

To Kill a Mockingbird by HARPER LEE (Heinemann; Pan)
Scout, the narrator, tells the story of three years of her childhood in a southern American town where her father, the lawyer Atticus, attempts to defend a Negro accused of rape. This novel paints a sympathetic picture of the children and their relatives and neighbours, and the dangers and tensions arising from prejudice.

The Proud American Boy by RUSSELL BRADDON (Hutchinson)
This story is similar in theme to Harper Lee's novel and although perhaps less well-written, it is even more shocking since it is based directly on fact. An eight-year-old child (accused of rape!) becomes the victim of racial prejudice and hate.

CHAPTER FOUR

Prejudice - II

THE RESULTS OF PREJUDICE

CAST: SHIRLEY ROBINSON, *the hotel receptionist.*
MISS MOLLY JONES, *a teacher on a walking tour.*
MISS DORA SMITH, *her friend, lame with blistered feet.*
MRS. BLAKE, *an elderly permanent hotel resident.*
MISS BROWN, *manageress of the hotel.*

SCENE: The entrance hall of a small country hotel one wet evening in late October. The receptionist has just called in the manager to explain that there is no booking for MISS SMITH. MRS BLAKE *is seated by the coffee table to the right of the fireplace.*

JONES: Nonsense. I booked 'em. For Jones and friend.
BROWN: But not for Miss Smith. We didn't reserve that room for Miss Smith.
SMITH: It doesn't matter. I'll be satisfied with any other room.
BROWN: Ah, there's the pity. We have no other room. I'm sure you'll find another hotel. One able to accommodate you.
JONES: Oh, talk sense.
BROWN: I hoped I had made the situation quite clear.
JONES: That you refuse to . . .
BROWN: That the hotel is quite full.
JONES: You should keep your staff in the picture. She told us that you were empty.
SHIRLEY: But they didn't say.
BROWN: Shirley, you may go.
SHIRLEY: Yes, Miss Brown.
JONES: Disposing of the evidence? You stay here . . . I said stay.
BROWN: I accept all responsibility. I am in full control here.
JONES: You refused. That's the situation, isn't it? My friend Miss Smith . . . You refused to . . .
BROWN: I haven't said so.
JONES: Then say it now.
BLAKE: Yes.

SMITH: I don't believe it.

(*She goes to a chair by the coffee table*).

SMITH: I don't . . .

(*She sits. As she does so, Mrs. Blake gets up*).

BLAKE: Excuse me.

(*She crosses to the settle, and sits. There is a slight shocked, pause*).

BLAKE: One has principles. Not that I hold anything against the young woman personally. She may be a sweet girl, devoted to her parents, and fond of animals. But a line must be drawn somewhere.

JONES: Will someone translate?

BLAKE: The gesture was melodramatic, I admit. But now you understand the position of the manager. She has others to consider.

SMITH: Suddenly I'm untouchable?

BLAKE: It's a question of standards. Other hotels are not so particular. Forgive my speaking so bluntly: I've no wish to hurt anyone.

JONES: I'm allowed, but she's not. Where's the logic? Where's the difference between us? Miss Brown, the manager . . .

BROWN: We are always open. Winter and summer. To anyone. With absolutely no discrimination. We have a reputation. But when the hotel is full, what more is there to say?

JONES: Would you recognize a lie if you saw it face to face?

BROWN: Please accept the situation. Feelings can be hurt so easily.

JONES: Do I have to shout to make myself understood? Why?

BLAKE: As if it weren't obvious. She is a . . . a . . . (*She struggles with a word which is obviously distasteful*) A Smith!

JONES: A what?

BLAKE: You can hardly expect me to repeat the word.

SMITH: My name? Because of my name you refuse to . . .

BROWN: I have never refused. I made that quite clear.

JONES: I'm losing my grip on reality. You're not real. You're only delirium—a touch of fever. A couple of aspirins, and a good night's rest, and you'll vanish.

SMITH: But my name's only a word—a sound. Smith.

BLAKE: Ugh.

SMITH: Smith. What does that mean? Nothing. Except that my father's name was Smith.

BLAKE: It runs in the blood. A Smith is a Smith, and you can't get away from it.

54

SMITH: I never wanted to.

BLAKE: The arrogance of the tribe!

JONES: Since when have Smiths been untouchable?

BROWN: There's nothing to be gained by an inquisition.

JONES: You there.

SHIRLEY: Me?

JONES: What does the name Smith mean to you?

SHIRLEY: I'd rather not say, miss.

JONES: Why not?

SHIRLEY: I was always told it wasn't very nice.

JONES: Told! What were you told?

SHIRLEY: I'd rather not say.

JONES: Why?

SHIRLEY: Because it's not very nice.

BLAKE: Have you ever consulted a telephone directory? Have you ever looked at the pages devoted to Smiths? Have you ever considered how they outnumber the rest of us? Think it over some time. When you've thought long enough, you'll realize why some of us are concerned. They're a powerful group—the Smiths.

SMITH: You're afraid—of me?

SHIRLEY: When I was a little girl, I was told never to play with the boys in the next yard. They weren't our sort. They were taken away in the end, and I never heard what happened to them. Their name was Smith. I think. At least, when I think of Smiths, I think of them.

BLAKE: Everywhere one turns, one meets them. They crawl through our daily life like an unmentionable disease.

SHIRLEY: I was always told that if I wasn't a good girl, the Smiths would come for me.

BLAKE: There are Smiths in the law, Smiths in medicine, Smiths in politics, Smiths in the church, Smiths in the army, navy, and air force, in the police, in the prisons, in the Commons, in the Lords, Smiths in the B.B.C. . . .

SHIRLEY: I was always told never to trust a Smith. They'll do you down as soon as look at you.

BLAKE: Commerce is riddled with them—W. H. Smith, Smith's Clocks, Smith's Crisps . . .

SHIRLEY: I was always told that Smiths never use a handkerchief.

BLAKE: Make no mistake: Smiths are a menace to the English way of life.

SMITH (*jumping up*): Stop it. Stop it!

SHIRLEY: I was told they ought never to have been let in the country in the first place.

BROWN: That will do, Miss Robinson.

SHIRLEY: Yes, Miss Brown. (*Turns to go.*)

BROWN (*to* MISS JONES): With your permission of course.

(*She nods to* SHIRLEY, *who goes.*)

JONES: She makes me ashamed of being a teacher. "I was told". If we can't teach them to think for themselves, what's the use of trying to teach anything?

SMITH: She did offer to find a bandage.

BROWN: Will you be taking your pack now?

(MISS SMITH *limps over to* MRS. BLAKE. MRS. BLAKE *shrinks to the end of the settle.*)

SMITH: Why should you want to hurt me?

BLAKE: Typical. Typical.

SMITH: I never hurt anyone knowingly.

BLAKE: Kindly stop molesting me.

SMITH: We're human. Two eyes, two arms, two legs, one head, one heart. What else matters?

BLAKE: The government ought to take a stand. It would if it weren't corrupted from within. Whitehall is riddled with Smiths.

SMITH: What harm have I ever done to you?

BLAKE: You? Your crew! . . . When my husband died, I was provided for. We had both been careful: our generation was taught the value of thrift. We had prepared for a quiet old age. Even without him, life offered compensations; a small place of my own, with a garden, maybe—not so large as to be a burden, but enough to show the changing seasons. For the rest—books, firelight, and muffins for tea. It was provided for, in safe investments. The money was there. Only it wasn't quite enough. A few years ago perhaps . . . But now—dear me, no. The price of property, the cost of domestic help . . . The money is still there—on paper. But year by year, the figures mean less and less. And here I am, with no place of my own: only a hotel with special rates for permanents out of season: and in the summer, a top back room, with no running water. Why here? you may ask. Why not South Kensington or Bournemouth with the rest of the flock? I'm not a beggar: I prefer not to display my sores. But each year the money buys less and less. And what is the forecast for the year after

57

next? A charitable institution for faded gentlewomen? . . .
Who tainted the money? Who stole my Indian Summer?

SMITH: You poor dear . . .

(*She stretches out her hand to* MRS BLAKE. MRS BLAKE. *shrinks from her.*)

SMITH: Why shrink from me?

BLAKE: You smell.

(MISS SMITH *recoils with a cry.* MRS. BLAKE, *slightly embarrassed by her outburst, crosses to the coffee table.*)

BLAKE: I can smell out a Smith anywhere.

(MISS SMITH, *struggling to keep her composure, hurries across the room as well as she can, and picks up her pack.* MISS JONES *catches her arm.*)

JONES: Where do you think you're off to?

SMITH: Let me go.

JONES: How can you go like that?

SMITH: If I stay, I'll end by believing them.

JONES: You're not leaving them the last word. (*Urges* MISS SMITH *back to the settle.*) You've been walking all day remember? You're not splashing through the dark for three more miles.

BROWN: But if there's no alternative?

JONES: There is. Here.

SMITH: What they believe is twisted, but they believe it. They believe that I—that I . . .

JONES: You're not. Now will you sit, or do I have to make you?

BLAKE: I warn the management that I could not possibly stay in a place that harbours a Smith. No matter how favourable the out of season rates . . . Smiths! I've seen them in their long, shiny cars. Where does all that money come from, eh? How can they afford long, shiny cars when I wear the same coat year after year?

SMITH: Please, Molly.

BLAKE: Vice.

JONES: Sit.

(MISS SMITH *sits.*)

BROWN: Can't you let well alone?

JONES: That would suit you fine, wouldn't it? You nearly won. She was on her way out. . . .

BLAKE: There's no room for a Smith anywhere. We're better off without them. They're responsible for . . . They're responsible.

BROWN: However . . .

BLAKE: You're not weakening?

BROWN: We may be able to reach a compromise.

SMITH: Compromise?

BLAKE: What did you say?

BROWN: Compromise.

JONES: What does that mean?

BROWN: We have the annexe.

SMITH: The annexe?

BROWN: It used to be the boathouse—on the far side of the grounds. I had it converted. It is waterproof and draught-proof.

JONES: I see. Or think I see.

BROWN: It is used in the season for our overflow. It hasn't quite the amenities of the hotel, but it provides a useful second best.

JONES: Second best?

BROWN: But all our guests receive full attention. You could have your breakfast brought to your room. For the sake of the other guests, such as Mrs. Blake, I would prefer you not to use the dining-room.

JONES: Naturally they must be considered.

BROWN: I am making an effort. Aren't you willing to meet me half-way?

JONES: It's a compromise.

BROWN: It's a solution.

BLAKE: It's the thin end of the wedge.

BROWN: Do you object?

BLAKE: The only good Smith is a dead Smith. However, I wouldn't want the girl to catch pneumonia.

BROWN: Miss Jones? Shall I have a bed made up over there?

JONES: Two beds. We stick together.

BROWN: Thank you. I'll show the way. Don't bother about the packs: I'll have them brought straight over. We can pick up an umbrella on the way out. (*She leads the way to the left archway*) Will you come this way, Miss Smith?

SMITH: No.

BROWN: I beg your pardon?

SMITH: I'm afraid I had to say no.

BROWN: But we've just come to an agreement.

SMITH: My friend agrees. I didn't.

JONES: Dora!

SMITH: Sorry, Molly. But I do have a mind of my own.

BLAKE: You see. You see. Typical.

SMITH: I cannot take your second best.

BROWN: I don't think you understand. There is no room in the hotel, but I am offering alternative accommodation.

59

SMITH: And I am declining. It was a kind gesture: I appreciate what it must have cost you—after all, you have to live here with your permanent guests.

BROWN: The annexe is very comfortable. We've never had a complaint.

SMITH: I'm sure of that. But it's the division, you see. Sheep from goats. I can't agree with that.

JONES: But I'm coming with you. We're friends.

SMITH: Some of my best friends are Smiths.

JONES: That was uncalled for.

SMITH: Do I sound ungrateful? I'm sorry. I don't mean to be. But I have no intention of accepting the second class label. I can be turned out into the wet, but I cannot be forced into accepting your second-rate accommodation.

(from *Incident* by David Campton)

Appreciation and Discussion

1. Was the hotel full? In what circumstances was Shirley supposed to say it was full up?

2. Study Miss Brown's part in the dialogue in this extract. Does she in fact show any prejudice against Smiths? What other reasons might she have for refusing a Smith accommodation in her hotel?

3. Why does Miss Jones accuse Miss Brown of "disposing of the evidence" when she dismisses Shirley? What kind of evidence could Shirley give?

4. When Miss Smith accuses Miss Brown of refusing her a room only because of her name, Miss Brown says: "I have never refused . . ." Is this true, either literally, or by implication?

5. In what various ways does Miss Brown seek to calm down the situation during this argument?

6. Why does Shirley make Miss Jones feel ashamed of being a teacher?

7. On two separate occasions, Mrs. Blake refers to Miss Smith's behaviour as "typical". Typical of what? How does Mrs. Blake use Miss Smith's words or actions to support her own prejudice against Smiths?

8. (a) Why is Miss Smith willing to go when she picks up her pack? (b) Why does Miss Jones persuade her to stay and stick it out? (There are at least two reasons.)

9. (a) Why is Miss Jones willing to accept the "compromise" of the annexe? (b) Why does Miss Smith now refuse to accept this?

10. What contrasts are there between the prejudiced opinions of Mrs. Blake and those of Shirley? Would either attitude be easier to alter than the other? Can you divide their statements into "attitudes" and "beliefs" along the lines suggested by Allport in the passage in Chapter Three?

11. Which of the two school-teachers is more forthright and outspoken? What other contrasts are there between Miss Jones and Miss Smith?

12. Discuss some of the beliefs and attitudes about Smiths that are expressed here as examples of prejudiced thinking. Give examples from your own experience of similar condemnations of Jews or coloured immigrants or other foreigners or minorities (gipsies, for instance). Which statements would you describe as contradictory or circular arguments?

13. This play was first produced on television in 1965 and has been printed as a one-act play suitable for groups of amateur actresses. Is this an effective way of emphasizing the absurdity of racial prejudice? Would seeing this play, or acting in it, really change people's attitudes?

14. How do you think the play continues? Will Miss Smith leave? Will Miss Jones go with her, or will she argue that Miss Smith is a fool not to take the offer of a bed in the annexe? Will Miss Brown or Mrs. Blake make any further concessions?

Techniques

Exercise 1. Read the following passage carefully, and answer the questions below:

The subject of conflict between social groups and races is complex, but one important aspect of such conflict is undoubtedly "scapegoating". The word "scapegoat" was used in the Bible to describe a ritual under the Mosaic Law, during
5 which a goat was ceremoniously driven out into the wilderness. On the Day of Atonement, the high priest confessed all the sins of the people over the head of this goat, and then released it into the desert, so that the people could see this as a symbol of all their guilt being carried away. In modern times, a scapegoat
10 has come to mean any person or group of people that is blamed or punished for other people's faults or failures. The victims of scapegoating are not always completely innocent, but they are blamed for many things they are not in fact responsible for. Usually a scapegoat is a person or group that appears different
15 from other people and so can be easily picked out and criticized. They may speak a different language or have a distinctive accent. They may wear unusual clothes or have a different colour of skin or hair, or may have inherited peculiar features such as a short nose or narrow eyes. Or their whole culture,
20 religion or way of life may be conspicuously different from their neighbours'. Scapegoats are also people who are assumed to be inferior or underprivileged in some way, possibly physically weak, or poor, or ignorant; this assumption is often false, but it is probably widely held by the majority.
25 When do people turn against scapegoats? Scapegoating seems most likely to occur in times of stress; when a group of people (or a whole social class or nation, even) feel frustrated and defeated or are in prolonged fear for their lives or property, or have strong feelings of guilt. After defeat in war a nation may well turn on
30 weak individual leaders or on a minority group in the population. When a nation or a social class is in the midst of economic diffiulties, with much unemployment and poverty, class conflict or race hatred are very likely to occur. A group of recent or coloured immigrants, for instance, may well be blamed for all
35 the trouble. In Germany in the nineteen thirties, one effect of repeated defeat and economic depression was to encourage anti-Jewish feeling. The persecution of Christians in Ancient Rome is probably another example. At times of unemployment, or when there is conflict between class interests or war between nations,
40 people are naturally reluctant to blame themselves for their troubles. In any very repressive society, where men are always being made to feel guilty or find it very difficult to maintain the

high standards expected of them, they will be tempted to take
their sense of failure out on anyone who is weak or different
45 from themselves. In addition, the leaders of a community may
well encourage the persecution of scapegoats in order to direct
blame and criticism away from their own failures and crimes.

(a) What usually characterizes the persons or groups of people
chosen as scapegoats?
(b) What examples are given in the passage of groups persecuted as scapegoats? Add at least one other example from your
own knowledge of history or current affairs.
(c) Explain in a word or short phrase the meaning of the
following, as used in this passage:

(i)   a ritual (line 4);   (ii) a symbol (line 8);
(iii) inferior (line 22);   (iv) a minority group (line 30);
(v)   reluctant (line 40);   (vi) a community (line 45).

(d) After studying the passage, write *three* definitions of
"scapegoating" or a "scapegoat":
   (i) as an Old Testament ritual,
   (ii) as a word in modern English (an ordinary dictionary
        definition); and
   (iii) as a psychologist might define it, including brief
         reference to the way it arises and is practised.
(e) Make a summary of the main information in this passage in
not more than 170 of *your own words*. The passage is mainly
about "scapegoating" in the modern sense, and you can omit
examples as long as the information they illustrate is clearly
stated.

Exercise 2. When (in the extract from the play) Miss Brown
offers Miss Smith accommodation in the boathouse annexe, the
same offer is described in four different ways:

JONES: It's a compromise.
BROWN: It's a solution.
BLAKE: It's the thin end of the wedge.
SMITH: I cannot take your second best.

Each of the women chooses words to match her own attitude
or prejudice. A phrase like "thin end of the wedge" is an
emotionally toned equivalent to "compromise"; "second best"
indicates a different attitude from "alternative accommodation".

63

(a) Write out a suitable neutral or objective word or phrase that would be equivalent to the following emotionally toned words or phrases from the extract printed in *italics*. Discuss the associations of the original word or phrase used.

e.g. Not that I hold anything against the young woman personally. . . . But *a line must be drawn* somewhere.

The clause means "there are some matters about which I am not prepared to compromise".

1. It *runs in the blood*. A Smith is a Smith.
2. The *arrogance of the tribe*!
3, 4. They *crawl through* our daily life *like an unmentionable disease*.
5. Commerce is *riddled* with them.
6. Kindly stop *molesting* me.
7. You? Your *crew*! . . .
8. Who *tainted* the money?
9. I can *smell out* a Smith anywhere.
10. I could not possibly stay in a place that *harbours a Smith*.

(b) "Whitehall is riddled with them".

Short, emotive statements such as this are very persuasive. They make an impact because they are vivid, simple and easy to remember. Many people therefore accept them without thinking about their meaning. If we expand them, however, our reasoning powers at once begin to operate. Consider this expanded version of the quotation above.

I think that there are far too many people with the surname "Smith" working in the civil service.

It is now much easier to see what an absurd and over-simplified argument is being put forward. The condensed version is much more dangerous because it can slip past our critical faculties so easily.

Shirley, the receptionist, is a perfect example of a person who accepts short, emotive statements without ever thinking about them.

e.g. "I was told they ought never to have been let in the country in the first place".

Such statements do not convey thought. They avoid it.

Expand all the following statements in writing; and then in discussion point out the emotionally-loaded words, the over-simplifications, the sweeping assumptions, and the illogicalities of the views expressed in them.

1. Jews are a menace to the English way of life.
2. The only good Chink is a dead one.
3. Once a thief, always a thief.
4. Scratch a Socialist hard enough, and underneath you'll find a dirty Commie.
5. If we didn't have trade unions, we wouldn't have strikes.
6. Black and white don't mix.
7. Mixed marriages make mongrels.
8. Roman Catholics have too much power.
9. Writers and artists are pansies; they don't know what an honest day's work is.
10. We should leave the wogs to their own devices.

(c) Write a short neutral, factual or objective description of ten of the following, and then rewrite it so that it is biased first in favour of and then against the subject. Make your statements as closely paralleled as you can, allowing the emotive language to colour the biased versions, rather than altering the evidence itself.

e.g. The Police

(i) The duties of the 116 000 policemen and policewomen in England and Wales include the maintenance of public order and the prevention, detection and punishment of all crime and breaches of the law.

(ii) This small, stalwart band of reliable public servants have a multitude of duties to perform, including keeping the streets peaceful and safe for ordinary citizens, protecting the innocent victims of crime, and relentlessly pursuing criminals and law-breakers to bring them to justice.

(iii) The state employs a vast force of 116 000 police officers mainly to impose its authority over the general public and to hunt down and persecute not only criminals but also those who oppose any of the laws dictated by the establishment.

1. very rich people
2. gipsies
3. apartheid
4. Jesus Christ
5. pet dogs
6. communism
7. pacifists
8. the royal family
9. rugby football
10. tax avoiders
11. research scientists
12. poets
13. a hospital matron
14. steam locomotives
15. civil servants

Exercise 3. The cast list that heads the extract from the play contains several phrases *in apposition*.

Shirley Robinson, the hotel receptionist.

Simply by placing nouns or noun equivalents alongside one another, we can make them share the same function, e.g.

I'm sure you'll find another hotel, one able to accommodate you. Here "hotel" is the object of the verbs "find", and the pronoun "one" is also the object, repeating the same idea in a different context.

(a) Study and discuss the words, phrases and clauses in apposition in the following — both elements are printed in italics in each case.

1. *We British* are already a mixed race.
2. *The earliest inhabitants of these islands, the Celts,* have intermingled with many later invaders.
3. Even *the Principality* of *Wales* includes many people of mixed descent.
4. *The claim that we are pure-bred English* is almost meaningless.
5. *Saxons, Vikings, Normans, Flemings, Huguenots, Jews, Anglo-Indians, Poles, West Indians, all these* have illustrated *the principle that new blood adds new richness to our race and culture.*
6. *It* is virtually certain *that all of us have a mixed ancestry.*
7. *The purpose of the Race Relations Bill, to protect everyone from the effects of discrimination,* is clearly excellent.
8. *It* is the hope of many people *that we shall create truly multiracial communities throughout the world.*

(b) In four of the eight sentences in (a), a noun clause was in apposition to a noun or pronoun, and in numbers 6 and 8 the pronoun was "it". In clause analysis, noun clauses may often have this function, but this has to be distinguished from the adjectival function of a clause beginning with "that";

e.g. 1. The assertion that there was no prejudice in Britain seemed to be nonsense.

2. The assertion that the speaker made seemed to be nonsense.

Pick out the noun clauses in apposition in the following sentences, and in each case state what noun, pronoun or phrase it is in apposition to. Examine all other clauses introduced by "that" in the sentences.

1. One result of racial prejudice is the fact that coloured immigrants find that they cannot obtain good jobs.
2. It is often clear that they are quite sufficiently qualified for these jobs.
3. It is not their lack of qualifications that the employers object to.
4. However, the employers will often make assertions that the coloured applicants are less skilled.
5. The assertions that the employers make are all too often unfounded.

6. Coloured people also claim that they suffer from prejudice in housing.
7. It is often their experience that they are told that the accommodation has already been taken.
8. The landlords use the excuse that other tenants or neighbours would object.
9. This is the situation that is being satirized in the play *Incident*.
10. It is important that we should all be on our guard against groundless prejudices that we have accepted unthinkingly over the years.

(c) Compose noun clauses in apposition to complete the following sentences; be prepared to analyse the complete sentences.
1. It is quite obvious that..................
2. This suggestion that..................seemed the most reasonable.
3. I just had an idea that..................
4. It does not often happen..................
5. The hope..................proved groundless.
6. I find it difficult to accept the idea..................
7. The fact..................is not an excuse for what you did.
8. What you said makes it seem very likely..................

Topics for Written Work

1. Imagine yourself in the position of a "scapegoat", picked on by the majority because you are foreign, eccentric or different in colour, customs or creed. You are being treated as inferior, a second-class human being without the privileges or respect that other people enjoy. The majority of people hate or fear or despise you—they avoid you, make excuses for not letting you a room, not giving you a job, not sitting near you in the trains. What does it feel like to be discriminated against when you yourself are not guilty, not a criminal, not diseased, dirty, stupid or uncouth?

A number of writers, like David Campton, have explored this theme. At least one had his skin colour temporarily altered to see how it felt to be an American Negro. Coloured writers in

America and South Africa have explained their feelings. Plays and novels have looked forward to an age when coloured people have superiority in political and economic power, as they already have in total numbers, and when perhaps Europeans will become persecuted minorities.

Write an account of your attitudes and feelings in these circumstances, or the story of one day in the life of an immigrant in a hostile society that regards him as an inferior interloper.

2. (a) *Incident* was performed on television in 1965. Take part of the extract and work out a film shooting script for it, as we explained in Book Four. Begin like this:

VISION	SOUND
1. Long-distance shot of Jones, Smith, Brown, and Shirley in a group.	JONES: Nonsense .... friend. BROWN: But not .... Smith.
2. Close-up of Smith.	SMITH: It doesn't .... room.
3. Middle-distance shot of Jones and Brown, with Shirley in background.	BROWN: Ah .... you. JONES: Oh .... sense. BROWN: I hoped .... clear. JONES: That .... to. BROWN: That .... full. JONES: You .... empty.

(b) Alternatively, rewrite part of the dialogue of the play as the kind of direct speech used in a novel, adding suitable descriptive material.

Use a wide range of verbs to indicate tones of voice. Make sure that you paragraph and punctuate the direct speech correctly.

e.g. "Nonsense!" snapped Miss Jones. "I booked 'em. For Jones and friend."

"But not for Miss Smith," explained the manageress patiently.

"We didn't reserve that room for Miss Smith."

"It doesn't matter, "said Miss Smith, anxious to avoid any unpleasantness. "I'll be satisfied with any other room."

Miss Brown turned to her with a look of carefully composed regret.

68

Oral Work

1. *Incident* is an entertaining play, but it provides more than just entertainment. It sets out to make a point—to show how illogical are most forms of prejudice. Select a novel, play or film which comments on society on some way: explain what point it tries to put across and the approach it uses to do this. Prepare this as a talk to the class.

Give a *brief* outline of the plot and the characters, and state clearly what topic is being dealt with. What is the attitude of the novel, play or film to this topic, and what message is it putting across? Does it deal directly with the subject, or does it deal with it indirectly, as does *Incident*? Is the approach dramatic and serious? Are there humorous elements? Was it entertaining as well as thought-provoking? Did it serve to confirm your views or did it cause you to change them? You may include *Incident* as one of your three choices, and refer to other extracts in the *Art of English*, e.g. *Shot Actress—Full Story*, *The Prize of Peril*, *Animal Farm* or *The Grapes of Wrath* in Book Four.

2. Act or tape-record this extract from *Incident*. If necessary, adapt the play substantially to suit an all-male cast.

Activities and Research

1. The following films, which all deal with aspects of social and racial prejudice, are well worth seeing.

The Defiant Ones—Two convicts, one white and one coloured escape from a working party while chained together.

In the Heat of the Night—A coloured policeman and a white policeman are forced to work together on a murder case—a situation which leads to personal and racial conflict between them.

Sapphire—Another murder case, but this time set in England. Colour prejudice, on both sides, comes out during the questioning of suspects, after a half-caste girl has been killed.

The Fugitive Kind—Set in a small town in the Southern States of America, this film, based on Tennessee Williams' play *Orpheus Descending*, demonstrates the violent prejudice that that can exist against an "outsider".

The Loudest Whisper—Two young women teachers become the butt of false rumours, about their relationships, which tragically affect their lives.

Further Reading

Incident by DAVID CAMPTON (J. Garnet Miller) (822.91)
In an atmosphere that moves from wry comedy to near night-mare, the illogicalities, the fears and the frustrations behind all kinds of discrimination are uncovered.

Two other one-act plays by the same author are:
Soldier from the Wars Returning (J. Garnet Miller) (822.91)
A sentimental barmaid and a bartender reduce the morale of a gallant soldier, just back from active service, to such an extent that he becomes a self-pitying wreck.

Funeral Dance (J. Garnet Miller) (822.91)
Returning from her husband's funeral, Ida Hartshorne is accosted by a stranger, whose knowledge of the past can threaten her entire future.

The Crucible by ARTHUR MILLER (Heinemann; Penguin) (812.5)
This dramatic impression of the witch-hunt that took place in the American colony of Salem at the end of the seventeenth century is a powerful condemnation of social persecution and prejudice. It was written in 1953 when "McCarthyism" was prevalent in America and it therefore had a strong bearing on the contemporary situation.

Conflicting Generations edited by MICHAEL MARLAND (Longmans) (822.91)
The theme of conflict, misunderstanding and prejudice between the generations is the link between these five television plays. The authors are: John Mortimer, John Hopkins, Paddy Chayevsky, Ronald Eyre and David Turner.

Z Cars edited by MICHAEL MARLAND (Longmans) (822.91)
These four scripts, taken from the B.B.C. series, make a powerful and sensitive exploration of social tensions and prejudices.

CHAPTER FIVE

A Sense of Humour

Gulley Jimson is an old, drunken artist. He is also dedicated to his work, very poor, and rather eccentric. One of his eccentric habits is to make insulting telephone calls to his former patron, Hickson.

Just then I saw the telephone box and went in to try button B. And I thought: what a game to ring up old Hickson again. I rang him up, and he answered before I'd finished speaking his name. A big surprise. So I told him I was the Home Secretary. Put a ball of paper in my mouth. To give the official tone. Told him I had instructed Scotland Yard to set inquiries in motion relative to certain dealings in the matter of the artistic productions of the late Gulley Jimson. The late was a good idea. After all, you wouldn't expect one of these high officials to know anything about art or artists. He would be acting on a report.

"I beg your pardon," said Hickson, and I did the piece again.

"Excuse me, sir," said Hickson, "are you referring to works which I bought after the Exhibition of 1921, or the small unfinished canvasses acquired from Mrs Monday in 1926," and spoke so humbly and politely he might have been a contractor with a battleship to sell. And I thought, could he really be taken in? For, of course, all this telephoning to old Hickson was a bit of a game. He nearly always spotted me, even if he pretended not to. And then he would try to get in a nasty one, on the side. Like telling me to warn myself against being a nuisance. And I would try to give the old man a prod or two, to keep him thinking. After all, he had got those pictures pretty cheap.

But this time he really seemed to be taken in. And I thought it must be the newspaper. Perhaps the Home Secretary really has adenoids; and these big bugs are always on the telephone to someone or other, especially millionaires. So I went on to say that the whole of his transactions *re* Mr. Gulley Jimson's artistic output was under the gravest consideration by my technical advisers who took the most serious view of the legal anomalies involved by and for the same. I was prepared, I said, to allow for the time-factor, but I was led to think that according to my

71

legal department, and the appropriate acts, there was at least a prima facie case —

"I beg your pardon, sir," said Hickson. The paper was too big and made me so heehaw that the old man couldn't catch my words, and said, "I beg your pardon," every minute.

So we went on for some time. And Hickson even asked me to hold the line while he found a letter from Sara which he wanted to read to me.

And I was just putting my hand over the receiver in case he came back too soon and heard me laughing, when there was a tap on the glass. Made me jump a foot. And when I opened, a young chap I didn't know pulled me out by the arm and said, "They're after you. Plain-clothes cop. Been asking down at the Feathers if you had been using their box. Alfred sent me to look for you."

I didn't stop to argue. I got out and ran for it. I saw now why Hickson had been so sweet and reasonable and deaf for the last half-hour. Been on to the local police station to look round the telephones. Probably sent out the butler to the street 'phone.

What surprised me, my legs were so shaky. Kept on trembling so I could hardly run. And my head was buzzing round. Why, I said, I'm not upset or anything. I'm not angry with Hickson. Or am I. Funny thing if a chap can get in a state without knowing it. And I was half-way along Greenbank, puffing like a stream car, when I thought: Why you damned old fool, you're running right into jug. That's just where they'll come for you.

And when I stopped I felt so queer I had to lean against the wall. Heart doing a hanged man's jig. Knees shaking like an old horse at the knacker's. Cheeks jumping up and down all by themselves.

Anybody would have thought I was frightened to death. Funny, I thought, if a chap's body can be frightened and he not able to stop it. I don't care a blast for anybody. Let 'em jug me if they like. Let 'em put me away for five years—that will about finish me. It's only what I've got to expect. I'm ready for anything. But my face isn't. It'll give me away to the first copper. He'll take me up even if he doesn't know who I am. Loitering with a face. And I sat down on a garden wall to give my insides a rest.

Surrey all in one blaze like a forest fire. Great clouds of dirty yellow smoke rolling up. Nine carat gold. Sky water-green to lettuce-green. A few top clouds, yellow and solid as lemons. River disappeared out of its hole. Just a gap full of the same fire, the same smoky gold, the same green. Far bank like a magic island floating in the green. Rheumatic old willows trembling and wheezing together like a lot of old men, much alarmed at the turn of things were taking, but afraid to say so out loud.

I could do that, I thought. Those round clouds and the island in the sky, heavy as new melted lead. But what's the good of thinking about it. They've got me. For I saw that they had got me. And I began to feel better. That's that, I thought. They've got me. Here, I said to myself, that's all about it. Who are you to make all this fuss about yourself? Things are moving, that's all.

(from *The Horse's Mouth* by Joyce Cary)

Appreciation and Discussion

1. What is "button B" for, in the older type of 'phone-box? Why might Jimson make a habit of trying button B when he is passing a 'phone-box?

2. What suggests that Jimson was expecting a servant to answer the 'phone? How do you know that Hickson was rich?

3. What effect would the ball of paper have on Jimson's speech, and why did he use it?

4. What does "the late" mean when prefixed to a name, and why did Jimson think it a good idea to say it now?

5. Apart from the fun of it, what else might Jimson hope to get from telephoning Hickson in this way?

6. What do you think Hickson and Mrs. Sara Monday might have done to annoy Jimson?

7. (a) How did Hickson usually behave when he knew it was Jimson telephoning? (b) Why did he go on pretending to be taken in by this call? At what point do you think he got in touch with the police?

8. Give a brief explanation of each of the following: unfinished canvasses; on the side; adenoids; the legal anomalies; a prima facie case; heehaw; to hold the line; a hanged man's jig; Let 'em jug me; nine carat gold.

9. Was Jimson really frightened when he was running away? Why was he surprised at his own reaction? How did he calm himself down?

10. What did Jimson mean by "I could do that"? Why was it no good thinking about it? Why did he begin to feel better at this stage?

11. What effect does the style of this narrative have, with its many brief, incomplete sentences? Does it seem particularly appropriate to the narrator's train of thought?

12. Do the descriptive passages suggest a painter's eye view of the landscape? Discuss the comparisons used. What vocabulary might you expect from a composer, or an engineer?

13. Is this a kind of poetic prose? What characteristics make it like poetry?

14. Are practical jokes ever justifiable? Have you played jokes of a similar kind? Jimson had recently been in prison for a month for "uttering menaces" against Hickson; was Hickson justified in taking police action?

The Practical Joker

Oh, what a fund of joy jocund lies hid in harmless hoaxes!
    What keen enjoyment springs
    From cheap and simple things!
What deep delight from sources trite inventive humour coaxes,
    That pain and trouble brew
    For everyone but you!
Gunpowder placed inside its waist improves a mild Havana,
    Its unexpected flash
    Burns eyebrows and moustache.
When people dine no kind of wine beats ipecacuanha,
    But common sense suggests
    You keep it for your guests—
Then nought annoys the organ boys like throwing red hot coppers.
    And much amusement bides
    In common butter slides;

And stringy snares across the stairs cause unexpected croppers.

           Coal scuttles, recollect,
           Produce the same effects.
              A man possessed
                Of common sense
              Need not invest
                At great expense—
              It does not call
                For pocket deep,
              These jokes are all
                Extremely cheap.

If you commence with eighteenpence—it's all you'll have to pay;
You may command a pleasant and most instructive day.
A good spring gun breeds endless fun, and makes men jump like rockets—

           And turnip heads on posts
           Make very decent ghosts.

Then hornets sting like anything, when placed in waistcoat pockets—

           Burnt cork and walnut juice
           Are not without their use.

No fun compares with easy chairs whose seats are stuffed with needles—

           Live shrimps their patience tax
           When put down people's backs.

Surprising, too, what one can do with a pint of fat black beetles—

           And treacle on a chair
           Will make a Quaker swear!
              Then sharp tin tacks
                And pocket squirts—
              And cobbler's wax
                For ladies' skirts—
              And slimy slugs
                On bedroom floors—
              And water jugs
                On open doors—

Prepared with these cheap properties, amusing tricks to play
Upon a friend a man may spend a most delightful day.

SIR W. S. GILBERT

Discussing the Poem

1. Discuss any of the words and references that may prove puzzling: e.g. jocund, ipecacuanha, the organ boys, cobbler's wax.
2. Examine the effect of the rhyme: find examples of internal rhyme and feminine rhymes. Is the generous use of ryhmes, sometimes of unexpected words, appropriate to comic verse?
3. This is a song from a light opera. Does the rhythm seem appropriately regular? How does it fit with the rhyme?
4. Do Gulley Jimson's false 'phone calls come into the same category as these "harmless hoaxes"? Are practical jokes really harmless or are they justified in some circumstances and cruel in others?

ART OR HOAX?

Techniques

Exercise 1. Does our society make sufficient provision for talented eccentrics like Gulley Jimson? Would a less competitive society give more, or less, opportunity to exceptional individuals? Study the following passage with these questions in mind.

Some psychologists and social philosophers say that it is natural to compete, that human beings are bound to be com-

petitive and that without the spur of competition a society is
doomed to decline and be overthrown. They see the whole his-
5 tory of mankind as a kind of race between individuals, and between societies and nations, towards the goal of "progress", in
fierce competition to reach prosperity and comfort first.

This argument is easily disproved by anthropologists, who
can point to many cultures and tribes in the world where com-
10 petition is not encouraged and the individuals have no desire to
engage in any serious struggle to do better than their neighbours.
The Hopi tribe of American Indians, for example, teach their
children to cooperate and not to compete, and they make fun of
the individual whose aim is to win more property, honour or
15 power than his fellows. Competition, it can be shown, is not an
"instinct" that every person is born with, but an attitude to life
that he may—or may not—learn as he grows up.

In our society, here in England in the 1970s, we still encourage rivalry rather more than we encourage cooperation.
20 In school the child who does best or passes more subjects in
examinations than the others is given the prize. In sport the
individual's achievement is glorified according to the strength
of his opponents. In the world of work we compete for well-paid
jobs, we agitate for wage increases, we encourage firms to go all
25 out for more business than their trade rivals. A child in our
society grows up believing that he or she must do better than
other children, must try to earn more and own more and prove
himself more clever, if he is to have the respect of his family and
friends.

30 This competitive atmosphere may be a spur to much invention and progress, and it may often bring those with the best
abilities to the forefront of our society; but it has two opposite but
equally unfortunate results. On the one hand, for every successful person in any competition, there have to be several failures;
35 and for many people repeated failure in different directions
becomes disheartening, and rapidly puts them in a mood when
they no longer want to try, and do not even want to do well
what they can do. On the other hand, even the successful may
not be happy when they succeed, for they may be envied by
40 their friends who are not so clever or so skilful, and feel cut off
socially. They will then often feel that it is better not to do their
best in competition, but to pretend to be only mediocre; and
consequently the competition will not have completely suc-
ceeded in bringing forward the best talent after all.

(a) Comment on the use of the word "natural" (line 2) as used
here, and in the light of the discussion about what is "normal"
or "natural", in Chapter Two, on page 32.

77

(b) Explain the point the writer is making in the second paragraph of this passage, and show how the Hopi tribe exemplifies it.

(c) From this passage, give (in your own words) two advantages and two disadvantages of competition.

(d) Sum up in your own words the various ways in which (according to this passage) our society is competitive.

(e) Take any obvious metaphor from this passage and comment on its effectiveness.

(f) Explain what is meant by the following in this passage: prosperity (line 7); anthropologists (line 8); cultures (line 9); honour (line 14); an "instinct" (line 16); agitate (line 24); disheartening (line 36); mediocre (line 42).

(g) The passage contains about 470 words. Summarize it in between 140 and 160 words, avoiding the original language as far as possible. Give at the end the exact number of words you use.

(h) Sometimes you are asked to give a suitable title to a passage or your précis of it. Discuss what would be wrong with these possible titles for this passage:

(i) Competition.
(ii) Anthropologists Attack Prize-Giving.
(iii) Can we Learn from the Hopis?
(iv) Fame is the Spur.

Discuss the difference between an informative title and, on the one hand, a book title and, on the other hand, a newspaper headline. Note the proper punctuation of titles.

Make up a suitable title to sum up the theme of this passage in a few words.

Précis Rule 10. TITLES:
A title should sum up briefly the main theme of the passage. When you are asked to give a title, use more than one word, but less than a sentence; aim at about six words, and do not make it sensational.

Exercise 2. When Gulley Jimson is pretending to be the Home Secretary, he adopts what he thinks is a bureaucratic or civil service style of speaking, full of *jargon, circumlocution* and *redundancy.* Those who have to write business letters, reports and legal documents have to guard against this tendency to wrap up plain statements in language that they think impressive, or in clichés that obscure real meaning. Thus, we could paraphrase Jimson's message as:

78

"My advisers were seriously investigating all his dealings in Mr. Jimson's paintings, and they were disturbed because these seemed unusual. I said I was willing to be generous because it was a long while ago, but my legal advisers thought that he might be found guilty under present laws."

If Gulley Jimson had gone so far as to forge a letter from the Home Secretary, and had written it in this pompous style, it might perhaps have been like this:

Herbert Hickson, Esq.,   10th October, 1938.
98 Portland Place,
London, W.1.

Sir,

Re Artistic Works by the late Gulley Jimson

I regret that I have to inform you, with reference to your enquiry of the 29th ultimo, that certain anomalies not unconnected with your purchase of some ten of the above-mentioned works at the retrospective Exhibition of 1921 have now come to light.

On the 6th inst. investigations were put in hand with a view to ascertaining the truth of allegations of conspiracy to defraud the said Mr Gulley Jimson of his lawful fees for the items designated in the schedule herewith attached.

It is the considered opinion of His Majesty's legal 'advisers that, under the Conspiracy Acts of 1894 and 1896, sub-sections 300 and 462, paragraphs 24, 25 and 30 (as varied in the Fourth Schedule thereto, "Revaluation of Undervalued Works in the Medium of Oil-paint"), there is a prima facie case against you. The Minister takes the gravest view of your conduct in this connection, notwithstanding the lapse of time during which the works herein referred to have been in your possession. Your title to these artistic works now being in question, it should be noted that you must, of course, refrain from any attempt to offer the latter in whole or in part for public exhibition or private sale, pending the hearing of this case in the appropriate Courts of Justice.

I, remain, Sir,

Your obedient servant,

J. O. BULLDOG

Personal assistant.

For and on behalf of: E. Thompson Leaf, B.A., under-secretary to the Secretary of State for the Home Office.

Rewrite this as a plain business letter, without jargon or circumlocution, but conveying the same information and the same warning to Mr. Hickson.

Exercise 3. The "breathless" style that Gulley Jimson uses is largely achieved by omitting subjects or auxiliary verbs. When he is describing the landscape, it has the effect of a series of quick notes made as an aid to memory—like an artist's quick sketches done as a preliminary stage before attempting the main work.

(a) Mr. Jingle, one of Charles Dickens' characters in *Pickwick Papers*, employs a similar style when telling his stories. Here is one of his anecdotes, told as he swept under a low arch on top of a coach:

"Heads, heads—take care of your heads," cried the loquacious stranger. "Terrible place—dangerous—other day—five children—mother—tall lady—eating sandwiches—forgot the arch—crash—knock—children look around—mother's head off—sandwich in her hand—no mouth to put it in."

Rewrite the above in a more connected and coherent style, using complete sentences and the correct punctuation.

(b) Now rewrite the following anecdote twice, using markedly different styles. Firstly, combine the short jerky sentences into longer, well constructed units, so that the passage reads smoothly. Then, make it even more compressed and staccato by writing it as it might have been told by Mr. Jingle. Compare the different effects created by the different styles of writing.

A practical joke was played in Piccadilly Circus, London. A gang of navvies arrived. They fenced off half the road. They put up warning signs. They began to dig up the road. Traffic was thrown into confusion. Police arrived to direct it. The navvies worked furiously. Crowds stopped to watch them. At six o'clock the navvies left. A night-watchman remained. No navvies appeared the next day. The authorities were informed. They were amazed at the state of the road. They had not given orders for it to be dug up. The navvies were students. They had done it for a joke.

(c) Finally, rewrite the penultimate paragraph of the extract from *The Horse's Mouth*; use complete, smooth-flowing sentences. What effect does this have upon the tone of the paragraph?

Topics for Written Work

1. "Laughter can be cruel as well as kind". Either discuss this statement in an essay, or write a short story to illustrate it.

The ideas in Oral Work 1 may be of particular use if you decide to write the essay. Try to include examples to illustrate your arguments.

2. Select humorous incidents from *three* novels, plays or films and compare the ways in which the humorous effects are produced. The incidents should present strong contrasts in type, style or sense of humour. For example, slapstick, parody, situation comedy, verbal wit, comic characterization, the comedy of the absurd and satire can all be amusing, and are all well represented in books, plays and films.

Oral Work

1. Read the following passage and quotations aloud, and use these as a basis for discussion on "laughter and levels of humour". Illustrate points you wish to make with jokes and funny situations.

Most people think of laughter as a demonstration of delight, a joyful response to a humorous or pleasurable stimulus. But this relaxed form of laughter is produced only by civilized man. On a lower level, the function of laughter is often to provide a release from tension or frustration. Young children may giggle when being reprimanded, not because they intend to be disrespectful but because in this way they are able to ease the strain which the situation imposes on them. Similarly, poorly educated people may guffaw and jeer when somebody uses "long" words which they do not understand, or when they are faced with an unfamiliar situation. Even further down the scale we have the hysterical cackles of the lunatic and the frenzied screams of primitive savages.

Another distinction that can be made is between laughing *at* and laughing *with* a person. Laughter which is directed at somebody is predominantly cruel, derisive and lacking in good humour. When we laugh with somebody, however, we are showing that we are in sympathy, that we are putting ourselves on equal terms with him.

Humour itself, of course, varies enormously in kind and in quality. It ranges from intellectual repartee to raucous slapstick; it can evoke a wry smile or a hearty belly laugh. But underlying all genuine humour is a genuine humanity.

"Hazlitt desires that comedy should make him think better of mankind, whereas I demand of comedy only that it shall make me think."—JAMES AGATE.

"There is a cruelty, a heartlessness about much of the older humour which is sometimes shocking, sometimes, in its less extreme forms, pleasantly astringent and stimulating."—ALDOUS HUXLEY, writing about Ben Jonson's plays.

81

"This world is a comedy to those that think, a tragedy to those that feel."—HORACE WALPOLE.

"A sense of humour, and above all the capacity to laugh at oneself, is the basic ingredient of successful personal relationships."

"The French practise *wit*, a public, intelligent game with an element of cruelty; the English are *humorous* and enjoy their jokes privately with a sympathetic sense of fun."

2. Think of enough jokes to make up a three-minute script. Jot down the jokes in note form and then, working from these notes, tell your jokes to the rest of the class. Try to link the jokes together and, if possible, rehearse your script beforehand. Telling jokes requires very precise timing; it is worth studying the styles of well-known comedians.

Activities and Research

1. Make a survey of the styles used by different cartoonists. Select two or three really good examples from newspapers and magazines to represent each of the cartoonists now working, and mount these on a sheet together with some comment on the particular interests and the sense of humour of that cartoonist. Are some cartoons directed more at some sections of the population than at others? Are some cartoons so "satirical" that they cease altogether to be humorous?

2. In 1957, *The Observer* published a "brief guide" to the "—isms" of Modern Art. The list then included: Realism (from 1845), Impressionism (from 1869), Neo-Impressionism (from 1884), Symbolism (from 1888), Intruism (from 1890), Post-Impressionism (from 1885), Expressionism (from 1890), Fauvism (from 1905), Cubism (from 1907), Naïve Painting (from 1908), Non-figurative Art (from 1911), Futurism (from 1909), Surrealism (from 1925), Neo-Romanticism (from 1936), Social Realism (from 1945), Tachism (from 1950).

One might now add such movements as "Op-art", "Pop-art", "Psychedelic art" and "Destructive art". And all such labels are in some ways misleading generalizations—some artists fit no category, and others fit several.

Make a study of modern art and artists, using some of the categories given above as a starting point.

For the film of *The Horse's Mouth*, John Bratby painted a number of pictures that were supposed to be the work of Gulley Jimson. Find out more about John Bratby's work.

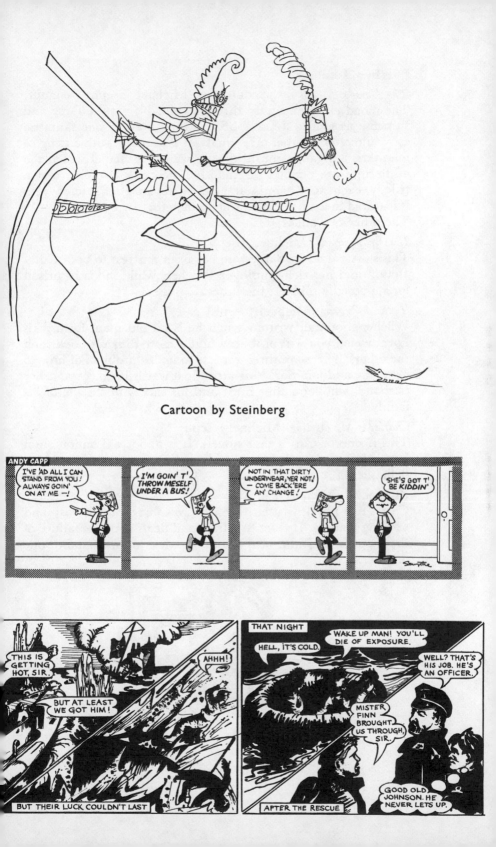

Cartoon by Steinberg

Further Reading

The Horse's Mouth by JOYCE CARY (Michael Joseph; Penguin)
The mood changes swiftly through comedy, pathos, farce and suspense as Gulley Jimson becomes involved in one fantastic escapade after another. His final act is to paint, with a gang of followers, a gigantic mural on the wall of a chapel which the authorities are about to demolish. The book is the first of a trilogy, each story being narrated by a central character, who is featured in a more minor role in the other two.
The other two books are:

Herself Surprised (Michael Joseph)
This story is told by Sara, who has been mistress to both Gully Jimson and her rich employer Wilcher, while she is in prison for supposedly robbing the latter.

To be a Pilgrim (Michael Joseph)
Wilcher's journal, written when he is an old man, forms this novel which you will probably find a more difficult book than the others. There are three aspects to it: his problem of how to get away and join Sara; his attitude towards his niece and her husband, who look after him; and his survey of the life of his family.

Charley is My Darling (Michael Joseph)
This is one of Cary's best novels. It is about a London slum boy, evacuated to Devon during the war, who ends up as a delinquent.

Aissa Saved (Michael Joseph)
Cary's first novel, written when he was forty-four, is easy and exciting reading. It is set in Africa and deals with the failure of the natives and the white missionaries to understand one another.

CHAPTER SIX

Attitudes - I

DIFFERENT VALUES

Maggie's father had been broken in health and spirit when his neighbour, Mr. Wakem, forced him to sell up the mill that the Tullivers had worked for generations. Her brother Tom hated the Wakems, and discovered that Maggie was secretly meeting Philip Wakem, an intelligent young man whom she found attractive despite his weak health and his twisted back.

"Is that all?" said Tom, looking straight at her with his frown.

Maggie paused a moment; then, determined to make an end of Tom's right to accuse her of deceit, she said, haughtily—

"No, not quite all. On Saturday he told me that he loved me. I didn't think of it before then—I had only thought of him as an old friend."

"And you *encouraged* him?" said Tom, with an expression of disgust.

"I told him that I loved him too."

Tom was silent a few moments, looking on the ground and frowning with his hands in his pockets. At last, he looked up, and said coldly—

"Now, then, Maggie, there are but two courses for you to take; either you vow solemnly to me, with your hand on my father's Bible, that you will never have another meeting or speak another word in private with Philip Wakem, or you refuse, and I tell my father everything; and this month, when by my exertions he might be made happy once more, you will cause him the blow of knowing that you are a disobedient, deceitful daughter, who throws away her own respectability by clandestine meetings with the son of a man that has helped to ruin her father. Choose!" Tom ended with cold decision, going up to the large Bible, drawing it forward, and opening it at the fly-leaf, where the writing was.

It was a crushing alternative to Maggie. . . .

"I *must* speak to Philip once more."

"You will go with me now and speak to him."

"I give you my word not to meet him or write to him again without your knowledge. That is the only thing I will say. I will put my hand on the Bible if you like.". . .

She felt it was in vain to attempt anything but submission. Tom had his terrible clutch on her conscience and her deepest dread: she writhed under the demonstrable truth of the character he had given to her conduct, and yet her whole soul rebelled against it as unfair from its incompleteness. He, meanwhile, felt the impetus of his indignation diverted towards Philip. He did not know how much of an old boyish repulsion and of mere personal pride and animosity was concerned in the bitter severity of the words by which he meant to do the duty of a son and a brother. Tom was not given to enquire subtly into his own motives, any more than into other matters of an intangible kind; he was quite sure that his own motives as well as actions were good, else he would have had nothing to do with them. . . .

Her heart beat with double violence when they got under the Scotch firs. It was the last moment of suspense, she thought; Philip always met her soon after she got beyond them. But they passed across the more open green space and entered the narrow bushy path by the mound. Another turning, and they came so close upon him that both Tom and Philip stopped suddenly within a yard of each other. There was a moment's silence, in which Philip darted a look of enquiry at Maggie's face. He saw an answer there, in the pale parted lips, and the terrified tension of the large eyes. Her imagination, always rushing extravagantly beyond an immediate impression, saw her tall strong brother grasping the feeble Philip bodily, crushing him and trampling on him.

"Do you call this acting the part of a man and a gentleman, sir?" Tom said, in a voice of harsh scorn, as soon as Philip's eyes were turned on him again.

"What do you mean?" answered Philip, haughtily.

"Mean? Stand farther from me, lest I should lay hands on you, and I'll tell you what I mean. I mean, taking advantage of a young girl's foolishness and ignorance to get her to have secret meetings with you. I mean, daring to trifle with the respectability of a family that has a good and honest name to support."

"I deny that," interrupted Philip impetuously. "I could never trifle with anything that affected your sister's happiness. She is dearer to me than she is to you; I honour her more than you can ever honour her; I would give up my life to her." . . .

86

"I should be very sorry to understand your feelings," said Tom, with scorching contempt. "What I wish is that you should understand *me*—that I shall take care of *my* sister, and that if you dare to make the least attempt to come near her, or to write to her, or to keep the slightest hold on her mind, your puny miserable body, that ought to have put some modesty into your mind, shall not protect you. I'll thrash you—I'll hold you up to public scorn. Who wouldn't laugh at the idea of *your* turning lover to a fine girl?"

"Tom, I will not bear it—I will listen no longer," Maggie burst out in a convulsed voice.

"Stay, Maggie!" said Philip, making a strong effort to speak. Then, looking at Tom, "You have dragged your sister here, I suppose, that she may stand by while you threaten and insult me. These naturally seemed to you the right means to influence me. But you are mistaken. Let your sister speak. If she says she is bound to give me up, I shall abide by her wishes to the slightest word."

"It was for my father's sake, Philip," said Maggie, imploringly. "Tom threatens to tell my father—and he couldn't bear it: I have promised, I have vowed solemnly, that we will not have any intercourse without my brother's knowledge."

"It is enough, Maggie. *I* shall not change; but I wish you to hold yourself entirely free. But trust me—remember that I can never seek for anything but good to what belongs to you.". . .

Tom and Maggie walked on in silence for some yards. He was still holding her wrist tightly, as if he were compelling a culprit from the scene of action. At last Maggie, with a violent snatch, drew her hand away, and her pent-up, long-gathered irritation burst into utterance.

"Don't suppose that I think you are right, Tom, or that I bow to your will. I despise the feelings you have shown in speaking to Philip: I detest your insulting unmanly allusions to his deformity. You have been reproaching other people all your life—you have been always sure you yourself are right: it is because you have not a mind large enough to see that there is anything better than your own conduct and your petty aims."

"Certainly," said Tom, coolly. "I don't see that your conduct is better, or your aims either. If your conduct, and Philip Wakem's conduct, has been right, why are you ashamed of its being known?"

"I don't want to defend myself," said Maggie, still with vehemence: "I know I've been wrong—often, continually. But yet, sometimes when I have been wrong, it has been because I have feelings that you would be the better for, if you had them. If *you* were in fault ever — if you had done anything very wrong, I should be sorry for the pain it brought you; I should not want punishment to be heaped on you. But you have always enjoyed punishing me—you have always been hard and cruel to me: even when I was a little girl, and always loved you better than anyone else in the world, you would let me go crying to bed without forgiving me. You have no pity: you have no sense of your own imperfection and your own sins." . . .

Maggie went up to her own room to pour out all that indignant remonstrance, against which Tom's mind was close barred, in bitter tears. . . . If she had felt that she was entirely wrong, and that Tom had been entirely right, she could sooner have recovered more inward harmony; but now her penitence and submission were constantly obstructed by resentment that would present itself to her no otherwise than as a just indignation. Her heart bled for Philip: she went on recalling the insults that had been flung at him with so vivid a conception of what he had felt under them, that it was almost like a sharp bodily pain to her, making her beat the floor with her foot, and tighten the fingers on her palm.

And yet, how was it that she was now and then conscious of a certain dim background of relief in the forced separation from Philip? Surely it was only because the sense of deliverance from concealment was welcome at any cost.

(from *The Mill on the Floss* by George Eliot)

Appreciation and Discussion

1. Explain in your own words why Maggie did not want to go on deceiving Tom.
2. Why did Tom force Maggie to give up Philip? Was he only thinking of the blow to his elderly and embittered father, if he heard of their friendship?

3. How did Maggie's promise in fact differ from the promise Tom wanted her to make?

4. (a) What did Maggie imagine Tom might do to Philip? (b) Does Tom make it seem likely that he will act in the way she imagines?

5. Maggie says she despises the feelings Tom shows in speaking to Philip—what feelings *does* he show? Is his attitude to Philip despicable?

6. Why does Tom reply to Maggie's outburst "coolly"? Why does he close his mind to her remonstrations?

7. What particularly does Maggie resent about Tom's attitude and behaviour?

8. What still gives Maggie some sense of relief after this incident?

9. What kind of person does Tom appear to be from this incident? What various feelings does Maggie apparently have for him as a brother?

10. Find evidence in this passage that, in addition to her love for Philip and her wish to spare her father, Maggie has a great respect and admiration for her brother.

11. What kind of girl is Maggie, as seen in this incident?

12. Does Philip emerge well from this incident? What do you respect about him or his behaviour?

13. What do the following words and phrases mean in this passage? exertions; clandestine; demonstrable; the character he had given to her conduct; the impetus of his indignation; repulsion; animosity; intangible; honour her; in a convulsed voice; intercourse; insulting unmanly allusions; vehemence; indignant remonstrance; obstructed by resentment.

14. Comment on the figurative language in the following:

(a) a crushing alternative to Maggie;

(b) Tom had his terrible clutch on her conscience and her deepest dread;

(c) she writhed under the demonstrable truth;

(d) with scorching contempt;

(e) her pent-up, long-gathered irritation burst into utterance;

(f) Tom's mind was close barred;

(g) it was almost like a sharp bodily pain to her, making her beat the floor with her foot, and tighten her fingers on her palm.

Techniques

Exercise 1. The following passage is an extract from one of the 1967 "Reith Lectures" by Edmund Leach, in which he is discussing tensions on our society, particularly between young people and their elders. It is in the style of a radio talk, rather than a formal lecture or written article.

Just now with moralists and politicians, high court judges and Fleet Street journalists all teaming up together, the adolescent is having a pretty rough time. The youth of Britain, we are told, is hell-bent for self-destruction. . . . The young are talked about
5 as if they were an anarchist fifth column. The old react with consternation. Should they exact summary vengeance or offer appeasement in the form of votes at 18? This is all very odd.

Tension between the generations is normal for any society; every son is a potential usurper of his father's throne; every
10 parent feels under threat; but the present anxiety of British parents seems altogether out of proportion. Young people are being treated as an alien category: "wild beasts with whom we cannot communicate". They are not just rebels but outright revolutionaries intent on the destruction of everything which
15 the senior generation holds to be sacred. . . .

You must be on your guard against cliché explanations. Some people will tell you that youthful disorder is just a symptom of the breakdown of family life. I can see no justification for this view. Nearly all the large-scale social changes which
20 have been taking place over the past century have been of a kind that should have brought the children closer to their parents rather than the other way about. The shortening of hours of work, improvements in housing standards, paid holidays, the prohibition of child labour, the extension of formal day-school
25 education, the disappearance of domestic servants should all, on the face of it, have helped to intensify family cohesiveness. But in practice it seems to work out the other way: the adults are now inclined to treat the teenagers as alienated ruffians — and not wholly without cause. Teenage gang warfare and the
30 wrecking of public amenities is a reality. What has gone wrong?

Well, up to a point the old seem to be simply responding to visual signals. The young quite systematically and quite consciously go out of their way to look unconventional, and the old react by believing that the young really are unconventional.
35 Quite a lot of the alarm is generated by sheep in wolves' clothing! But even if you should agree that the young are not really as rebellious as they look, you may still demand an explanation. What are the young people getting at? Why do they try to be so outrageous?

40　Well, mostly, of course, they don't know, they are just imitating one another. But the leaders, who *do* know, have a perfectly good political case. They argue that they are the involuntary heirs to a generation of incompetents. Their seniors, who still keep all the power in their own hands, have made a total mess

45　of things. It is these incompetent adults who manage the educational system and lay down rules about what young people are supposed to learn. The whole set-up is rigged to fit the belief that, when the young grow up and come to power, they too will carry on running the show just as before. But this assumption

50　makes cooperation impossible. If the old expect the young to participate in planning the future, then they might at least take the trouble to find out what sort of future the young would actually like to have.

(from *The Listener*, Nov. 1967)

(a) Discuss or write explanations of the following words or phrases:

an anarchist fifth column (line 5); consternation (line 6); exact summary vengeance (line 6); offer appeasement (lines 6–7); out of proportion (line 11); an alien category (line 12); cliché explanations (line 16); intensify family cohesiveness (line 26); alienated (line 28); public amenities (line 30); outrageous (line 39); involuntary heirs (lines 42–43); incompetents (line 43).

(b) Discuss the use of the following examples of colloquial language. What does each mean? Is the use of this kind of language justified in a radio talk?

having a pretty rough time (line 3); hell-bent for self-destruction (line 4); fifth column (line 5); getting at (line 38); made a total mess of things (lines 44–45); the whole set-up is rigged (line 47); carry on running the show (line 49).

(c) Apart from phrases quoted in (b), there are some interesting metaphors in this passage. What is the comparison in each of the following, and how effective is it?

with moralists (etc.) ... all teaming up together (lines 1–2); every son is a potential usurper of his father's throne (line 9); youthful disorder is just a symptom of the breakdown of family life (lines 17–18); alarm is generated by sheep in wolves' clothing (line 35–36).

(d) If you were asked to make notes in answer to the question "What are the explanations given here of the particularly serious rift now to be found between young people and their elders?", would you agree with the following headings?

(i) Not simply that parents have no time for children.
(ii) Not simply because teenagers dress unconventionally.
(iii) Articulate youth dissatisfied with mismanagement by elders.
(iv) Adults assume world will not change and do not consult youth about their future.

Notice that the notes are not an outline summary of the *whole* passage. Expand them into a fully written summary of the answer to this one question only, as given by this passage. You should not use more than *120 words* in all. *Begin as follows,* and then add up to 100 more of your own words.

> Edmund Leach does not think that the present serious rift between young people and their parents is explained simply by . . .

Exercise 2. In reading novels and plays from the nineteenth century or earlier, one finds many examples of words that are shifting in meaning, so that in modern English rather different interpretations of these words have become the standard ones. Even in our extract from *The Mill on the Floss* (published in 1860), the words "trifle", "intercourse", "irritation" and "conception" are used in senses that have been overtaken by others in common, modern usage.

(a) The following sentences use words of this kind in their older sense. The words or phrases in each case are printed in italics. Explain briefly the old-fashioned meaning of each, and then compose a sentence using each in one of its more common modern senses:

e.g. While Keats was slowly dying of *consumption*, he wrote some of his finest poetry.
consumption—tuberculosis
Britain's consumption of sweets is the highest per head of population in the world.

1. The squire's son was a man of *singular* habits who was often seen alone.
2. Without an *independence* he was scarcely eligible as a prospective wooer.
3. He was in fact destined *to take orders* in the church upon the death of the local *incumbent*.
4. When *agreeable* young men came to stay, the squire's young daughters could only hope one of them would *make an offer*.

93

5. The girls had no fresh *intelligence* from their brother in Yorkshire:
6. Too *reserved* in manner, he *wanted* the polish and style to be considered a real gentleman.
7. The newcomer's whole *address* was charming.
8. They would be very *sensible* of the honour done to them by his lordship.
9. For a small *consideration*, the servants would be discreet.
10. The ghost's appearance in that *habit* created an *awful sensation* in the *breasts* of the ladies present.
11. Since I have no *interest* in whether or not you accept his *suit*, having a *competence* of my own, I shall endeavour to accept your decision with *resignation*.

(b) Sometimes English from even earlier periods requires to be *paraphrased* before it is fully comprehensible to a modern reader. Make a paraphrase of the following translation of a passage from Sir Thomas More's book *Utopia* (published in Latin in 1516) in which he gives the views of the inhabitants of his ideal, imaginary country on the subject of hunting. A paraphrase is a translation, not a summary. It should neither add nor omit anything, although it may have to be slightly longer than the original in order to be clear.

What delight can there be, and not rather displeasure, in hearing the barking and howling of dogs? Or what greater pleasure is there to be felt when a dog followeth an hare than when a dog followeth a dog? For one thing is done in both, that is to say, running, if thou hast pleasure therein. But if the hope of slaughter and the expectation of tearing in pieces the beast doth please thee, thou shouldest rather be moved with pity to see a silly innocent hare murdered of a dog: the weak of the stronger, the fearful of the fierce, the innocent of the cruel and unmerciful. Therefore all this exercise of hunting, as a thing unworthy to be used of free men, the Utopians have rejected to their butchers, to the which craft (as we said before) they appoint their bondmen. For they count hunting the lowest, the vilest and most abject part of butchery, and the other parts of it more profitable and more honest, as bringing much more commodity, in that they kill beasts only for necessity, whereas the hunter seeketh nothing but pleasure of the silly and woeful beast's slaughter and murder. Which pleasure in beholding death they think doth rise in the very beasts, rather of a cruel affection of mind, or else to be changed in continuance of time into cruelty by long use of so cruel a pleasure.

(translated by Ralph Robinson, 1551)

Exercise 3. Read and compare these two articles about young people, and answer in discussion or writing the questions that follow.

I LIKE TEENAGERS

Don't get the idea that I dislike teenagers. I don't. I think they're very quaint. I like 'em. But when I look at them teeming around me, I can't help having a few doubts sometimes. Can you?

CHEAP TRIMMINGS

For a start, take the clothes they wear. We're constantly being told that the kids today are more fashion conscious than we were when we were minors. All this means, of course, is that they waste a lot of money getting through more trends faster.—The kindest way to describe their cheap trimmings is probably "original". (A favourite word with the glossy little magazines that cater for their adolescent egos.) Certainly, "graceful", "pretty", and "elegant" are OUT!

MUSIC?

Then there's their "music". An astonishing mixture of tarted-up spirituals and 1930s sob stuff. With just an occasional dash of strangled Stravinsky or beaten-up Bach to make it seem intellectual. Need I say more?

CONFUSED

But perhaps the most alarming thing about the present batch of juniors is what goes on inside their "minds". Buttressed by their bulging money belts, working-class youngsters now believe they're as good as anybody else. And their contemporaries further up the social scale actually agree with them. Which is all RUBBISH—if you're honest about it! Your dustman may be a very nice chap but you don't find him rubbing shoulders with members of the aristocracy. Social differences are something that, as adults, we accept. The under-twenty-ones, however, haven't even got around to recognizing this fact of life. Let alone accepting it.—Just because they may like the same kind of music, a public schoolboy and a junior roadsweeper will deliberately try to pretend there are no differences between them. How confused can you get?!

REFUSE TO LISTEN

Still it wouldn't be so bad if they just assumed they were equal with each other. But no! They also reckon they're as good as their elders and betters. They refuse to listen to adult advice, whether its about their personal habits, or wider issues such as politics. Now, I may be a little naïve, but I don't see how any sixteen-year-old can possibly be as mature or as knowledgeable as someone of our age.

TOOTHLESS MONGREL

But what depresses me most of all is their wish to disown the country of their birth. They're not proud of being British. They don't want to uphold the British way of life. Instead they ape the customs of

95

every other country under the sun. Go to Spain these days and you can't tell the young British tourists from the rest. They might just as well be foreigners. Patriotism is a dirty word. The British bulldog has become a toothless mongrel.

HEAVEN HELP US IN THE NEXT WAR
Today's teenagers certainly won't!

* * * * *

(ii) A great deal has been written about the teenagers of today. Much of it consists of nothing more than prejudiced opinion, with no basis in fact. I do not claim to be an expert on the younger generation, but at least I shall try to be *objective*.

One fact that cannot be disputed is that they are *better-dressed* than previous groups of teenagers have been. And this is not simply because they spend more money on clothes: our children take more interest in their appearance; they are certainly more colourful; and they are probably cleaner.

Their musical tastes, as reflected by pop music, are more *advanced* than ours were when we were young. Highly respected music critics of such newspapers as the *Sunday Times* and *The Guardian* have confirmed this view. This is not to say that all modern pop music is worthy of serious attention, but it is a grave error of judgement to condemn it *in toto* as "rubbish".

But perhaps the most encouraging thing about young people today is their increased *maturity*. This is probably derived, in part, from their increased economic power, and it may, of course, be only superficial sophistication; but I personally believe it goes much deeper than that. For example, when I was a teenager, society was rigidly divided into social classes, which came into contact with each other only in jail or the army. Today's teenagers have *dismissed* these *class* barriers. They are not in the least self-conscious about it either. When I visited a local club recently and spoke to some of its members, I found that they came from widely differing social backgrounds. But when I asked them to comment on this, they were simply not interested. They regarded the question of class as completely unimportant, so trivial, in fact, that it was not worth discussing.

Their self-assurance asserts itself in other ways too. They don't accept that they should be *told* what to do by adults. In their private lives they expect to be able to determine, to a large extent, how they behave. On public issues they expect their opinions to be recognized, and quite rightly so. However much some of their "elders and betters" may disapprove of these opinions, I fail to see how they can be any more foolish or dangerous than the policies of our present rulers, who have created a world in which international tensions and the threat of nuclear war are the order of the day.

96

What I find most heartening, though, is their rejection of nationalism: their outlook is truly *international*. When they go abroad, they
are often much more at ease then their parents are. One factor here
is the international nature of teenage fashions, which immediately
creates a link. But it is not the basis of their attitude, which rests on a
genuine understanding of the phrase "the brotherhood of Man".

With a little luck, the chances of world peace twenty years hence
will be greater than they have ever been during our lifetime.

(a) Quote the phrases used by the two writers to establish the
idea that they are fair-minded and impartial. Do you think
that either of these articles is completely detached and
balanced?

(b) Which article is written in a colloquial style? Which has the more difficult vocabulary? Which has the more complex sentence structure? Which contains incomplete sentences. Which layout is more eye-catching, and how is this effect achieved?

(c) Bearing the above points in mind, say which article most people would find easier to read.

(d) To what sort of audiences would the first article appeal? What sort of people would prefer the second article?

(e) The two articles follow the same paragraphing plan. What points are dealt with in each paragraph?

(f) What is the purpose of the paragraph heading in the first article? What technique does the second writer use to achieve the same effect?

(g) What emotionally-toned names does the first writer use when referring to young people? What association do these names have? What expressions does the second writer use to refer to young people? Are these emotive expressions?

(h) Which article is the more dogmatic? Quote some of the words and phrases which make the other article more guarded in its statement of opinion.

(i) In what respects, according to the second article, are today's teenagers better dressed? What enables teenagers today to be "cleaner"?

(j) Which of these two meanings is the question mark intended to give to the third paragraph heading in the first article?

    i. What shall I say about their music?

    ii. Can the sounds they like be described as music?

(k) Both writers use the phrase *elders and betters*, but in the second article it is enclosed in quotation marks. What difference does this make? Where has the first writer used quotation marks for the same purpose?

(l) Which of these two writers uses sarcasm and ridicule more? Quote relevant phrases.

(m) Is there anything illogical in the following argument? If so, explain where the illogicality occurs.

"The under-twenty-ones, however, haven't even got around to recognizing this fact of life . . . a public schoolboy and a junior roadsweeper will deliberately try to pretend there are no differences between them."

(n) What conclusion does the second writer reach about teenagers and social class? Do you agree with this conclusion?

98

(o) Does either writer produce real evidence to substantiate his views?

(p) Compare phrases in each of the following pairs and explain the difference in implication:

    i. "They refuse to listen to adult advice";
      "They don't accept that they should be told what to do by adults";

    ii. "their wish to disown the country of their birth";
      "their rejection of nationalism";

    iii. "their bulging money belts";
      "their increased economic power".

(q) Do you think either of these articles is typical of a real newspaper or magazine? Consider both the views expressed, and the styles of writing.

(r) With which article are you in general agreement? With which points in it do you disagree?

Topics for Written Work

1. Write the script of a speech, or an article suitable for a newspaper, defending young people of today against the attacks upon them from "moralists and politicians, high court judges and Fleet Street journalists" (to quote Edmund Leach). Many of the arguments used appear in Exercises 1 and 3 in this chapter, and the rest of the ammunition used against modern teenagers is familiar enough.

Try to make your defence reasonable enough to convince an adult audience. Explain what it is that young people react against in contemporary society, and how and why many young people would like to change the world. Try to be objective about your own generation, and to avoid the sweeping generalizations that condemn them all as hooligans or as irresponsible and inconsiderate. If you wish, attack the adults and the press and television for painting a false picture, or even encouraging young people to be different or rebellious.

2. Describe a popular coffee bar, discotheque or club where young people of your age congregate. Take a typical evening and describe the place as the crowd comes and grows and finally disperses. Try to capture the atmosphere of the place: the sights, sounds, conversation, the refreshment, even the smell, but without undue exaggeration and avoiding a sensational story. This should be atmospheric description.

3. Take any incident in a book, film or play with a similar basic situation to that in the extract from *The Mill on the Floss*—that is, a couple in love and up against the opposition of their family or community to their friendship or marriage. Describe the characters and situation, and how it is resolved in the particular instance you have selected.

Oral Work

1. Read the following two passages. The first is an extract from Shakespeare's *Julius Caesar*—Anthony's funeral oration over Caesar's dead body. The second is a "translation" of this speech into the language of American "beat talk". Which of the idioms in the latter are you familiar with? Give their meanings. By checking them against the language of the first passage, work out the meanings of other expressions. Which of the two passages do you prefer?

   (i) Friends, Romans, countrymen, lend me your ears;
       I come to bury Caesar, not to praise him.
       The evil that men do lives after them,
       The good is oft interred with their bones;
       So let it be with Caesar. The noble Brutus
       Hath told you Caesar was ambitious;
       If it were so, it was a grievous fault,
       And grievously hath Caesar answer'd it.
       Here, under leave of Brutus, and the rest,—
       For Brutus is an honourable man;
       So are they all, all honourable men,—
       Come I to speak in Caesar's funeral.
       He was my friend, faithful and just to me:
       But Brutus says he was ambitious;
       And Brutus is an honourable man.
       He hath brought many captives home to Rome,
       Whose ransoms did the general coffers fill:
       Did this in Caesar seem ambitious?
       When that the poor have cried, Caesar hath wept;
       Ambition should be made of sterner stuff:
       Yet Brutus says he was ambitious;
       And Brutus is an honourable man.
       You all did see that on the Lupercal
       I thrice presented him a kingly crown,
       Which he did thrice refuse: was this ambition?
       Yet Brutus says he was ambitious;
       And, sure, he is an honourable man.
       I speak not to disprove what Brutus spoke,

But here I am, to speak what I do know.
You all did love him once, not without cause:
What cause withholds you then to mourn for him?
O judgment! thou art fled to brutish beasts,
And men have lost their reason. Bear with me;
My heart is in the coffin there with Caesar,
And I must pause till it come back to me.

(ii)   *The Ides of Mad*

Friends, Romans, hipsters,
Let me clue you in;
I come to put down Caesar, not to groove him.
The square kicks that some cats are on stay with them;
The hip bits, like, go down under;
So let it lay with Caesar. The cool Brutus
Gave you the message Caesar had big eyes;
If that's the sound, someone's copping a plea,
And, like, old Caesar really set them straight.
Here, copacetic with Brutus and the studs,—
For Brutus is a real cool cat;
So are they all, all cool cats,—
Come I to make this gig at Caesar's lay me;
He was my boy, the most and real gone to me;
But, like, Brutus pegs him as having big eyes;
And old Brutus is a real cool cat.
He copped a lot of swinging heads for home,
Which put us way out with that loot;
Does this give Caesar big eyes?
When the square cats bawled, Caesar flipped;
Big eyes should be made of more solid 'megillah';
Yet Brutus pegs him as having big eyes:
And Brutus is a real cool cat.
You all dug that scene at the Lupercal scene
Three times I bugged him with the king's lid,
And three times he hung me up; was this big eyes?
Yet Brutus pegs him with big eyes;
And, sure, he is a real cool cat.
I don't want to double-O what Brutus gummed,
But, like, I only dig what comes on straight.
You all got a charge out of him once,
So how come you don't cry the blues for him?
Man! You are real nowhere,
You don't make it anymore. Don't cut out on me;
My guts are in the pad there with Caesar,
And I gotta stop swinging till they round-trip.

(from *Mad* magazine)

2. Dramatize the incident in the extract from *The Mill on the Floss*, borrowing, adapting and improvising suitable dialogue and soliloquy.

Activities and Research

1. Investigate the extent to which manufactures and advertisers are aiming products specifically at a teenage market, and analyse some of the methods used and the appeals they are making. Look for the advertising techniques examined in Book Four.

Make a survey of shops and public places in the nearest shopping centre, examine newspapers and magazines with a special appeal to young people, and make a study of current advertisements on television.

What kind of products are being directed at this market, and within what price range? Are there any signs of "exploitation", such as selling rubbish simply for fashion's sake, or over-charging, or encouragement to smoke or drink heavily, or indulge in any kinds of anti-social behaviour?

Are a majority or large proportion of teenagers an easy market for commercial interests today?

Further Reading

The Mill on the Floss by GEORGE ELIOT (various publishers)
This is a powerful story that ends tragically—thwarted in her hopes of marrying Philip, the young man she really loves, Maggie runs off with a shallow young man called Stephen Guest, and find herself turned away for good by her unsympathetic brother Tom, whom she has always loved and respected. But the novel includes a number of amusing character studies and lighter incidents, as well as the fiercely intelligent, wilful and passionate Maggie.

Adam Bede by GEORGE ELIOT (various publishers)
The author based this story on an actual confession of a child-murder, and the plot revolves around Hetty Sorrel's tragic affair with the young squire when in fact she is loved by the worthy Adam. This powerful nineteenth-century classic has also some fine comic characterizations and a rich rural setting.

Absolute Beginners by COLIN MACINNES (Panther)

Although some of the language and references may now seem a little dated, this story is still a most perceptive and readable account of teenage attitudes, and its vivid pictures provide a firm basis for studying the changes that have taken place in teenage fashions and tastes. The climax of the plot revolves around the race riots which occurred in Notting Hill.

June in Her Spring by COLIN MACINNES (Panther)

Colin MacInnes's second novel is set in Australia, where he was brought up. It tells the tragic story of two young lovers whose innocent dream of eloping and starting afresh, away from their families, is finally destroyed in the grim finale of a fancy dress dance.

CHAPTER SEVEN

Attitudes - II

HIGHBROW, LOWBROW

CAST: BEATIE BRYANT, *aged 22, who has been living in London, under the influence of a young man of ideas, called Ronnie.*
MRS. BRYANT, *her mother.*
FRANK BRYANT, *Beatie's brother.*
PEARL, *Frank's wife.*
JIMMY BEALES, *Beatie's brother-in-law.*
MR. BRYANT (*Beatie's father*) *and* JENNY BEALES (*her sister*) *are also present.*

SCENE: A country cottage in Norfolk. It is Saturday afternoon in the Bryants' front parlour. A table is laid for tea. The family have gathered to welcome Ronnie, but a letter has just arrived to explain that he does not want to continue his friendship with BEATIE.

MRS. BRYANT: I suppose doin' all those things for him weren't enough. I suppose he weren't satisfied wi' goodness only.
BEATIE: Oh, what's the use.
MRS. BRYANT: Well, don't you sit there an' sigh gal like you was Lady Nevershit. I ask you something. Answer me. You do the talking then. Go on—you say you know something we don't so *you* do the talking. Talk—go on, talk gal.
BEATIE: (*despairingly*): I can't mother, you're right—the apple don't fall far from the tree do it? You're right, I'm like you. Stubborn, empty, wi' no tools for livin'. I got no roots in nothing. I come from a family o' farm labourers yet I ent got no roots—just like town people—just a mass o' nothing'.
FRANK: Roots, gal? What do you mean, roots?
BEATIE: (*impatiently*): Roots, roots, roots! Christ, Frankie, you're in the fields all day, you should know about growing things. Roots! The things you come from, the things that feed you. The things that make you proud of yourself—roots!
MRS. BRYANT: You got a family ent you?

BEATIE: I am not talking about family roots—I mean—the— I mean—look! Ever since it begun the world's bin growin' hasn't it? Things hev happened, things have bin discovered, people have bin thinking and improving and inventing but what do we know about it all?

JIMMY: What is she on about?

BEATIE (*Various interjections*): What do you mean, what am I on about? I'm talking! Listen to me! I'm tellin' you that the world's bin growing for two thousand years and we heven't noticed it. I'm telling you that we don't know what we are or where we come from. I'm telling you something's cut us off from the beginning. I'm telling you we've got no roots. Blimey Joe! We've all got large allotments, we all grow things around us so we should know about roots. You know how to keep your flowers alive don't you mother? Jimmy— you know how to keep the roots of your vegies strong and healthy. It's not only the corn that need strong roots, you know, it's us too. But what've we got? Go on, tell me, what've we got? We don't know where we push up from and we don't bother neither.

PEARL: Well, I aren't grumbling.

BEATIE: You say you aren't—oh yes, you say so, but look at you. What've you done since you come in? Hev you said anythin'? I mean really said or done anything to show you're alive? Alive! Blust, what do it mean? Do you know what it mean? Any of you? Shall I tell you what Susie said when I went and saw her? She say she don't care if that ole atom bomb drop and she die—that's what she say. And you know why she say it? I'll tell you why, because if she had to care she'd have to do something about it and she find *that* too much effort. Yes she do. She can't be bothered—she's too bored with it all. That's what we all are—we're all too bored.

MRS. BRYANT: Blust woman—bored you say, bored? You say Susie's bored, with a radio and television an' that? I go t'hell if she's bored!

BEATIE: Oh yes, we turn on a radio or a TV set maybe, or we go to the pictures—if them's love stories or gangsters—but isn't that the easiest way out? Anything so long as we don't have to make an effort. Well, am I right? You know I'm right. Education ent only books and music—it's asking questions, all the time. There are millions of us, all over the country and no one, not one of us is asking questions, we're all taking the easiest way out. Everyone I ever worked with took the easiest way out. We don't fight for anything, we're so mentally lazy we might as well be dead. Blust, we are dead! And you know what Ronnie say sometimes? He say it serves us right! That's what he say—it's our own bloody fault!

JIMMY: So that's us summed up then—so we know where *we* are then!

MRS. BRYANT: Well if he don't reckon we count nothin', then it's as well he didn't come. There! It's as well he didn't come.

BEATIE: Oh, *he* thinks we count alright—living in mystic communion with nature. Living in mystic bloody communion with nature (indeed). But us count? Count mother? I wonder. Do we? Do you think we really count? You don' wanna take any notice of what them ole papers say about the workers bein' all important these days—that's all squit! 'Cos we aren't. Do you think when the really talented people in the country get to work they get to work for us? Hell if they do. Do you think they don't know we 'ont make the effort? The writers don't write thinkin' we can understand, nor the painters don't paint expecting us to be interested—that they don't, nor don't the composers give out music thinking we can appreciate it. "Blust," they say, "the masses is too stupid for us to come down to them. Blust," they say, "if they don't make no effort why should we bother?" So you know who come along? The slop singers and the pop writers and the film makers and women's magazines and the Sunday papers and the picture strip love stories—that's who come along, and you don't have to make no effort for them, it come easy. "We know where the money lie," they say, "hell we do! The workers 've got it so let's give them what they want. If they want slop songs and film idols we'll give 'em that then. If they want words of one syllable, we'll give 'em that then. If they want the third-rate, BLUST! We'll give 'em THAT then. Anything's good enough for them 'cos they don't ask for no more!" The whole stinkin' commercial world insults us and we don't care a damn. Well, Ronnie's right—it's our own bloody fault. We want the third-rate—we got it! We got it! We got it! We . . .

(*Suddenly* BEATIE *stops as if listening to herself. She pauses, turns with an ecstatic smile on her face*—)

D'you hear that? D'you hear it? Did you listen to me? I'm talking Jenny, Frankie, mother—I'm not quoting no more.

MRS. BRYANT (*getting up to sit at table*) : Oh hell, I hed enough of her—let her talk awhile she'll soon get fed up.

(*The others join her at the table and proceed to eat and murmur.*)

BEATIE: (*as though a vision were revealed to her*) : God in heaven, Ronnie! It does work, it's happening to me, I can feel it's happened, I'm beginning, on my own two feet—I'm beginning . . .

(*The murmur of the family sitting down to eat grows as* BEATIES'S *last cry is heard. Whatever she will do they will continue to live as before and the* CURTAIN FALLS *as* BEATIE *stands alone—articulate at last.*)

(from *Roots* by Arnold Wesker)

Appreciation and Discussion

1. What does the saying "the apple don't fall far from the tree" mean here?

2. Why is Mrs. Bryant annoyed (a) with Ronnie, and (b) with Beatie? Does her attitude change at all as Beatie talks to the family?

3. What single adjective describes an attitude like Susie's: "She can't be bothered—she's too bored with it all."?

4. Why doesn't Beatie accept that radio, television and cinema will relieve this kind of boredom?

5. What is Beatie's idea of education? What kind of schools and lessons would result if this idea was applied to our educational system?

6. Did Ronnie make a distinction between working-class people in towns and those in the country? Does Beatie accept the distinction?

7. In what limited way (according to Beatie) are the workers more important today?

8. Beatie is pleased to find she is "not quoting no more". Who do you think she had been quoting before? *What* has happened to her, and *what* is she "beginning" at the end of this extract (which is also the end of the play)?

9. What, according to Beatie and Ronnie, is the main difference between "highbrow" and "lowbrow" standards in writing, painting, music, etc.? Do you agree that "the whole stinking commercial world insults us and we don't care a damn"?

10. Is it fair to assert that "pop" culture is simply taking the easiest way out (". . . you don't have to make no effort for

them, it come easy"), and therefore is "third rate"? What of the other argument, that there is good and bad "pop", good and bad "classical", and so on?

11. How would you define a "classic"?

12. Are "roots" important in the sense Beatie means (not family roots but cultural background)? Do schools do enough to pass on to the *majority* of their pupils their whole cultural heritage, and an understanding of the best in art, literature, music, philosophy and science?

13. (a) Ideally, what can or should be done by newspapers, radio and television and the entertainment industry to raise people's standards?
    (b) Do you agree that (for instance, through the Arts Council) taxpayer's money should be used to promote the arts when the majority of taxpayers do not enjoy the results?

14. Wesker wrote this play in Norfolk dialect. Find examples of its own vocabulary and its own grammar (especially verb forms that would be wrong in Standard English). What factors make Beatie's speeches so eloquent and vigorous?

Bad Taste

What line would ever hook a genuine craftsman
With shoddy workmanship? Joiner or draughtsman,
By virtue of knowing even one trade through,
Has insight into other standards, too.

But we—the poor clock-watchers, and floor-sweepers,
Minders of engines, makers of any old tack—
We have our reward: to be fooled by the first glib quack

That opens his bag and is gone as soon as paid.
Untaught to see through the ribs of anything made,
We eat bad films, bad novels, and bad songs—
A permanent taste of bad upon our tongues.

RAYMOND RICHARDSON

Discussing the Poem

1. What, according to this poet, has caused us to accept the third-rate?
2. What is a "glib quack" literally, and what kind of people does he stand for in this poem?
3. What is "bad" or "shoddy" about the films, novels, songs, etc. that we are now given?
4. Discuss the poet's choice of the following images and all the suggestions or implications behind them:

> What line would ever hook . . .
> poor clock-watchers, and floor-sweepers . . .
> any old tack . . .
> gone as soon as paid . . .
> to see through the ribs of anything . . .
> a permanent taste of bad . . .

Techniques

Exercise 1. The following passage offers a contrast with the point of view of Beatie (or Ronnie) in her outburst in the play. Study it carefully:

Certain changes in the world of popular music have been significant. In the period immediately following the second world war, it was easy for critics and intellectuals to sneer at the hit songs of the time. The music was simple and undemanding; the lyrics were contemptible. If the songs of that period offered anything at all, it was an escape into an unreal and softly romantic world where "you" might be "blue" but there would always be "love" "above" and a "moon" in "June". The vocabulary and the rhyme were as repetitive and as superficial as the dance rhythms of the music.

Rock 'n' roll music burst on that scene in the mid-1950s and turned many of our standards upside down. A new generation of young people with independence, improved education, more leisure and above all good weekly wages, was buying record players and discs and crowding round the juke boxes in the cafes and the new Espresso coffee bars. The music was loud and asserted itself—it demanded to be listened to, danced to, and played again. Many young people took up the guitar, or formed skiffle groups with any home-made instruments (like the washboard) that could beat out a rhythm. Promoters, record companies and the commercial machinery for the creation of new pop stars plunged into this new kind of music in a big way, and one must admit that much of what was produced was still phoney and ephemeral. But at least the music was geared to the lively tastes and interests of a younger age-group.

Out of this kind of pop-music has arisen a new interest in the feelings and attitudes of the young. We have therefore had protest songs, about the H-bomb and war, about people's loneliness and a more genuine, often quite unromantic kind of love, and about the lack of understanding between the older and the younger generations. Equally important, the music has become much more sophisticated, and demands a higher level of technical competence. Popular musicians have to be much more talented. One of the British stars of the early rock 'n' roll era, Tommy Steele (now an established entertainer with an international reputation) has admitted that he probably "wouldn't have stood a chance" had he started his career in the mid-1960s. We therefore have a number of gifted young musicians and writers who have a genuine artistic desire to express, in their own words and music, the fears and longings of the young people of their own place and time. This is more than just another aspect of commercialism and the shameless peddling of the third-rate. We now have a new kind of folk-music, with its own artistic integrity, striving to reinterpret and express the mood of a whole generation with real sincerity.

Summarize the argument of this passage—i.e. make a précis of it in not more than 160 of your own words. State the exact number of words you use.

Give your précis an appropriate *title* of the kind discussed in Chapter Six.

Exercise 2. (a) Beatie's Norfolk dialect preserves a number of forms that are not considered correct in Standard English. What is the more correct equivalent to the following?

1. The apple don't fall far from the tree, do it?
2. I got no roots in nothing.
3. We don't bother neither.
4. She say she don't care if that ole atom bomb drop and she die.
5. We go to the pictures—if them's love stories or gangsters.
6. You don' wana take any notice of what them ole papers say.
7. Anything's good enough for them 'cos they don't ask for no more.
8. I'm not quoting no more.

(b) A number of these are examples of double negatives. There was once a time when English made full use of double negatives; Chaucer wrote about the Friar among his Canterbury Pilgrims:

There nas no man nowhere so virtuous.

(nas = ne was = was not)

and even in Shakespeare's *Hamlet,* we find the Prince saying:

It is not nor it cannot come to good.

But standard modern English has adopted the rule that two negatives in one construction cancel each other out, so that:

I don't know no one.

should mean: I do know someone.

The following sentences illustrate a number of muddled constructions and difficulties with negatives. Discuss them, and write improved versions.

1. I don't want to go and I won't go neither.
2. We should not be surprised if Beatie was not rather intelligent after all.
3. We are none of us really sure how far we are not in danger of compromising over this.
4. The causes of the many accidents on that corner are sometimes never discovered.
5. All English people do not speak a foreign language.
6. Everyone can never be certain that he will not make a mistake sometime.
7. He would not admit that he belonged either to the middle class nor to the working class.
8. Beatie had little reason to be proud of her family on this occasion, or felt anything but relief that Ronnie was not going to see them arguing like this.
9. Philip was not only more intelligent than Tom, but Tom feared that Maggie did not love him as much as she loved Philip.
10. He really liked neither the original Bach, played in the classical style, or the jazz version based or the original.

(c) The negative form of a word—or its antonym—does not always simply reverse the original meaning. Discuss the following three cases:

i. responsible—irresponsible

The captain was responsible for the loss of his ship, but the official enquiry could not agree that his behaviour had been irresponsible, nor even that (as some of the crew alleged) he had shown a lack of responsibility.

ii. common—uncommon

It was common for girls with strong London accents to be

told they were common, and not uncommon for them to be asked to leave certain expensive restaurants.

iii. opposite — what does it mean in a sentence like the following?

Some critics say that these writers are the product of their society; others say the opposite.

Exercise 3. Beatie Bryant assumes a considerable gulf between her family — the "workers", the "masses", "us" — and the "really talented people", the writers, painters and composers, or indeed ". . . the whole stinkin' commercial world . . ." — "them" — who are the people who really count and really have status and power.

She assumes, in fact, that she is living in a class-divided world, and that only a few people, like Ronnie and perhaps (at the end of the play) herself, can cut across class barriers. Britain is indeed a class-conscious society, and the different ways in which people speak, dress and behave tend to reinforce this stratification all the time. In the book *Sense and Nonsense in Psychology*, H. J. Eysenck writes:

"Let us begin by noting certain facts about the society in which we grew up, facts which every youngster learns in the course of his early life. The first fact we must know is that people differ with respect to their social status. By status we mean such things as the amount of money a man earns, the kind of education he has had, or which he can afford for his children, the kind of house he lives in, and the part of the town in which he lives, his accent, the kind of people he mixes with, and so on and so forth."

The way people talk has a great deal to do with social and geographical differences in Britain.

(a) What can you say about the probable social backgrounds of people who use the following terms?

Mumsie	Mummy	Mum	Mam	Mamma
Ma	Mother	Mater	the old woman	

Which name do you use?

(b) What social distinctions are suggested by the following terms?

> drawing-room—lounge—sitting-room
> living-room—front room—parlour
> dining-room—backroom—eating room

(c) Describe the social environment (status and class) which best suits each of the following statements. Consider both the speaker's choice of words and the actions mentioned. Read the statements aloud, using appropriate accents.

(i). 1. "A glass of sherry before dinner," suggested the Colonel. "Sweet or dry?" he asked his guest, leading the way to the library.

2. "Let's pop round to the local for a couple of pints of wallop. Then we can bring a pork pie and a bottle of stout for the missis," said George.

3. "What about a drink before we eat? I've got some light ale," John said, opening the cocktail cabinet, which he had made himself from a Handyman kit.

(ii). 1. "Mum usually has the dinner ready at about one o'clock. Then we have our tea at half-past five, and sometimes Mum and Dad have a bit of supper before they go to bed."

2. "We normally have lunch at one. Tea is at four; and dinner is served at eight."

(iii). 1. "My youngest boy is at Cambridge University for three years, doing Biology."

2. "My son is at Cambridge, studying for a degree in Botany and Zoology."

3. "My son is up at Trinity, reading Natural Sciences."

Topics for Written Work

1. After studying the views given in the passage in Exercise 1 on page 110, write an article giving your own views on popular music of today.

If you agree with the writer of the article, reinforce his arguments by stating examples. Quote the titles of and lines from contemporary and past songs. Give the names of singers and song writers. Provide examples of songs about war, loneliness, unromantic love, and misunderstanding. Explain what "fears and longings" are expressed in modern pop songs and what "moods" they portray. If you disagree with any of the views put forward, explain clearly what you think is wrong with them and provide evidence to support your case.

2. Attack or defend what you understand as "highbrow" tastes in art, music, literature, entertainment and design.

Look carefully at Beatie's argument in her speech in the play and the ideas of the poem *Bad Taste*. Is it true that people who can make things for themselves—with creative talents—are the ones who develop the soundest judgement? Is the difference between "good" and "bad" simply the difference between what is hand-made and what is mass-produced? What qualities are there in a "classic" in any of the arts: is what lasts likely to be better than what will not endure? In the play *Death of a Salesman*, Arthur Miller puts these words into the mouth of the typical American householder:

> "Once in my life I would like to own something outright before it's broken! I'm always in a race with the junkyard! I just finished paying for the car and its on its last legs. . . . They time those things. They time them so when you finally paid for them, they're used up."

Is this idea true of popular music or literature as well as of mass-produced gadgets with "built-in obsolescence"?

3. A wealthy, upper-middle class woman, a poorly educated and impoverished tramp, and an intelligent, well-educated young man from a working-class background are trapped together in a broken lift for several hours. Write a short play showing how they react to one another.

Oral Work

The way people speak can affect their economic as well as their social prospects. Look at this excerpt from an article in the *Daily Mirror* by Audrey Whiting:

> Six promising sixteen-year-old school-leavers, having gained 4 "O" levels in the G.C.E. examination applied for their first jobs recently and were turned down flat. Their parents were distressed, their former teachers dismayed. Why? A member of the firm's selection board explained: "Half the time we simply couldn't understand a word they said. Frankly, we can no longer afford to employ people who speak in such a slovenly fashion."
>
> Tragically, many school-leavers in Britain have never been told that the way they speak can mean success or failure in a highly competitive age where fast business deals require fast understanding. Neither school nor home, in most cases, has attached any importance to speech. Indeed, one-third of intending graduate teachers were found to speak inadequately.
>
> No one urges affected speech or wants to lose the variety and warmth of our many regional dialects, but speech must be understandable by anyone, anywhere, at once.

The transformation of a person's character and attitudes that may accompany a fundamental change in his speech habits was the subject of Bernard Shaw's play *Pygmalion*. Professor Higgins, an expert in phonetics, discusses the point with his friend Colonel Pickering, using a Cockney flower girl who is standing nearby as his illustration:

COLONEL. But is there a living in Speech Training?

PROFESSOR. Oh yes, quite a fat one. This is an age of upstarts. Men begin in Kentish Town with £80 a year and end up in Park Lane with £100,000. They want to drop Kentish Town; but they give themselves away every time they open their mouths. Now I can teach them.

FLOWER GIRL. [*upset because he has been mimicking her*]. Let him mind his own business and leave a poor girl. . . .

PROFESSOR. Woman, leave this detestable boohooing instantly or else seek the shelter of some other place of worship.

FLOWER GIRL. I've a right to be here if I like, same as you.

PROFESSOR. A woman who utters such depressing and disgusting sounds has no right to be anywhere—no right to live. Remember that you are a human being with a soul and the divine gift of articulate speech: that your native language is the language of Shakespeare and Milton and the Bible; and don't sit there crooning like a bilious pigeon.

FLOWER GIRL. [*overwhelmed*]. Ah-ah-ah-ow-ow-ow-oo!

PROFESSOR. Heavens! What a sound! [*reproducing exactly*] Ah-ah-ah-ow-ow-ow-oo!

FLOWER GIRL. [*laughing in spite of herself*]. Garn!

PROFESSOR. You see this creature with her kerbstone English: the English that will keep her in the gutter to the end of her days. Well sir, in three months I could pass her off as a duchess at an ambassador's garden party. . . .

Probably there is more snobbery attached to the accent and structure of speech in Britain than in any other part of the world. Are both the following variations on standard pronunciation equally to be condemned?

"As a maddererfacd, I fort it was a reely nyce slycer kyke I ad wiv me cuppa tea yisterdiy."

"As a metter of fect, I thot it was a rahly naice slaice of cek I hed with my cup off teh yesterdeh."

Discuss the whole matter of regional and social variations in the way we speak:

(a) Which dialects and accents do you find (i) most pleasant to listen to, and (ii) most easy to understand?

(b) What regional dialects are reckoned the funniest or the most difficult to understand by people in London and S.E. England? How do those in the regions feel about this?

(c) Has an employer any right, under any circumstances, to take an applicant's speech into account when considering him for a job? Is it more important in some jobs than in others?

(d) Should we preserve either regional or social differences in the English language? Are differences dying out? What is the job of the schools in dealing with this problem?

(e) Should people be "bilingual", having one standard of speech at home and among friends, and another for their school work or their dealings with the general public?

(f) What should the BBC and the television companies have as their standards? Do you approve of the idea of a common "BBC English" for the whole country?

(g) Is there a difference between "elocution" and "oral English"? Which (if either) have you been taught? Should schools do more to help pupils improve their standards of (i) expression and fluency with words, (ii) interesting conversation, (iii) recitation and reading aloud, or (iv) articulation and pronunciation?

(h) How far do you agree with, or how would you reply to, the following statement?

"The high standards in speech, writing and behaviour that schools once set out to achieve are now being thrown aside. Young people are no longer trained to speak properly; they are given novels and plays to read which are written in appalling, colloquial styles, and which contain swear words and filthy references; they are encouraged to talk about sex, crime and violence. These influences at school inevitably corrupt young people."

Activities and Research

Conduct a survey of musical tastes and knowledge in your school. To help suggest the kind of questions you might ask and the form in which your final report might appear, here are some extracts from an article in the magazine of Wandsworth School recording the results of a survey conducted by senior boys.

Our survey covered sources of musical entertainment, music making, favourites, and opinions about music in school, and the same questionnaire was given to 25 boys in the Upper Sixth, and to 5 Pi, 5 Omega, 5 Iota/Kappa, 3 Alpha, 3 Omega, 3 Kappa, 1 Gamma, 1 Iota and 1 Tau. We hoped in this way to discover the views and habits of a cross-section of the school, but we were sometimes more surprised at the similarities than at the differences. . . .

The following table shows in percentages the replies to the questions "Have you a record player of *your own*?" and "Have you a tape-recorder of *your own*?": —

Record player:

U6	5Pi	5Ome	5Io/Ka	3Al	3Ome	3Ka	1Ga	1Io	1Ta
60	44	65.2	45.8	41.4	28	25	27.6	30	25

Tape-recorder:

U6	5Pi	5Ome	5Io/Ka	3Al	3Ome	3Ka	1Ga	1Io	1Ta
40	27.7	17.5	20.8	20	3.4	3.4	3.4	3.1	8.1

In a number of cases boys owned both, and it is clear that a lot of money is represented by these figures. We also found that it was not uncommon for boys to own 100 or more discs (in 5Ome one boy claimed to own 250). And yet many have never been to a "live" concert of any kind of music.

No very obvious pattern emerged from the answers to the question about ability to play any instrument. Percentages were never large: 28% of the U6th, 37.9% of 3Al, 20% of 1Io, only 11% of 5Pi and 4% 1Ta. The guitar, piano and violin were the most common; there was one player of the Jew's harp and one of the washboard. Membership of groups, bands and choirs outside the school was not common. Clearly, the vast majority of boys are skilled only in playing the gramophone.

Boys were asked to choose their favourite kinds of music from a given list.

In the next four questions, boys were asked to name their favourite groups, orchestras, instrumentalists, singers and composers. These questions posed a real problem to upper sixth formers, many of whom felt it was unreasonable to narrow their tastes down to one or two choices, and nearly half of them refused to answer questions in this section. Yet it was clearly the most popular section with members of other forms, and here it is the analyst who faces the problem, in sorting out the many favourites proposed. . .

When we asked in what years music should be taught, we found a widespread belief that it should be taught to any and every year but one's own! Thus in 5Pi only 11.1% wanted it taught to the fifth forms, but 38.9% wanted it taught to the 1st and 2nd years; while in 1Io 70% wanted to see music taught to the 3rd and 4th year boys, but only 10% wanted it taught to the first year! 1Ta and the U6th both overwhelmingly agree that music should be taught to sixth formers (perhaps mainly to *Lower* Sixth formers?).

Finally, what should be included in the music curriculum? Much the most popular choice was learning to play an instrument. Only in the U6th and 3Ome were there more boys wishing to learn about jazz than wishing to learn an instrument. Over the whole sample an average of 53.8% of each class (more than half) would like to learn to play an instrument in school music lessons, and among the first formers and 3Al (an exceptional form, as we have noted already), the figure is nearly 70%. Learning about jazz was also popular (44%), and 88% of the U6th group wished this to be included. 25% of the whole sample were in favour of learning to appreciate classical music, a desire that 1Ta seem to have in common with 3Al and the U6th!

Further Reading

Roots by ARNOLD WESKER (Longmans; Penguin) (822.91)
When Beatie Bryant returns from working in London to see her working-class family in Norfolk, she is forever talking about Ronnie Kahn, the man she hopes to marry and who has attempted (unsuccessfully, she has to admit) to make her "really aware and alive". All her family resent her preaching and react in their different ways. The climax of the play is the extract quoted in this chapter.

Chicken Soup with Barley and *I'm Talking About Jerusalem* (Longmans; Penguin) (822. 91)
Are two other plays by Wesker which, with *Roots* as the central play, form a trilogy about members of the Khan family and their changing attitudes to social questions, both in the 1930s and after the Second World War. Each is an interesting and well-constructed play to read separately.

Chips With Everything (822.91) and *The Kitchen* (822.91)
(Which we recommended in Book Four) are two other plays
by ARNOLD WESKER that are well worth reading or acting. *Chips
With Everything* is about another intellectual "rebel", the well-
educated young idealist who tries to resist the assumptions of the
officer-class in the RAF, when on his preliminary training, but
is subtly absorbed into the society he rebels against.

Look Back in Anger by JOHN OSBORNE (Evans; Faber) (822.91)
When this play was first produced in the 1950s, it shocked critics
and audiences alike with its savage ideas and dialogues; but it
came to be regarded as an outstanding play, and one which has
had a profound effect on modern drama.—The "hero"
Jimmy Porter, is a young man with a passionate hatred of the
Establishment, which frequently leads him to lash out at
members of the middle class, and their values. Since his wife,
Alison comes from a typically middle-class background, she and
her family often serve as targets for his attacks.

The Entertainer by JOHN OSBORNE (Evans; Faber) (822.91)
Archie Rice, an unsuccessful, middle-aged, seaside entertainer is
an older version of Jimmy Porter—a man who is convinced he
can no longer feel anything. The dialogue is again violent and
brash.

CHAPTER EIGHT

Violence - I

DESTRUCTION

Mr. Thomas ("Old Misery") lived alone in a once beautiful Wren house near Wormsley Common that had barely survived the war-time bombing. The "Wormsley Common Gang" of twelve boys usually met on the empty bomb-site next door, under Blackie's leadership.

The new recruit had been with the gang since the beginning of the summer holidays, and there were possibilities about his brooding silence that all recognized. He never wasted a word even to tell his name until that was required of him by the rules. When he said "Trevor" it was a statement of fact, not as it would have been with the others a statement of shame or defiance. Nor did anyone laugh except Mike, who, finding himself without support and meeting the dark gaze of the newcomer, opened his mouth and was quiet again. There was every reason why T., as he was afterwards referred to, should have been an object of mockery—there was his name (and they substituted the initial because otherwise they had no excuse not to laugh at it), the fact that his father, a former architect and present clerk, had "come down in the world" and that his mother considered herself better than the neighbours. What but an odd quality of danger, of the unpredictable, established him in the gang without any ignoble ceremony of initiation? . . .

Next day T. astonished them all. He was late at the rendezvous, and the voting for that day's exploit took place without him. . . .

"Where have you been, T. ?" Blackie asked. "You can't vote now. You know the rules."

"I've been *there*," T. said. He looked at the ground, as though he had thoughts to hide.

"Where?"

"At Old Misery's." . . .

The gang had gathered round: It was as though an impromptu court were about to form and to try some case of deviation.

121

T. said, "It's a beautiful house," and still watching the ground, meeting no one's eyes, he licked his lips, first one way, then the other. . . .

"What did you do it for?" Blackie asked. He was just, he had no jealousy, he was anxious to retain T. in the gang if he could. It was the word "beautiful" that worried him — that belonged to a class world that you could still see parodied at the Wormsley Common Empire by a man wearing a top hat and a monocle, with a haw-haw accent. He was tempted to say, "My dear Trevor, old chap," and unleash his hell hounds. "If you'd broken in," he said sadly — that indeed would have been an exploit worthy of the gang.

"This was better," T. said. "I found out things." He continued to stare at his feet, not meeting anybody's eye, as though he were absorbed in some dream he was unwilling — or ashamed — to share.

"What things?"

"Old Misery's going to be away all to-morrow and Bank Holiday."

Blackie said with relief, "You mean we could break in?"

"And pinch things?" somebody asked.

Blackie said, "Nobody's going to pinch things. Breaking in — that's good enough, isn't it? We don't want any court stuff."

"I don't want to pinch anything," T. said. "I've got a better idea."

"What is it?"

T. raised eyes as grey and disturbed as the drab August day. "We'll pull it down," T. said. "We'll destroy it.". . .

On Sunday morning all were punctual except Blackie. . . .

There was no sign of anybody anywhere. The loo stood like a tomb in a neglected graveyard. The curtains were drawn. The house slept. Blackie lumbered nearer with the saw and the sledge-hammer. Perhaps after all nobody had turned up: the plan had been a wild invention: they had woken wiser. But when he came close to the back door he could hear a confusion of sound, hardly louder than a hive in swarm: a clicketyclack, a bang bang bang, a scraping, a creaking, a sudden painful crack. He thought: It's true, and whistled.

They opened the back door to him and he came in. He had at once the impression of organization, very different from the old happy-go-lucky ways under his leadership. For a while he wandered up and downstairs looking for T. Nobody addressed him: he had a sense of great urgency, and already he could begin to see the plan. The interior of the house was being carefully demolished without touching the outer walls. Summers with hammer and chisel was ripping out the skirting-boards in the ground floor dining-room: he had already smashed the panels of the door. In the same room Joe was heaving up the parquet blocks, exposing the soft wood floorboards over the cellar. Coils of wire came out of the damaged skirting and Mike sat happily on the floor, clipping the wires.

On the curved stairs two of the gang were working hard with an inadequate child's saw on the banisters—when they saw Blackie's big saw they signalled for it wordlessly. When he next saw them a quarter of the banisters had been dropped into the hall. He found T. at last in the bathroom—he sat moodily in the least-cared for room in the house, listening to the sounds coming up from below.

"You've really done it," Blackie said with awe. "What's going to happen?"

"We've only just begun," T. said. He looked at the sledge-hammer and gave his instructions. "You stay here and break the bath and the wash basin. Don't bother about the pipes. They come later.". . .

"What are you going to do?" Blackie asked.

"I'm looking for something special," T. said.

It was nearly lunch-time before Blackie had finished and went in search of T. Chaos had advanced. The kitchen was a shambles of broken glass and china. The dining-room was stripped of parquet, the skirting was up, the door had been taken off its hinges, and the destroyers had moved up a floor. Streaks of light came in through the closed shutters where they worked with the seriousness of creators—and destruction is after all a form of creation. A kind of imagination had seen this house as it had now become. . . .

"Did you find anything special?" Blackie asked.

T. nodded. "Come over here," he said, "and look." Out of both pockets he drew bundles of pound notes. "Old Misery's savings," he said. "Mike ripped out the mattress, but he missed them."

"What are you going to do? Share them?"

"We aren't thieves," T. said. "Nobody's going to steal anything from this house. I kept these for you and me—a celebration." He knelt down on the floor and counted them out—there were seventy in all. "We'll burn them," he said, "one by one," and taking it in turns they held a note upwards and lit the top corner, so that the flame burnt slowly towards their fingers. The grey ash floated above them and fell on their heads like age. "I'd like to see Old Misery's face when we are through," T. said.

"You hate him a lot?" Blackie asked.

"Of course I don't hate him," T. said. "There'd be no fun if I hated him." The last burning note illuminated his brooding face. "All this hate and love," he said, "it's soft, its hooey. There's only things, Blackie," and he looked round the room crowded with the unfamiliar shadows of half things, broken things, former things. "I'll race you home, Blackie," he said.

(from *The Destructors*, a short story by Graham Greene)

Appreciation and Discussion

1. Why do you think the other members of the gang would have found T.'s full name funny? What *other* evidence is there that Trevor came from a different kind of background from the other members of the gang?
2. What is a "ceremony of initiation", and why might T. have had to go through one?
3. What does . . . "some case of deviation" mean? In what way had T. deviated from the usual behaviour of the gang?
4. What do you imagine were T.'s secret thoughts as he stared at the ground after his first view of Old Misery's house?
5. Blackie said, "We don't want any court stuff" and Trevor said, "We aren't thieves." What laws *were* they breaking, (a) in entering Old Misery's house, and (b) in demolishing it from the inside?
6. At what point is it clear that T. has taken over the leadership of the gang from Blackie? How and why do you think this happened?
7. What was Blackie's attitude to T. and his plan when he arrived on Sunday? Was he jealous of T., then or earlier?
8. (a) How did T. set about the demolition job? (b) What made the rest of the gang work so hard and seriously?
9. In what ways does the burning of the pound notes seem like a "celebration"?
10. What does T. mean by (a) "There'd be no fun if I hated him" and (b) "There's only things"?
11. (a) What do the following words mean, as used in this passage? rendezvous; monocle; parquet; a shambles. Look up the *derivation* of these words.
    (b) Why is the phrase "come down in the world" and the word "beautiful" (when not actually part of direct speech) in inverted commas?
12. (a) Comment on the comparison in each of the following figurative phrases, and its effectiveness in this passage:
    (i) unleash his hell hounds;
    (ii) eyes as grey and disturbed as the drab August day;
    (iii) The loo stood like a tomb in a neglected graveyard;
    (iv) The house slept;
    (v) a confusion of sound, hardly louder than a hive in swarm;
    (vi) The grey ash floated above them and fell on their heads like age.

(b) Comment on the meaning and effectiveness of the words in italics in the following quotations from the passage: his *brooding* silence; the *dark* gaze of the newcomer; an odd quality . . . . . of the *unpredictable*; any *ignoble* ceremony of initiation; an *impromptu* court; a *haw-haw* accent; Blackie *lumbered* nearer; a sudden *painful* crack; *streaks* of light came in; room crowded with the *unfamiliar* shadows.

13. Does T.'s attitude seem to you incomprehensible? Is he mentally unbalanced? What signs does he show of a gloomy abnormality, and what hints does the extract give that his home background might be responsible?

14. Is there an "art" of destruction? Is "destruction. . . . a form of creation"? Does T. show a "kind of imagination?" Do you think people *enjoy* breaking things, or need to have a chance to destroy occasionally, or is this a perverted, unhealthy tendency?

Incendiary

That one small boy with a face like pallid cheese
And burnt-out little eyes could make a blaze
As brazen, fierce and huge, as red and gold
And zany yellow as the one that spoiled
Three thousand guineas' worth of property
And crops at Godwin's Farm on Saturday
Is frightening, as fact and metaphor:
An ordinary match intended for
The lighting of a pipe or kitchen fire
Misused may set a whole menagerie
Of flame-fanged tigers roaring hungrily.
And frightening, too, that one small boy should set
The sky on fire and choke the stars to heat
Such skinny limbs and such a little heart
Which would have been content with one warm kiss,
Had there been anyone to offer this.

VERNON SCANNELL

Discussing the Poem

1. What is the poet implying was the *motive* for this act of arson by a small boy?
2. What kind of boy is he? Discuss the adjectives used: ". . . face like *pallid* cheese", ". . . *burnt-out* little eyes" . . . ". . . *skinny* limbs", etc.
3. How is the size, beauty and glory of the fire emphasized? Again, examine the poet's *diction*: "brazen, fierce and huge", "zany yellow", "set the sky on fire and choke the stars". Look also at the *figurative language*.
4. The poet says this incident is "frightening, as fact or metaphor". What does he mean by "metaphor"—is the fire a metaphor to describe or explain something about the boy's state of mind?
5. Does the poet imply that this act of wanton destruction is a kind of perverted creation, in any way similar to T.'s careful demolition of the beautiful old house?

Techniques

Exercise 1. Study the following passage carefully:

Desmond Morris in his book, *The Naked Ape*, looks at human beings as they appear to a zoologist, rather than from the point of view of a psychologist or a historian looking at man in the context of his own civilizations. For man is still basically an animal, biologically very like the other species of primates, even if his brain has enabled him to modify his environment to an astonishing degree. His aggressive tendencies, therefore, are basically like those of other animals, and serve the same purposes; and yet it is known that almost no other species of animal will fight its own kind to the death in normal circumstances.

Desmond Morris argues that human beings have developed from apes that lived in loose communities, moving through the forests eating fruit, where one male was normally dominant over the group. They then became hunting animals with a more definite sense of their home territory and closer-knit family units. Both these kinds of society allowed for displays of anger and aggression: the leader exacted submission from any follower who challenged his authority; the male hunter threatened any intruder who entered his home or endangered his family or property. But the aim of that aggression was not to kill; it was to assert (or to challenge) someone's status or his ownership, and then to exact a display of submission.

Human beings therefore show their aggression or anger by very clear outward signs: we stare fiercely, we frown, we turn pale; we may stamp our foot or advance with shaking fist; and we breathe harder and faster and adopt a fierce tone of voice. Equally important, we have inherited and developed a pattern of signs to indicate submission—when we look away, or fidget nervously, when we relax and smile, or bow our heads, and when we make placatory speeches, we are signalling clearly that we do not wish to challenge our opponent's rights. Much of our polite behaviour in company consists of such submission signals.

Normally, as among other animals, there is no need for individual humans to come to blows, and certainly there would be little to be gained from killing your opponent. But man has used his intelligence to develop very sophisticated tools, and unfortunately some of these are highly aggressive weapons that allow him to threaten without even seeing his enemy closely. He is, secondly, very strongly motivated by loyalty to the groups to which he belongs: originally these were hunting packs that demanded this full cooperation from every member of the group. Thirdly, the human population has grown enormously, and tends now to live in crowded conditions. Aggression by an armed gang or a national army is not, in these circumstances, simply assuaged by seeing the submission signals from the enemy. Man's conflicts with his own kind are more bloody and destructive than those of any other species, and the overcrowding of most of the earth's desirable living areas with yet more human beings can only increase the dangers of bloodshed and violence.

(a) Discuss or look up the meaning of words or phrases that are at all puzzling, including:

The context of his own civilization; species of primates; to modify his environment; dominant over the group; exacted submission; placatory speeches; sophisticated tools; motivated by loyalty; assuaged.

(b) Discuss or write an explanation of the difference between:

   (i) a zoologist and a psychologist;
  (ii) loose communities and family units;
 (iii) status and ownership;
 (iv) invented and developed;
  (v) armed gang and national army.

(c) Make *notes* summarizing the argument of each of these paragraphs; here are some possible notes on the *first* paragraph —continue on these lines:

Desmond Morris's *Naked Ape*: zoologists' view of man—essentially animal (with superior brain)—aggression like animals, yet only man fights to death.

(d) Select one *title* from the following list which seems to sum up most clearly the theme of this whole passage:

A Review of *The Naked Ape*
How and Why Animals Fight
The Dangers of Violence Among Men
How we Show our Anger
A Zoologist's View of Human Aggression
Aggression Without Submission
A History of War and Violence.

(e) Using your notes, write a complete *summary* of this passage in good, continuous English, of between 160 and 180 words. State at the end the number of words you use; give your summary the most suitable title selected from the list in (d).

Exercise 2. (a) Look carefully through the passage examining sentence structures and the sentences which begin with something other than the subject and main verb.

Discuss the following paragraph: notice how the sentences become longer, culminating in the last-but-one sentence with its series of onomatopoeic words, and the simplicity of the last sentence:

There was no sign of anybody anywhere. The loo stood like a tomb in a neglected graveyard. The curtains were drawn. The house slept. Blackie lumbered nearer with the saw and the sledge-hammer. Perhaps after all nobody had turned up: the plan had been a wild invention: they had woken wiser. But when he came close to the back door he could hear a confusion of sound, hardly louder than a hive in swarm: a clicketyclack, a bang bang bang, a scraping, a creaking, a sudden painful crack. He thought: it's true, and whistled.

Examine also the last paragraph, and notice there the *repetition* of that significant word "things":

"All this hate and love," he said, "it's soft, it's hooey. There's only things, Blackie," and he looked round the room crowded with the unfamiliar shadows of half things, broken things, former things. "I'll race you home, Blackie," he said.

Repetition is not necessarily effective—consider the following excerpt from a speech:

I believe that this honour which you have done me today is a greater honour than any which I have had done to me by anyone who has done me such an honour since I last had such an honour done to me.

On the other hand, repetition of particular words and parallel constructions can make very powerful writing. In Book Four we referred to the famous passage in *Ecclesiastes* in the Old Testament (the opening of Chapter 3) beginning:

To everything there is a season, and a time to every purpose under the heaven: A time to be born, and a time to die; . . .

In this the phrase "a time to" is repeated four times in each of seven verses. *Psalm 150* has a similar construction depending upon the words "praise him". In twentieth-century prose, one example is this from *For Whom the Bell Tolls*:

Dying was nothing and he had no picture of it nor fear of it in his mind. But living was a field of grain, blowing in the wind on the side of a hill. Living was a hawk in the sky. Living was an earthen jar of water in the dust of the threshing with the grain flailed out and the chaff blowing. Living was a horse between your legs and a carbine under one leg and a hill and a valley and a stream with trees along it and the far side of the valley and the hills beyond.

(b) Examine the six ways in which the following four statements have been combined. The simplest way would be to use "and . . . but . . . and".

Most artists are creative people.
They create beautiful things.
A minority enjoy destroying.
A few experts consider this art.

1. Although most artists are creative people who create beautiful things, a minority enjoy destroying which a few experts consider art.
2. Most artists being creative people who create beautiful things, only a few experts consider it art when a minority enjoy destroying.
3. Whereas most artists create beautiful things, a minority enjoy destroying which is considered art by a few experts.
4. Because most artists are creative people creating beautiful things, a minority enjoy destroying what a few experts consider art.
5. While a minority enjoy destroying and while a few experts consider this art, most artists are creative people creating beautiful things.
6. In so far as they create beautiful things, most artists are creative, yet a few experts consider it art when a minority enjoy destroying.

Now add four more constructions, beginning as suggested:
7. A few experts consider it art when . . .
8. The fact that they create beautiful things makes . . .
9. Since a minority enjoy . . .
10. In spite of the fact that a few experts consider it art . . .
Make up at least two other examples as well.

Attempt a similar series of sentences combining each of the following groups of four statements in various constructions.

T. had joined the gang that summer.
He brooded in silence.
This brooding had possibilities.
All the gang recognised this.

They took it in turns.
Each held up a pound note.
He lit the top corner.
The flame burnt slowly towards his fingers.

Exercise 3. The repetition and parallelism discussed in Exercise 2 is often in the form of clauses building up compound or complex sentence structures. COMPOUND sentences contain several main clauses (joined by coordinating conjunctions like "and", "but", "or", or by commas or semi-colons); COMPLEX sentences contain one or more subordinate clauses in addition to the main clause:

> *Compound*: Most artists are creative people and they create beautiful things, but a minority enjoy destroying and a few experts call this art.
>
> *Complex*: Although most artists are creative people who create beautiful things, a minority enjoy destroying which a few experts consider art.

Analyse the clauses in these two examples. Notice that number 6, in Exercise 2(b) is "compound-complex", since it has two main clauses joined by "yet" (an adverb, not a subordinating conjunction) as well as two subordinate clauses; and note that number 5 has two coordinate subordinate clauses, both introduced by "while" and both being adverb clauses of time modifying the verb "are" in the main clause.

(a) What clauses are coordinated, or paralleled, in the following sentences? State whether each sentence is compound, complex or compound-complex.

1. The facts that he was called Trevor, that his father was a failed architect and that his mother thought herself superior, all made him an object of mockery.
2. The long slender aircraft moved smoothly on to the tarmac, accelerated with effortless power down the runway and lifted gracefully into the air.
3. Although he was still young, although he had had little training, although he had still produced no significant work, the boy's talents as an artist were quite outstanding.
4. This then is the man who left home at the age of twelve, who worked long hours for his qualifications, who struggled for years as a student, who ruined his eyesight with reading, who dedicated his life to study, and whom now you would condemn for his poverty.
5. We knew where we were going; we knew what we wanted; we knew who were our friends; and we were so certain we were right.
6. I speak of an age that is long dead, an age before aeroplanes roared in our skies, before cars cluttered our roads, before trains sped through the countryside, before we could transmit news round the earth, before men had conquered disease or banished dirt, before men had discovered the secrets of life and of devastating destruction.

(b) Extend the following by adding parallel clauses:

1. When I had.............................I was at last ready for the journey.
2. Make time for travel while you.........................
3. He hardly recognized him because...................
4. The place had changed beyond recognition: the walls were ....
5. Because...................I finally gave up hope.
6. I just cannot stand people who...................

(c) Make up similar sentences, using paralleled phrases or clauses for a stylistic effect, to describe the following:

1. A long, hot, tiring day.
2. Waiting for someone who is very late.
3. Climbing to the summit of a mountain.
4. An older person's opinion of the younger generation.
5. The scoring of a goal.
6. The behaviour of a crowd.

Topics for Written Work

1. Write a discussion composition on one of the following topics. Ideas for material should be suggested by the passages, questions and other material in this chapter, including the Oral Work and Activities and Research sections.

(a) "Destruction is a form of creation." Is there any sense in this remark? Are there some people who need to destroy, or is aggressive behaviour a sign that something has gone wrong, either with the individual or with the society in which he lives? Should we plan to give young people more opportunities to fight, to find adventure, and more outlet for their aggressive energies?

(b) "When a young person hurts, breaks or destroys, he is really crying for help." Is this a reasonable description of much juvenile delinquency? Can you explain how someone's need for love and encouragement might be perverted into an outburst of violence and aggression? What "punishment" or "treatment" should be given in such a case?

(c) "Man is an animal . . . he cannot with impunity allow the natural environment of living things from which he has so recently emerged to be destroyed." (Lord Shackleton.) What is the case for nature conservation? What species of animals are in danger of extinction and what is being or should be done about them? Is it in our own interests to preserve the natural world?

(d) "Man has lost the capacity to foresee and to forestall. He will end by destroying the earth." (Albert Schweitzer.) What has led to this danger? (Compare the passage from *Silent Spring* in Oral Work.) Did man ever have the capacity to foresee, or is it only recently that men have advanced so much as to be able to destroy on this scale? Should scientists take more care to see that their discoveries are put only to strictly controlled use?
(e) Litter. (Consider the picture below as an example.)

2. Write a story in which you imagine someone (possibly yourself) in one of the following situations:

(a) Faced with a child of about ten years old who has been caught in some act of wanton and apparently pointless destruction.
(b) A scientist who has discovered an immensely powerful new drug with incalculable potential for good or for evil.
(c) A naturalist fighting big business interests to save the wild life of an area of marshland wanted as a site for a factory, including a unique species of some insect.
(d) A game-keeper on a big-game reserve who has to try to persuade a hunter that one particular animal is *not* dangerous and must *not* be shot.
(e) A public health official who has just discovered that the "health-giving" waters of a well-known spa, with hundreds of hotels and clinics, are in fact poisonous and positively harmful.

Oral Work

1. Practise reading aloud the following passage:

The most alarming of all man's assaults upon the environment is the contamination of air, earth, rivers, and sea with dangerous and even lethal materials. This pollution is for the most part irrecoverable; the chain of evil it initiates not only in the world that must support life but in living tissues is for the most part irreversible. In this now universal contamination of the environment, chemicals are the sinister and little-recognized partners of radiation in changing the very nature of the world—the very nature of its life. Strontium 90, released through nuclear explosions into the air, comes to earth in rain or drifts down as fallout, lodges in the soil, enters into the grass or corn or wheat grown there, and in time takes up its abode in the bones of a human being, there to remain until his death. Similarly, chemicals sprayed on croplands or forests or gardens lie long in the soil, entering into living organisms, passing from one to another in a chain of poisoning and death. Or they pass mysteriously by underground streams until they emerge and, through the alchemy of air and sunlight, combine into new forms, that kill vegetation, sicken cattle, and work unknown harm on those who drink from once-pure wells.

(from *Silent Spring* by Rachel Carson)

Discuss the implications of this passage in the context of man's relationship to his environment, and the responsibility we now have because we know how to alter our environment so radically. What has led men to pollute rivers with detergent, to spray the land with chemicals (many of them poisonous), kill off wild life, and release radioactive materials into the atmosphere? Discuss other examples of man's short-sightedness, in cutting down forests or turning fertile grass-lands into dust-bowls. What can and should men do now to control their own environment and work with nature, rather than arbitrarily destroying natural life?

2. Discuss the more "emotional" aspects of man's relationships with animals, including his treatment of pets, domestic and farm animals, and animals used in scientific experiments. Has man the "right" to keep animals in cages or train them to do tricks for his own amusement? What about pets, so often bought and then neglected, or pampered and forced to live "unnatural" lives? Is the case very different when we consider the intensive breeding of animals for our food supply: battery hens, "factory farming" applied to pigs or cattle, and the wide-

135

spread use of hormones and drugs in a closely controlled environment to fatten the animals rapidly and economically? Is it wrong to treat animals in these ways; indeed, are these methods necesssary or desirable to produce our food? (Many people complain that the result is less tasty or less nutritious.)

Finally, there is the very controversial question of vivisection and the use of living animals in scientific experiments. No one can deny that the development of vaccines and drugs has saved countless human lives, but nearly all such new methods of treatment, or surgery, have meant the use of many animals in dangerous experiments. How much control should be exercised in these researches? What is the law now, and how would the opponents of vivisection (represented by the British Union for the Abolition of Vivisection and the National Anti-Vivisection Society) wish it to be changed? The R.S.P.C.A. and the League Against Cruel Sports also have points of view on the use of animals for science and for recreation.

Activities and Research

1. Find out what you can about the following organizations that are concerned with combating threats of destruction to the natural life in various parts of the world. This research might be undertaken by groups; only one letter should be sent to each address requesting information, with a large stamped, addressed envelope:

> The World Wildlife Fund
> Panda House, 29 Greville Street, LONDON, EC1N 8AX
>
> The Nature Conservancy,
> 19 Belgrave Square, LONDON, SW1X 8PY
>
> The Council for Nature,
> Zoological Gardens, Regent's Park, LONDON, NW1 4RY
>
> The Royal Society for the Protection of Birds,
> The Lodge, SANDY, Beds., SG19 2DL
>
> The British Trust for Ornithology,
> Beech Grove, TRING, Herts.

From these organizations and reference books in the library, magazine articles, documentary programmes on television, etc., find out which species of animals are most in danger of extinction, what is being done to create nature reserves, to promote the welfare of rare species and to protect threatened creatures (seals, whales, ospreys and other species of birds, land animals, such as bison, etc.). Find out also about control of pests that threaten the natural balance in certain areas, such as mink and coypu.

It should be easy to find illustrations from magazines and pamphlets, so that accounts could be attractively presented in folders or wall displays.

2. For wider aspects of threats to our "heritage", it would be worth writing to the following organizations:

The National Trust for Places of Historic
Interest or Natural Beauty,
42 Queen Anne's Gate, LONDON, SW19 9AS

The Countryside Commission,
1–2 Cambridge Gate, LONDON, NW1 4JY

The Council for the Protection of Rural England,
4 Hobart Place, LONDON, SW1W 0HY

The Commons, Open Spaces and Footpath
Preservation Society,
166 Shaftesbury Avenue, LONDON, WC2H 8JH

Under this heading, consider the threats today to our countryside as a whole, when towns are being constantly expanded and new roads, pipelines and electricity transmission lines are cutting up rural areas. What is done to preserve particular areas of outstanding beauty or to make available certain parts of the country for recreation?

Include research into the problems of litter and the disposal of unwanted junk in unofficial tips in the countryside, or for that matter in the streets and vacant plots in our towns. What restrictions govern the erection of unsightly or unsuitable buildings or hoardings in town or country?

Further Reading

"The Destructors" appears in *Twenty-one Stories* by GRAHAM GREENE (Heinemann; Penguin)
This collection includes other psychological studies of boys ("The Basement Room" and "The End of the Party"), and

other stories against a background provided by the Second World War ("When Greek meets Greek" and "Men at Work"). An interest in men and women and their feelings and motives shines through all these short stories, written between 1929 and 1954.

Silent Spring by RACHEL CARSON (Hamish Hamilton; Penguin) (574.65)
This book is a famous landmark in the study of man's relationship to his natural environment. In 1962 it came as a shock to many to realize how serious was the danger that man might be destroying the natural world of which he is an integral part. But the author is an outstanding writer as well as a scientist, and this book (like her others: *The Sea Around Us*, *The Edge of the Sea*, and *The Sea*) is extremely readable as well as disturbing.

Brighton Rock by GRAHAM GREENE (Heinemann; Penguin)
This novel is set in pre-war Brighton, where gangs of criminals, many of them young, terrorize the race-track. "The Boy", Pinkie, and his gang are guilty of murder and an innocent young waitress, Rose, is drawn in because she knows too much. But the novel is more than a crime story: it is a study of Pinkie's sense of guilt and Rose's love and trust, and the twisted relationship between them.

Our Man in Havana by GRAHAM GREENE (Heinemann; Penguin)
The author calls this an "entertainment" rather than a novel, and it is certainly a story of espionage and intrigue in the West Indies full of comic invention. But Graham Greene is an accomplished novelist, and offers interesting characterization and an intelligent undercurrent of ideas as well.

The Naked Ape by DESMOND MORRIS (Cape; Corgi) (572)
This fascinating book takes a fresh look at man as an animal and shows how in his sexual and his social life, in his aggressions and affections and even in his eating habits and his religious beliefs, he still follows patterns of behaviour that go back to his hunting-ape ancestors. It provides an exciting insight into the secret motivations of our behaviour, and explains much that might otherwise puzzle or disturb us.

CHAPTER NINE

Violence - II

BRUTALITY

Richard Hoggart's book "The Uses of Literacy" is a well-known analysis of the attitudes of working-class people in Northern England, and the books and magazines that were popular among them. In the chapter entitled: "The Newer Mass Art: Sex in Shiny Packets" he deals with "Spicy Magazines" and then "Sex-and-Violence Novels".

These are novels of violent sex, in which sex seems to be regarded as thrilling only when it is sadistic. There must be violence all the time: between the men, prolonged arm-twistings, razor-slashings, long-drawn-out beatings with rubber tubes: "He had a wound in his cheek that looked like a mouth that wouldn't stop bleeding." When man meets woman the air is heavy with violence, with drug-inspired moans, with embraces ending in bloody bites on both sides (the usual number seems to be two violent sexual contacts in each novel, as well as a few single-sex beatings-up); tongues get fiercely to work and finger-nails claw: "all the time her hips kept going like they had a dynamo inside there . . . she'd pull away, then she'd purr like a pussy when I snatched her back again."

There has been a literature of sexual adventure for centuries; one thinks of Nashe's *Unfortunate Traveller*, in one of its aspects, or of Defoe's *Moll Flanders*. There has been a literature of violence: there has been, on a small and esoteric scale, a literature of sadism and masochism. But this new form is rather different. This is not produced for a small and perverse set such as made their own use of the works of the Marquis de Sade. It has a wider appeal at its own level. It differs from the sex and violence of Nashe and Defoe in its ingrown quality: it is violent and sexual, but all in a claustrophobic and shut-in way.

Further, and here it contrasts strikingly with the writing of such as Pierre Laforgue, it exists in a world in which moral values have become irrelevant. The Laforgue books have often titles like, *Should He Forgive?*, *Shameful Payment*, *Fallen Beauty*, *Sullied*

Madonna, Bought Kisses, and *Retributions.* Such titles would be almost impossible for these later works, since "forgiveness", "shame", "retribution", and "to be sullied", "to fall", or "to pay" are concepts outside their moral orbit. In a list of fifty-five works by one author I found only one title which had a moral reference. . . .

The aim of the later writers is to make their readers feel the flesh and bone of violence. They cannot invoke the stock and formal thrills of anti-code behaviour, since there is no code: they must directly stir their readers' senses. They are, therefore, oddly enough and in a very limited way, much more in the situation of the truly creative writer towards his material than are writers of the Laforgue type, or the writers of love-stories in the women's magazines, or the writers of naughty stories in the "spicy" magazines. The gangster writers have to ensure that the physical thrill is actually communicated:

Suddenly Fatsy brought his knee hard up into Herb's groin. Herb's face came down sharp and Fatsy met it with his ham-like fist. The knuckles splintered the bone and made blood and flesh squelch like a burst pomegranate. Herb fell back to the tiled floor, retching teeth. He was bubbling gently as he lay there, so Fatsy gave him one in the belly with his steel-shod shoe. Then—just for luck—Fatsy ground his foot straight on the squelchy mess that useter be Herb's face. . . .

Gangster-fiction writing is in large measure dead, full of trite simile, weak imitation of tough American talk, and flatly photographic description. It moves in jerky, short-winded periods which match the thinness and one-sidedness of the imaginative presentation. Yet it undoubtedly has in parts a kind of life. When it is describing the thrill of inflicting pain, it sometimes moves closely along the nerve. It moves then with a crude force as it creates the sadistic situation; the images cease to be clichés and catch the nerve-thrill. It turns directly on to its objects and immerses itself in the detail of pain. At such moments it has the life of a cruel cartoon, and presents a similarly two-dimensional and lop-sided picture of experience. . . .

It seems probable that the cheap sex-fiction has developed in the way illustrated partly because our great cities have become more crowded, and because a sense of direction has become harder to find in them. This is the popular literature of an empty megalopolitan world. It is related, in its submerged sense of a great hollow where some purpose might be, to elements in Ernest Hemingway. *A Farewell to Arms* closes with Henry leaving the hospital where Catherine has died:

"You can't come in now," one of the nurses said.
"Yes, I can," I said.
"You can't come in yet."
"You get out," I said, "the other one too."

But after I had got them out and shut the door and turned off the light it wasn't any good. It was like saying goodbye to a statue. After a while I went out and left the hospital and walked back to the hotel in the rain.

A typical gangster-novelette is likely also to close with the narrator leaving the dead body of his love behind:

When I saw Fan was dead and cold, I just turned away. Spikey was saying something over and over, but I only knew there was a great hollow inside of me. I left the joint and started walking. I walked a mighty long way in the cold night. In the end, Spikey overtook me. "Come on, pal," he said, "there's a gang of us going on to Mike's place. The girls'll be glad to see you." I didn't answer. Maybe I didn't really hear. I only knew I wanted to go on walking, walking alone in the night.

In both books that final emptiness, though it is in each case specifically related to a death, symbolizes also a much wider and more pervasive emptiness. Indeed, the girls can only mean so much because they have seemed the only meaningful things in a whole disillusioning world. The parallels of tone are in most cases striking. I ought to add, perhaps, that the efforts made by each type of passage are not so much alike as this comparison suggests. The effects are decided by all that has gone before in each novel. The similarities are illuminating here; but Hemingway's world, I need hardly say, is much more mature than that of the gangster-novelette authors.

In the world of gangster-fiction there can be no happy endings, nor any endings which are really beginnings, attempts to restart life by staying in the same spot and doing what you can to build the city. You either end in the flat emptiness just illustrated, or induce the temporary impression of a new start by getting into a fast machine and roaring away down a concrete highway (the characters are usually rootless, without homes or permanent work). The tyres scud on the surface, the demands of the city are left behind; the demands on the personality are —you continue to hope—left with it; you are heading West, to a world where there may still be the childhood dream. Not that you really think so, but you go on—progressivism translated into an endless and hopeless tail-chasing evasion of the personality. This is the usual manner:

So we quit that city and headed down the turnpike for the next. I was dead sick of that joint and the countryside sure looked good to me with the sun on it. I let the old Chev. full out and she roared down the concrete at a steady eighty. I kept on like that for I don't know how many hours—biting off the miles—heading for I don't know what....

Running away from megalopolis; but in megalopolis's own product, the life-consuming machine. He'll be back; there is another town ahead, just the same as the others. After that, another escape; and so on, till sudden death puts an end to it.

(from *The Uses of Literacy* by Richard Hoggart)

Appreciation and Discussion

1. In what ways do the sex-and-violence novels differ from:
   (a) the older books of sexual adventure;
   (b) the literature of violence; and
   (c) the books of Pierre Laforgue? (Laforgue is an imaginary name, typical of the pen-names of authors of pre-war "spicy" books.)
2. (a) What does the author believe is "the situation of the truly creative writer towards his material"?
   (b) What accounts for the power of this writing about violence, according to the author?
   (c) Are gangster-novels of this kind consistently forceful?
3. What is wrong with our urban way of life (or sense of values), according to the author, that has led to the popularity of this kind of writing?
4. Why are there no happy endings in these novels?
5. (a) The author says gangster-fiction has much "flatly photographic description". What other phrase does he use later (in the same sixth paragraph of our extract) to explain the kind of writing he has in mind?
   (b) In what ways is this picture of the world like a "cruel cartoon", as the author suggests?
6. Hoggart writes of the gangster hero trying to leave behind —or evade—the "demands on the personality". What kind of demands do you think he has in mind?
7. This passage includes three short extracts from this kind of gangster-novelette writing (actually close imitations of the

typical style, written by Hoggart). From them, find examples of (a) "trite simile", (b) imitation of tough American talk, and (c) "images that cease to be clichés and catch the nerve-thrill". One feature of the transatlantic style slang is the invented or distorted word—"kinda" and "sorta" are common examples; (d) find an example of this slang from the three typical passages.

8. Elsewhere, the author describes the "tough", clipped style of these novelettes as "debased Hemingway". What other feature of the gangster-novels does he attribute to Hemingway's influence? What contrast does he make between Hemingway's work and that of his cheap imitators?

9. What do the following mean, as used in this extract? esoteric; sadism; masochism; claustrophobic; trite; short-winded periods; megalopolitan; pervasive; progressivism; evasion of the personality.

10. When Hoggart talks of these novelettes as "claustrophobic", "ingrown" and giving a ". . . lop-sided picture of experience," what kind of experiences or values are being left out? Are there other aspects of sexual relationships, or of physical effort, pain and violence, that the novelettes simply ignore?

11. These sensational novels convey the physical thrills of sex and violence in a cheap, popular form and against a background without any sense of right or wrong. Would such literature encourage crime and violence? Or do books simply supply a fantasy-world which readers do not confuse with the real world? Is it only a certain type of person who wants to escape into this kind of fiction?

12. Hoggart wrote this book in 1957. Have other kinds of popular literature taken the place of the sex-and-violence gangster-novelettes he was describing? For instance, has the spy taken over from the gangster? Give examples of the popular cheap novelettes you know. Are the attitudes to violence, death, sex or heroism changing? Is there a new vocabulary or a new kind of characterization in sensational literature now?

13. What, if anything, should be banned from our bookstalls (or film and television screens) by law? Where would you draw the line and say that literature is obscene or pornagraphic—likely to deprave and corrupt people who read it? Should children be protected by any special regulations —or is that simply the responsibility of their parents?

Hunting with a Stick

Once, ten years old, in the cobweb sun
I chased a rabbit on stiffening grass
Till it twinkled into its hole of sand.
Although I knew that the hunt was done
(For rabbits burrow deeper than fire)
I crouched and crept there, stretching my hand,
And kneeling my shadow on frost I saw
In a turn of the hole too tight to pass
Its fluffed fat haunches were firmly jammed,
Its white tail sat as still as a star.

The moment froze in a single breath:
Give me a second and I could be quick,
Having spent ten years in the ways of death,
And I wanted this death, not one planned.
I thrust at its buttocks with my stick
And felt the soft bone go under the fur,
The silence I knelt on echo and stir,
The green meat of mornings that made me sick . . .

I dragged it back by a fistful of hair,
Then flourished my prize with a dripping claw;
But dangling it upwards again I saw
Its face was bitten and muffled in blood
One eye was empty and showed the skull
The soft jaw was eaten into a snarl,
Death hung from its ears in a glistening hood.

And at ten years old I first understood
There were other deaths in the world than me,
More ways to kill than with stone and stick:
While my shadow falconed it from the air
A stoat had sat in its horror there
And bitten its borrowing bone to the quick.

MICHAEL BALDWIN

Discussing the Poem

1. Who really killed the rabbit—the stoat or the boy?
2. How did the boy (the poet) feel when he saw the rabbit
   "firmly jammed"? Do all three of the last lines of verse two

depend on the verb "and felt . . ."? Why do you think he mentions the "green meat of mornings?"

3. In what ways does he convey the impression that the stoat was cruel and its attack ugly? Discuss the words and phrases he uses.

4. What did the poet learn about death? Would he have been more sensitive and less cruel after this experience, do you think?

5. Discuss the interesting figurative language here—adjectives like ". . . the *cobweb* sun", ". . . *stiffening* grass", ". . . *muffled* in blood"—". . . *kneeling* my shadow . . .", verbs like "*twinkled*", "the moment *froze*"; and comparisons such as "deeper than fire", "as still as a star", "death hung from its ears in a glistening hood."

6. The poem makes interesting use of *rhyme* and *alliteration*, as well as having a clear *rhythm* pattern. Find and discuss examples of these.

Techniques

Exercise 1. The following is an extract from the *Pilkington Report on Broadcasting* and considers the possible effects of violence portrayed on television to an audience including children.

(a) Make two separate lists of notes, one of the different kinds of violence thought to do harm to children, and the other of the different reasons why such violence might do the children harm.

We deal first with violence. This was widely defined by those who criticized its portrayal as including not only physical violence, but also an unfeeling or cruel disposition of mind which might express itself in speech or apparently casual habits alone, and not necessarily in acts of overt violence. On the whole, the critics recognized that the stylized conventions to be found in Sherwood Forest or in Ruritania, or in the old-fashioned "Cowboys and Indians" programme, robbed violence of much of its effect, and thought that such programmes were in themselves harmless. But this could not be said of some of the newer "sophisticated" Westerns which depict recognizable psychological problems in an atmosphere of violence and brutality. And the constant repetition of even the most stylized scenes of violence was thought to be harmful.

Disquiet at the portrayal of violence was expressed on three main grounds. The first was that scenes of violence frightened small children, that small children were disturbed by any programmes which suggested a threat to the world which they knew and in which they felt secure; and that the most cruel threat was violence. The second was that such programmes might lead children to dangerous, and even disastrous, experiment. The third was that showing violence encouraged anti-social, callous and even vicious attitudes and behaviour. These three grounds were not always differentiated, for the same programme will affect different people differently. To show that it does not affect one part of the audience is not to show that it affects no other part. The disquiet was, then, about the general effect of violence, and it led to two main criticisms of programmes in which it featured. The first criticism was simply that too much violence was shown on television. Some put this criticism to us merely as an example of lack of balance—where time was limited it was given undue prominence. But most claimed that it was the constant repetition of violence, rather than the fact that it was shown at all, which was damaging. The second main criticism was of the treatment of violence. Many submissions recorded the view that it was often used gratuitously, that it often did little or nothing to develop plot or characterization and that it was, presumably, thrown in "for kicks". Another common opinion was that it was often unnecessarily emphasized by being shown in close-up and by being lingered over. The damage was not necessarily repaired by ensuring that, in the end, the good were seen to win and the bad to lose, and that crime did not pay: conventional endings of this sort did not penetrate to the level at which the portrayal of violence had its emotional effect. What mattered was that violence provided the emotional energy, the dramatic content, of the programme.

Though the damage was said to be to all age groups, submissions criticizing violence in television were almost without exception especially concerned about its effect on children. It was not enough to produce between the hours of 5 and 6 p.m. programmes suitable for children. Until 9 p.m. audiences, we were told, included a great many children. Children, particularly very young children, were especially defenceless. Self-evidently, they lacked experience and discrimination; for them the distinction between reality and make-believe was often obscured. When violence, through television with all its power of dramatic presentation, invaded the security of the home, and did so in a form which was not to the watching child a game being played, then the child suffered. For the Church of England, Bishop Cockin voiced a general view when he told us that the danger and damage lay in brutality in any form. "Most of what we might think is rather pernicious passes over a child's head, but brutality does not: it hits it".

(from *The Report of the Committee on Broadcasting*, 1960)

Discuss and compare your own notes: how far do they agree with the following headings?

Kinds

(i) Physical violence—especially when unnecessary and highly dramatic.
(ii) Cruelty in speech and attitudes.
(iii) Psychological problems leading to violent behaviour.
(iv) Even stylized violence when constantly repeated.

Reasons

(i) Small children may fear violent threats to a familiar world.
(ii) Children may copy weapons and brutal behaviour.
(iii) Children may grow up accepting callous attitudes as normal because:
    (a) there is too much violence in proportion to other viewing, and
    (b) it often has great emphasis and emotional impact.
(iv) Violence has a direct effect on children when they lack experience to distinguish fiction from fact.

(b) When you are satisfied with your notes, make *two* short summaries. The first summary, in not more than 70 words (of continuous prose, not notes), should explain what kinds of violence were thought harmful to children. The second should be not more than 120 words and should explain various ways in which violence on television may do harm to children. Write in complete sentences and use your own words as far as possible.

Exercise 2. (a) Discuss the different meanings of the words printed in italics in the following pairs, as suggested by the different contexts. The *first* example in each pair is taken from the passage from the *Pilkington Report on Broadcasting* printed in Exercise 1 above.

Write suitable sentences to illustrate the second meaning of each word in the pairs, as distinct from the first meaning from the passage.

e.g. We *deal*—a great *deal*
A great deal of the violence portrayed on television comes at a time when many children may be watching and be harmed by it.
casual habits—*casual* labour;
habits alone—monks' *habits*;

stylized *conventions*—political parties' *conventions*;
atmosphere of violence—the upper *atmosphere*;
callous attitudes—*callous* (or *calloused*) hands;
many *submissions*—the *submission* of an enemy;
recorded the view—*recorded* the interview;
develop plot—*develop* film;
to *produce* programmes—agricultural *produce*;
lacked *discrimination*—practised *discrimination*.

(b) The following words from the same passage (again in italics) are easily confused with the words paired with them; again, make up suitable sentences to make the distinction between them quite clear:

e.g. cruel *disposition*—cruel *dispossession*.

In this cruel case of *dispossession* and eviction by the authorities, the inhabitants of the dilapidated cottages were given no right to appeal.

casual habits—*causal* relationship;
overt violence—*avert* violence;
disquiet—*unquiet*;
vicious—*viscous*;
differentiated grounds—*differential* scales;
gratuitously—*graciously*;
conventional endings—*convectional* currents;
exception—*accession*;
its *effect* on children—to *affect* the children;
pernicious—*perverse*.

Exercise 3. In the Appreciation and Discussion questions about the passage, we noted the use of a tough, trite and rather slangy and distorted style in gangster-novelettes.

(a) Re-examine the examples quoted in the passage (both the shorter quotations at the beginning and the paragraphs in smaller type). Discuss all the faults or weaknesses of style.

(b) Collect or make up other examples of
   (i) typical trite similies;
   (ii) made-up words coined for this kind of writing.

(c) The most obvious weakness of the two passages overleaf is the use of short sentences, jerkily put together, some of them not grammatically sentences at all.

Rewrite the passages, combining the sentences into more balanced, longer ones, but do not add or omit any information, and keep a similar vocabulary.

(i) He saw Liz. She was lying on the floor. Her neck was twisted at an unnatural angle. The side of her face was covered in blood. He turned away. He knew she was dead. He suddenly felt cold. Cold and empty inside. Duke tugged his sleeve. But Harrison did not notice. He only knew what he felt inside. He pushed his way out. And started walking. Into the night. Only the night could understand. It was as cold and empty as he was. He didn't look back.

(ii) I pushed my foot down. The engine roared. I swung round the corner. And I headed straight down the highway. The needle crept round the clock. Eighty. Ninety. A hundred. I just kept going. The car ate up the distance. The hours slid past. Afternoon became dusk. Dusk became night. My head ached. My joints were stiff. But I didn't stop. I couldn't. Too much depended on this trip. Then it happened. I must have been half-asleep. A bend loomed up ahead. I jerked awake. I slammed on the brakes. The car left the road. It seemed to float through the air. Everything was in slow motion. A tree zoomed at me. I blacked out.

(d) Now discuss the comparisons, vocabulary and ideas in the passages, and see if you can rewrite one of the passages so as to express the same experience in a more effective way.

Topics for Written Work

1. Write a poem or a short prose description of a cruel or brutal incident that you have been involved in, that you have witnessed, or that you have seen reported. Bring out as vividly and as clearly as you can the effect that this had upon you.

This is not intended to be a sensational, make-believe description. Your poem or account should be a completely honest piece of reporting. However much we may disapprove of brutality and cruelty, we cannot ignore the fact that they take place and that many people, at some time or another, deliberately inflict suffering and pain. The incident itself may seem quite trivial but it should be something that affected you strongly. The cruelty need not be physical, of course; the poem *Mac*, by a pupil, shows that mental cruelty can be just as brutal. You may use a newspaper report or a photograph as the basis for your writing, as Michael has done in the poem *N.S.P.C.C.*, written after seeing photographic evidence of cruelty to a child.

Mac

They call him Mac and make fun of him.
He is too afraid to fight back.

Mac! Mac! they yell at him and he leaves
His set and goes to them.
They tease him and in the end they
Tease him so much that he strikes
With his fists but misses them.

They try to make him mad again.
Mac! Mac! you can't catch us Mac!
He comes to them again and
Catches a boy who he brings
Hurling to the ground.

When he gets up he goes for him
Again.
Mac! Mac! let go of me Mac.

The boy wears a tattered coat and
His unbrushed hair is blown in the
Wind.   JOHN

N.S.P.C.C.

The bloody strap
across my back
whistles
through the air;
my back is blue,
my face is pale,
my teeth chatter as it strikes;
my toes curl up,
my fingers are stiff,
the buckle falls,
a second of rest after each strike,
the tears fall upon the ground
the echo of the screaming
the sweat squelches out of my pores,
the strap strikes
Again
And again.   MICHAEL

2. Write a discussion essay giving your views on censorship with special reference to books, plays, films and television programmes that may be considered offensive or contain too much brutality. Consider all the points raised in Exercise 1 of the Techniques section (page 146) and in the Oral Work section, and also the following extracts from an address given by Sir Hugh Greene, then Director-General of the BBC, in 1965. He is discussing the pressure that now comes from groups claiming to represent "ordinary decent people":

Such a censorship is the more to be condemned when we remember that, historically, the greatest risks have attached to the maintenance of what is right and honourable and true: honourable men who venture to be different, to move ahead of—or even against—the general trend of public feeling, with sincere conviction and with the intention of enlarging the understanding of our society and its problems, may well feel the scourge of public hostility many times over before their work is recognized. It is the clear duty of a public service organization to stand firm against attempts to decry sincerity and vision, whether in the field of public affairs or in the less easily judged world of the arts including the dramatic art.

I believe that broadcasters have a duty not to be diverted by arguments in favour of what is, in fact, disguised censorship. I believe we have a duty to take account of the changes in society, to be ahead of public opinion rather than always to wait upon it. I believe that great broadcasting organizations, with their immense powers of patronage for writers and artists, should not neglect to cultivate young writers who may, by many, be considered "too advanced", even "shocking". Such allegations have been made throughout the ages. Many writers have been condemned as subversive when first published. Henrik Ibsen, for example, was at one time regarded as too shocking for his plays to be staged in Britain. . . .

I do not need to be reminded that broadcasting has access to every home, and to an audience of all ages and varying degrees of sophistication. We must rely, therefore, not only on our own disciplines but on those which have to be exercised by, among others, parents. Programme plans must, to my mind, be made on the assumption that the audience is capable of reasonable behaviour, and of the exercise of intelligence—and of choice. . . .

Relevance is the key—relevance to the audience, and to the tide of opinion in society. Outrage is impermissible. Shock is not always so. Provocation may be healthy and indeed socially imperative.

(from *The Listener*)

Oral Work

Discuss the topic of censorship in the arts; the following questions are relevant:

1. Has "society" (the majority of us?) the right to impose certain standards of behaviour on everybody—at least in public?
2. If so, what kinds of behaviour are to be forbidden, and why? Should artists, for instance, be prevented from showing publicly any work that might be considered offensive? Who should judge or "censor" them?
3. How do censorship or other controls work now? Consider (separately) films, books and newspapers, plays, television.
4. At present in Britain, "obscene publications" can be prosecuted. The prosecution have to prove that the published work may "tend to deprave and corrupt" those who are likely to see it. It is no longer necessary for the defence to prove that the work has literary merit. How would you define "obscenity" and "pornography" in deciding what should be banned?
5. Is there an important distinction between violence (in works of literature or art), and sexual excitement? Is it for any reason (as the passage by Richard Hoggart seems to suggest) more important to discourage the vivid description of brutality than to discourage descriptions that are sexually exciting?
6. The difficult question is: do vivid descriptions, either of violence or of sexual contacts, lead the readers to imitation (e.g. in violent crime and sexual assault), or are these a "safety valve" for feelings that would otherwise lead to anti-social behaviour? What is your opinion? Perhaps it is only abnormal people, or those who are guilt-ridden, who *want* to be stimulated in this way?
7. Finally, it is often argued that the medium makes a great deal of difference—so that what is harmless in a written description becomes more harmful as a picture or a film, and most liable to corrupt people when on television. Television is of course in one's own home, a vivid picture thrust right into the family circle. Should there be different standards for (a) television, (b) films (e.g. "A" and "X" certificates), (c) stage plays and (d) books, magazines, etc.?

Activities and Research

1. Make a critical and comparative study of examples of brutality and violence in literature, both the "classics" and cheap modern paperbacks, magazines and also "comics" or picture-books. Include reference to the so-called "theatre of cruelty". Can you draw a clear distinction between the violence in *King Lear* (the blinding of an old man, Gloucester, takes place on stage in this play) or other established novels or plays, and the violence in the fiction that Hoggart was describing?

What are the "stock" situations and characters that recur in "comics": the war stories, gangster stories, Westerns and spy thrillers? (Look at the example on page 83.)

Examine the "James Bond" series of stories that were so popular in the 1960s. What is the usual "formula" and what "ingredients" are required to make these novels successful?

2. Carry out a survey of the amount of violence shown on television between the hours of 5 p.m. and 11 p.m. in any one evening or one week. Organize a rota so that every programme can be covered, and work out how you will record the results of your viewing. e.g. (a) Killing (methods—shooting, stabbing, strangling etc.?), (b) Woundings (c) Fights (types?) etc. If possible, make notes on the way the violence was treated. Was it "shown in close-up" or "lingered over"?

Further Reading

The Uses of Literacy by RICHARD HOGGART (Chatto and Windus; Penguin) (301.44)
The author begins his Preface: "This book is about changes in working-class culture during the last thirty or forty years, in particular as they are being encouraged by mass publications." First published in 1957, it retains its fascination as a detached and yet extremely vivid and well-informed picture of popular entertainments in the context of urban Northern England.
Dr. No by IAN FLEMING (Jonathan Cape; Pan)
Fleming is a writer in the tradition of Edgar Wallace and Raymond Chandler—thrills, gimmicks, suspense, violence, glamour and sex are combined in fast-moving stories that are, to quote one reviewer "irresistibly, mercilessly readable". Other critics have deplored the attitudes, particularly towards violence, that are found in his books. These, all published by Cape and Pan, include: *Goldfinger*; *Moonraker*; *Thunderball*; *Live and*

Let Die; *Diamonds are Forever*; *Casino Royale*; *From Russia with Love*.

Fleming's hero is James Bond, a suave Secret Service Agent, Number 007, "licensed to kill", who has been made even more famous by the film versions of Fleming's stories.

The Spy Who Came in from the Cold by JOHN LE CARRÉ (Victor
  Gollancz)

This book provides an excellent contrast to the escapist spy thrillers of Ian Fleming, where real emotion is almost totally lacking. Here the emotions *are* real, and the plot is completely credible. The central character, Alec Leemas, is not a magnificent hero like James Bond; he is a "small man". The action is complex and to summarize it here would spoil the story. The book, and the film, are strongly recommended.

Billy the Kid—A poetry anthology compiled by MICHAEL
  BALDWIN (Hutchinson Educational) (821.8)

Those of you who think poetry is concerned only with sweet sentiments, (even after reading Michael Baldwin's *Hunting with a Stick*) should try this anthology of tough poetry. Not all the poems are of a high standard and some of them are very brutal, but they will certainly set you thinking about the implications of violence and cruelty.

CHAPTER TEN

Far Away Places

In 1914 Arthur Grimble, a young and inexperienced cadet in the Colonial Service, was sent to the Gilbert and Ellice Islands in the Pacific, where he lived for the next six years. Here he describes an octopus hunt.

The Gilbertese happen to value certain parts of it as food, and their method of fighting it is coolly based upon the one fact that its arms never change their grip. They hunt for it in pairs. One man acts as the bait, his partner as the killer. First, they swim eyes-under at low tide just off the reef, and search the crannies of the submarine cliff for sight of any tentacle that may flicker out for a catch. When they have placed their quarry, they land on the reef for the next stage. The human bait starts the real game. He dives and tempts the lurking brute by swimming a few strokes in front of its cranny, at first a little beyond striking range. Then he turns and makes straight for the cranny, to give himself into the embrace of those waiting arms. Sometimes nothing happens. The beast will not always respond to the lure. But usually it strikes.

The partner on the reef above stares down through the pellucid water, waiting for his moment. His teeth are his only weapon. His killing efficiency depends on his avoiding every one of those strangling arms. He must wait until his partner's body has been drawn right up to the entrance of the cleft. The monster inside is groping then with its horny mouth against the victim's flesh, and sees nothing beyond it. That point is reached in a matter of no more than thirty seconds after the decoy has plunged. The killer dives, lays hold of his pinioned friend at arms' length, and jerks him away from the cleft; the octopus is torn from the anchorage of its proximal suckers, and clamps itself the more fiercely to its prey. In the same second, the human bait gives a kick which brings him, with quarry annexed, to the surface. He turns on his back, still holding his breath for better buoyancy, and this exposes the body of the beast for the kill. The killer closes in, grasps the evil head from behind, and wrenches it away from its meal. Turning the face up towards himself, he plunges his teeth between the bulging eyes, and bites down and in with all his strength. That is the end of it. It dies on the instant; the suckers release their hold; the arms fall away; the two fishers paddle with whoops of delighted laughter to the reef, where they string the catch to a pole before going to rout out the next one.

Any two boys of seventeen, any day of the week, will go out and get you half a dozen octopus like that for the mere fun of it. Here lies the whole point of this story. The hunt is, in the most literal sense, nothing but child's play to the Gilbertese.

As I was standing one day at the end of a jetty in Tarawa lagoon, I saw two boys from the near village shouldering a string of octopus slung on a pole between them. . . . Then they began whispering together. I knew in a curdling flash what they were saying to each other. . . . I was already known as a young Man of Matang who liked swimming, and fishing, and laughing with the villagers; I had just shown an interest in this particular form of hunting; naturally, I should enjoy the fun of it as much as they did. Without even waiting for my answer, they gleefully ducked off the edge of the reef to look for another octopus—a fine fat one—*mine*.

I hope I did not look as yellow as I felt when I stood to take the plunge; I have never been so sick with funk before or since. "Remember, one hand for your eyes," said someone from a thousand miles off, and I dived.

I do not suppose it is really true that the eyes of an octopus shine in the dark; besides, it was clear daylight only six feet down in the limpid water; but I could have sworn the brute's eyes burned at me as I turned in towards his cranny. That dark glow—whatever may have been its origin—was the last thing I saw as I blacked out with my left hand and rose into his clutches. Then I remember chiefly a dreadful sliminess with a herculean power behind it. Something whipped round my left forearm and the back of my neck, binding the two together. In the same flash, another something slapped itself high on my forehead, and I felt it crawling down inside the back of my singlet. My impulse was to tear at it with my right hand, but I felt the whole of that arm pinioned to my ribs. In most emergencies the mind works with crystal-clear impersonality. This was not even an emergency, for I knew myself perfectly safe. But my boyhood's nightmare was upon me. When I felt the swift constriction of those disgusting arms jerk my head and shoulders in towards

the reef, my mind went blank of every thought save the beastliness of contact with that squat head. A mouth began to
nuzzle below my throat, at the junction of the collar-bones. I
forgot there was anyone to save me. Yet something still directed
me to hold my breath.

I was awakened from my cowardly trance by a quick, strong
pull on my shoulders, back from the cranny. The cables around
me tightened painfully, but I knew I was adrift from the reef.
I gave a kick, rose to the surface and turned on my back with
the brute sticking out of my chest like a tumour. My mouth was
smothered by some flabby moving horror. The suckers felt like
hot rings pulling at my skin. It was only two seconds, I suppose,
from then to the attack of my deliverer, but it seemed like a
century of nausea.

My friend came up between me and the reef. He pounced,
pulled, bit down, and the thing was over—for everyone but me.
At the sudden relaxation of the tentacles, I let out a great breath,
sank, and drew in the next under water. It took the united help
of both boys to get me, coughing, heaving and pretending to
join in their delighted laughter, back to the reef. I had to
submit there to a kind of war-dance round me, in which the
dead beast was slung whizzing past my head from one to the
other. I had a chance to observe then that it was not by any
stretch of fancy a giant, but just plain average. That took the
bulge out of my budding self-esteem. I left hurriedly for the
cover of the jetty, and was sick.

(from *A Pattern of Islands* by Sir Arthur Grimble)

Appreciation and Discussion

1. What *two* motives do the young islanders have for hunting octopus?
2. What *one* fact about an octpous makes this way of killing it possible? Quote a *noun clause* from the first paragraph as your answer.
3. Where do the octopus live and what keeps them in the same position?
4. (a) List all the different nouns used to name the octopus in this passage (for instance, in the seventh line of the first paragraph it is called their "quarry").
   (b) Comment on the "emotional tone" of these words, as compared with the plain word "octopus".
5. Two men hunt the octopus together; one man is the "killer". List at least *five* names (nouns) given to the killer's partner in the course of the first two paragraphs.
6. What quality of the water makes this form of hunting possible, and why is it so necessary? (Two synonymous adjectives are used to describe the water, one in the second and one in the sixth paragraph: what are they?)
7. (a) Why is it important for the killer to "wait for his moment"?
   (b) How does he finally kill the octopus?
8. Judging from the evidence throughout the passage, work out how long the whole kill would take from the moment the decoy plunges into the sea.
9. Where were the author's hands while he was in the clutches of the octopus?
10. What various words and phrases does the author use to describe (a) the arms of the octopus, and (b) its mouth?
11. What words and phrases prepare the reader for the fact that the author is sick at the end of this incident?
12. Why had he little reason to be proud of himself by Gilbertese standards?
13. What details here show (a) that Grimble was conscious of his reputation and position as a British District Officer, and (b) that he overcame a genuine horror of the octopus for the sake of his pride? Would you have acted as he did in the circumstances? Do you think he would gain the respect of the islanders by this kind of behaviour?

The World is Too Much with Us

The world is too much with us; late and soon,
Getting and spending, we lay waste our powers:
Little we see in Nature that is ours;
We have given our hearts away, a sordid boon;
This sea that bares her bosom to the moon;
The winds that will be howling at all hours,
And are up-gathered now like sleeping flowers;
For this, for everything, we are out of tune;
It moves us not. — Great God! I'd rather be
A Pagan suckled in a creed outworn;
So might I, standing on this pleasant lea,
Have glimpses that would make me less forlorn;
Have sight of Proteus rising from the sea;
Or hear old Triton blow his wreathèd horn.

WILLIAM WORDSWORTH

Discussing the Poem

1. Make sure you understand the language and allusions in this
   poem: a "boon", for instance, means a blessing or a gift;
   and since Proteus and Triton are both sea gods according to
   Greek and Roman mythology (find out more about them
   from a classical dictionary), we may assume that the
   "outworn Pagan creed" is the worship of Greek and Roman
   gods.
2. Where is the poet standing as he thinks these thoughts? Why
   would he rather have been a Greek or Roman?
3. What was it that Wordsworth believed his generation (in the
   early nineteenth century) were out of touch, or "out of tune"
   with? Is it significant that he gives the word "nature" a
   capital N?
4. This poem is a *sonnet*. It contains fourteen lines rhymed
   together in one of the limited number of patterns used by
   Petrarch, an Italian poet of the fourteenth century, and by
   many English sonnet writers, including John Milton.
   Notice how one set of rhymes carries the poem through eight
   lines (the "octave") and another takes over for the final six
   (the "sestet"). Is there a corresponding break in the sense of
   of the poem?

Techniques

Exercise 1. The following passage is adapted from an article in *The Guardian* about a visit to the annual Festival of Ancient Greek Drama at Epidaurus in Greece. Study it and answer the questions below.

The evening sunshine came slanting over the tops of the pines at Epidaurus into the fan-shaped amphitheatre. Promptly at half past seven, as if by perfect stage management, the sun sank behind the trees, a great gong boomed and echoed in the hills, and the audience of 14,000 were silenced. Bronze doors at the back of the stage opened and the rich vibrant voice of Katina Paxinou took command. The Festival of Epidaurus had begun.

The ancient Theatre of Epidaurus, designed and built by Polyclitus in the middle of the fourth century BC, is the best preserved and most beautiful in Greece. It sits comfortably and naturally on the western slopes of Mount Kynortion. The seats rise steeply in 55 rows, divided horizontally into two concentric zones by a gangway. . . . The acoustics are so good that even the faintest whisper of an actor's voice is audible everywhere.

Every summer the National Theatre of Greece stages at Epidaurus a festival of ancient Greek drama. This year the festival offered Euripides's *Phoenissae, Oedipus Rex, Hercules Furens, Hecuba, Lysistrata,* and Menander's *Misanthrope.* It is organized by the National Tourist Organization and the Hellenic Touring Club.

The problems which the National Greek Theatre had to face were, as Anghelos Terzakis, the Director of Repertory puts it, first, "whether the classical play itself is, in fact, a prisoner of its times or can burst through these bonds and make direct contact with the broader spirit of man; and secondly, assuming the validity of the ancient drama outside the limits of its own time, what is the best method of interpreting it? Should its manner be drawn from the artistic, social, and intellectual climate of its own times? Or should it be adapted to present-day sensibilities, thus bridging the centuries, but without altering the substance or spirit of the classical dramatic type?"

For myself I am glad that they have rejected the "museum piece" type of presentation. I have little Greek, but with the English translation to help out, I was moved beyond words. Katina Paxinou as Iocasta dominated *Phoenissae* in such a way that even when she was offstage her presence was felt. Alexis Minotis, who played the blind Oedipus, held the vast audience breathless on his every word.

Not until now have I known what the Greek chorus was all about. But at Epidaurus I felt it spoke for me and said the things I wanted to say. Here it expressed for me the emotions I was too shy to express for myself.

After the performance came the hundred-mile drive back to
Athens, past floodlit ancient monuments at Mycenae and Corinth
and all the way along the route—but my mind was still on what I
had seen and heard at Epidaurus and I knew the meaning of catharsis.

RONALD LLOYD

(a) Summarize, in not more than 100 of your own words, all
that this article tells you of the location, date, shape and design
of the theatre at Epidaurus. (State at the end the number of
words you have used.)

(b) Sum up, in not more than 40 of your own words, the *two*
problems facing directors of ancient Greek plays in considering
them for production before a modern audience. (State the
number of words you use.)

162

(c) Which solution did this production adopt to the second of these two problems?

(d) What was the function of the chorus in a production of the kind described here?

(e) Why does the author mention the floodlit ruins of Mycenae and Corinth?

(f) Look up the plays mentioned here in the *Oxford Companion to Classical Literature*, or a similar reference book.

  (i) Which ancient Greek authors are represented in this selection of plays?

  (ii) Which of the plays are tragedies and which are comedies?

  (iii) Which particular play did this writer see? What part do Oedipus and Iocasta play in the story of that play?

(g) Find out the meaning and origin of the term "catharsis" and explain what this has to do with Greek tragedy.

Exercise 2. Study the following account of the octopus.

The octopus is a mollusc that has a soft body and eight tentacles, each clad in powerful suckers, which radiate from its mouth. The name comes from Greek and means "eight feet". On its head it has two eyes and it breathes through gills. The horny jaws of its mouth resemble a parrot's beak, and inside there is a long armoured tongue or radula, with which food can be grated into small fragments. The octopus eats crabs, lobsters and fish, which are caught by the power-ful sucker discs on its arms and drawn into the mouth.

The octopus usually rests quietly in a niche among rocks on the sea-bed during the day, and is more active at night. On the sea-bed, it walks head downwards on its eight legs, but it can swim by means of a "siphon" or funnel beneath the head, which ejects water out and propels the creature backwards very rapidly. When either frightened or very excited, the octopus will emit an inky fluid through this same tube, which confuses its enemy as a smoke-screen would. This black fluid is secreted from a gland near its liver. As a further protection, the octopus can change its own colour to match its surroundings.

Octopuses are found especially in the Mediterranean, the China Seas, the Hawaiian Islands and parts of America. They vary greatly in size, with arms of up to 10 metres span in the Giant Octopus in the Pacific. In several parts of the world they are hunted and eaten as a delicacy.

The octopus reproduces by laying large clusters of eggs which are carefully guarded by the female. Young octopods are about 2 cm long, with their arms as mere buds round the minute head.

In what kind of context would you expect to find such a description? The account of an encounter with an octopus in the passage from *A Pattern of Islands* is *subjective* (what does that mean?). Arthur Grimble's feelings about the creature influence his choice of words:

"the lurking brute—the beast—every one of those strangling arms—the monster inside is groping with its horny mouth against the victim's flesh—clamps itself more fiercely to its prey—grasps the evil head . . . and wrenches it away from its meal—the bulging eyes—the brute's eyes burned—a dreadful sliminess with a Herculean power—I felt it crawling— those disgusting arms—the beastliness of contact with that squat head—the brute sticking out of my chest like a tumour —some flabby moving horror—the suckers felt like hot rings —a century of nausea"

In contrast, what word describes the style of the account we have reprinted in this exercise? Which of the two accounts is more reliable as evidence of what an octopus is like? Which is more vivid or more likely to fire your imagination?

Write your own description of an octopus, basing it on the vocabulary and imagery that Grimble uses. In fact, write a short subjective description (not the story of an incident, as in the case of the extract from *A Pattern of Islands*), to contrast with the objective or scientific account given above.

Exercise 3. Notice how many times the word "octopus" appears in the fictional account in Exercise 2. Compare this with the number of times the word is used in the three paragraphs of the passage from *A Pattern of Islands*, which is almost as full of factual information. Note how the words "quarry", "brute", "beast" and "monster" are used partly to convey the writer's attitude to the creature, but also to avoid monotonous repetition of the word "octopus". Pronouns and other references (for instance, "grasps the evil head" instead of "grasps the octopus by its head"), or other constructions, are also used to add variety and interest to the style of the passage.

The following passages are written in a poor style, with too little variety in their sentence structure and vocabulary. Rewrite each, improving its style without adding to or altering the context of the passage:

(a) All the cups in the office were all cracked and dirty. I cannot stand a cracked cup: at home we always throw away cracked cups because the cracks harbour germs. So I took my own cup to the office to use instead of the cracked cups.

(b) There are many different ideas of an ideal holiday. For one person the ideal may be a holiday abroad, in exotic surroundings. For another the ideal holiday may be an active holiday; for another person the ideal holiday may be a holiday doing nothing. Perhaps the ideal holiday for most people is to do something quite different from what they do when not on holiday.

(c) There are two different kinds of turtles: marine turtles live in the sea and mud turtles live in fresh water. Marine turtles are divided into five species of turtles, but the leathery turtle is noticeably different from the other four species of turtles. The leathery turtle is the largest of all turtles, and the leathery turtle can reach a length of $2\frac{1}{2}$ m. The leathery turtle is rarely seen because these turtles live in the deepest waters, but leathery turtles do come ashore to breed. Leathery turtles lay their eggs in holes in the warm sand. The young turtles escape to the sea as soon as they are hatched.

In a recent article in *The Listener*, Nancy Mitford objected to certain faults of style that are becoming common. The following examples embody these faults. What is wrong with each of them and how could they be improved?

(d) The Prime Minister has been undergoing character assassination.
(e) In this day and age we have more works of book length than ever before.
(f) This I believe to be true, that experts will think up many new

theories, read up the research that has been done already, and meet up with other experts to discuss their ideas.

(g) Well now, we have in fact been fortunate enough to obtain a personal television interview with a personal friend of the person in question, and in fact we now hope to contact all those who have had recent personal contact with him.

Similarly, George Orwell, in his essay *Politics and the English Language*, wrote the following imitiation of a politician's jargon. What does this really mean?

(h) While freely conceding that the Soviet régime exhibits certain features which the humanitarian may be inclined to deplore, we must, I think, agree that a certain curtailment of the right to political opposition is an unavoidable concomitant of transitional periods, and that the rigours which the Russian people have been called upon to undergo have been amply justified in the sphere of concrete achievement.

Topics for Written Work

1. Write *two* accounts of an animal, a place, or a historical event or scene, (a) a clear, factual and objective account; and (b) a vivid, imaginative and subjective account.

Study the example given in Exercise 2 in the Techniques section and also both accounts of Hadrian's Wall in Oral Work. Notice the differences in style: the objective account should be in plain language, without figurative expressions or personal opinions, and with clear, logical sentences. The subjective account should use every possible means to convey a personal impression, with comparisons, original and fresh vocabulary and imagery, and a sense of the atmosphere or your emotional reactions.

2. "Far Away"—Use this title as the starting point for a piece of writing of any kind—poem, article, play, etc.

You may interpret this topic in any way you like: for example a description of a holiday abroad or in a distant part of this country, an article about a remote part of the world, a poem expressing ideas and feelings suggested by the title. You may follow any one of these, or you may use an entirely different approach.

3. Write about two travel books that deal with expeditions in remote parts of the world, or life in distant and little-known countries.

Choose books that relate true stories; do not refer to fictional accounts or to geography text books. *A Pattern of Islands* would be a suitable choice, as would *The Kon-Tiki Expedition* by T. Heyerdahl, *"Gipsy Moth" Circles the World* by Sir Francis Chichester, and other autobiographical accounts. With what impression of the journey or the country did the book leave you? What was the attitude of the narrator? If you can choose two books dealing with very different aspects of travel, bring out the comparisons and contrasts between them.

Oral Work

Practise reading aloud the following two descriptions of Hadrian's Wall:

1. Hadrian's Wall was built along the line of the Stanegate Road, from Carlisle for some 120 kilometres, across the hills to the Tyne estuary. In an effort to pacify the area, threatened by Picts and various anti-Roman exiles to the north and also by the Brigantes to the south, the Romans first built a chain of forts from Burgh-by-Sands to Newcastle. Then very soon a continuous wall was built (mostly of stone, although turves were used at the western end) from Bowness to Wallsend (Segedunum), to link most of these forts. This wall was mainly of concrete faced with stone, about 5 to 6 metres high (without the parapet), with a walk on top 1½ metres wide. The thickness ranged to over 3 metres. Mile-castles and turrets were built into the wall, and each of the mile-castles could house about 100 men. On the north side of the wall the frontier was further defended by a ditch 12 metres wide and over 3 metres deep (except where the ground already fell away steeply). To the south side of the Wall was another earthwork: a flat-bottomed ditch known as the Vallum, about 10 metres wide and over 2 metres deep. In addition to the mile-castles, there were seventeen of the larger forts, holding either 500 or 1000 men. It was particularly on the south side of these that settlements of "canabae", or camp-followers, grew up. Here, in time, parts of the Vallum were filled in to make room for shops, taverns, "married quarters" for those soldiers who took local wives, facilities for recreation and temples.

2. Just when you think you are at the world's end, you see a smoke from East to West as far as the eye can turn, and then, under it, also as far as the eye can stretch, houses and temples, shops and theatres, barracks and granaries, trickling along like dice behind—always behind—one long, low, rising and falling, and hiding and showing line of towers. And that is the Wall!. . . .

167

Along the top are towers with guard-houses, small towers, be-tween. Even on the narrowest part of it three men with shields can walk abreast, from guard-house to guard-house. A little curtain wall, no higher than a man's neck, runs along the top of the thick wall, so that from a distance you see the helmets of the sentries sliding back and forth like beads. Thirty feet high is the Wall and on the Picts' side, the North, is a ditch, strewn with blades of old swords and spear-heads set in wood, and tyres of wheels joined by chains. The Little People come there to steal iron for their arrow-heads.

But the Wall itself is not more wonderful than the town behind it. Long ago there were great ramparts and ditches on the South side, and no one was allowed to build there. Now the ramparts are partly pulled down and built over, from end to end of the Wall; making a thin town eighty miles long. Think of it! One roaring, rioting, cock-fighting, wolf-baiting, horse-racing town, from Ituna on the West to Segedunum on the cold eastern beach! On one side heather, woods and ruins where Picts hide, and on the other, a vast town—long like a snake, and wicked like a snake. Yes, a snake basking beside a warm wall!

The second of these passages is from Kipling's historical fantasy *Puck of Pook's Hill*. Discuss how it contrasts with the first passage. Which is the easier to read aloud, the easier to understand, and the more vivid? Is one more informative than the other? Find at least one contradiction or discrepancy between the two accounts—how can this be explained? What information is contained in 1 that is not matched in 2? In what ways is the second description confined to a particular view-point at a particular time?

Activities and Research

1. The fact that more and more people are going abroad for their holidays is only one of the changes that have taken place in the pattern of British holiday-making in the last twenty years. Work out a questionnaire which could be used to deter-mine where, how and why people go on holiday. Have this questionnaire filled in by as wide a cross-section of people as possible, and analyse the results.

2. Do some research into Greek drama, following up the work in Exercise 1 of the Techniques section (p. 161). Begin with the origins of tragedy and comedy in the ancient religious rites, and find out how the drama developed, with the number of actors growing as the role of the chorus becomes more sophisticated,

and with the changes in the physical structure of the theatres. Find out the main known facts about the chief Greek playwrights: Aeschylus, Sophocles, Euripides, Aristophanes, Menander. Do research into the main legends that are dramatised in Greek tragedies, and the differences in the way the tragedians treated them. How much has ancient Greek drama influenced the history of drama in western Europe?

Further Reading

A Pattern of Islands by SIR ARTHUR GRIMBLE (John Murray) (919.681)
Despite the fact that the Gilbert and Ellice Islands were one of the most remote and underdeveloped parts of the British Empire, and that living conditions were often appallingly bad, Arthur Grimble became very attached to the islanders and their territory. The book is basically a collection of "excellent yarns".

Return to the Islands (John Murray) (919.681)
"I borrowed £150 at the end of my leave to pay my way . . . back to the Pacific and leave the family in funds until I arrived there. I did not see them again for seven years. But that is another story."
So ends *Pattern of Islands*; *Return to the Islands* is the other story to which Sir Arthur Grimble refers.

Pacific Picture edited by L. M. M. MITCHELL (Angus & Robertson) (919.0)
An anthology containing contributions about the Pacific Ocean, its people and its islands, by such writers as Sir Arthur Grimble, D. H. Lawrence and Joseph Conrad.

Sailing Alone Around the World by J. SLOCUM (Adlard Coles; Dover) (910.4)
An exciting first-hand account of the author's famous voyage in the "Spray", a sloop that he rebuilt after finding her in a field.— Those of you who have read accounts of Sir Francis Chichester's single-handed voyage round the world will find this book particularly interesting.

CHAPTER ELEVEN

War

1. TRENCH WARFARE IN 1914–1918

These are extracts from letters written by Robert Graves from the trenches near Béthune in 1915. As a young officer taking responsibility in the front line for the first time, he was posted to a battalion of the Welsh Regiment.

May 28th. In trenches among the Cuinchy brick-stacks. Not my idea of trenches. There has been a lot of fighting hereabouts. The trenches have made themselves rather than been made, and run inconsequently in and out of the big thirty-foot high stacks of bricks; it is most confusing. The parapet of a trench which we don't occupy is built up with ammunition boxes and corpses. Everything here is wet and smelly. The Germans are very close: they have half the brick-stacks, we have the other half. Each side snipes down from the top of its brick-stacks into the other's trenches. This is also a great place for German rifle-grenades and trench-mortars. We can't reply properly; we have only a meagre supply of rifle-grenades and nothing to equal the German sausage mortar-bomb. . . .

"Sausages" are easy to see and dodge, but they make a terrible noise when they drop. We have had about ten casualties in our company today from them. I find that my reactions to danger are extraordinarily quick; but everyone gets like that. We can sort out all the different explosions and disregard whichever don't concern us—such as the artillery duel, machine-gun fire at the next company to us, desultory rifle-fire. But we pick out at once the faint plop! of the mortar that sends off a sausage, or the muffled noise when a grenade is fired. . . .

Last night a lot of German stuff was flying about, including shrapnel. I heard one shell whish-whishing towards me and dropped flat. It burst just over the trench where "Petticoat Lane" runs into "Lowndes Square". My ears sang as though there were gnats in them, and a bright scarlet light shone over everything. My shoulder got twisted in falling and I thought I had been hit, but I hadn't been. The vibration made my chest sing, too, in a curious way, and I lost my sense of equilibrium. I was ashamed when the sergeant-major came along the trench and found me on all fours, still unable to stand up straight.

A corpse is lying on the fire-step waiting to be taken down to the grave-yard tonight: a sanitary-man, killed last night in the open while burying lavatory stuff between our front and support lines. His arm was stretched out stiff when they carried him in and laid him on the fire-step; it stretched right across the trench. His comrades joke as they push it out of the way to get by. "Out of the light, you old bastard! Do you own this bloody trench?" Or else they shake hands with him familiarly. "Put it there, Billy Boy." Of course, they're miners, and accustomed to death. They have a very limited morality, but they keep to it. It's moral for instance, to rob anyone of anything, except a man in their own platoon. They treat every stranger as an enemy until he proves himself their friend, and then there's nothing they won't do for him. . . .

June 9th. I am beginning to realize how lucky I was in my gentle introduction to the Cambrin trenches. We are now in a nasty salient, a little to the south of the brick-stacks, where casualties are always heavy. The company had seventeen casualties yesterday from bombs and grenades. The front trench averages thirty yards from the Germans. Today, at one part, which is only twenty yards away from an occupied German sap, I went along whistling "The Farmer's Boy", to keep up my spirits, when suddenly I saw a group bending over a man lying at the bottom of the trench. He was making a snoring noise mixed with animal groans. At my feet lay the cap he had worn, splashed with his brains. I had never seen human brains before; I somehow regarded them as a poetical figment. One can joke with a badly-wounded man and congratulate him on being out of it. One can disregard a dead man. But even a miner can't make a joke that sounds like a joke over a man who takes three hours to die, after the top part of his head has been taken off by a bullet fired at twenty yards' range.

Beaumont, of whom I told you in my last letter, also got killed —the last unwounded survivor of the original battalion, except for transport men. He had his legs blown against his back. Everyone was swearing angrily, but an R.E. officer came up and told me that he had a tunnel driven under the German front line, and that if my chaps wanted to do a bit of bombing, now was the time. So he sent the mine up—it was not a big one, he said, but it made a tremendous noise and covered us with dirt—and we waited for a few seconds for the other Germans to rush up to help the wounded away, and then chucked all the bombs we had.

Beaumont had been telling how he had won about five pound's worth of francs in the sweepstake after the Rue du Bois show: a sweepstake of the sort that leaves no bitterness behind it. Before a show, the platoon pools all its available cash and the survivors divide it up afterwards. Those who are killed can't complain, the wounded would have given far more than that to escape as they have, and the unwounded regard the money as a consolation prize for still being here.

(from Goodbye to All That by Robert Graves)

Appreciation and Discussion

1. (a) Why didn't the author like the Cuinchy trenches?
   (b) What was even worse about the trenches to the south, where he was in June?
2. Noticing the terms used here ("front trench", "support trench", "sap", "fire-step", "parapet"), and using any previous knowledge you may have, describe the usual construction and layout of trenches at the front in the First World War. Illustrate with diagrams or sketch maps to make your description clear.
3. What indications are there here that the British were less well supplied with arms and ammunition than the Germans at this time?
4. What do the following terms mean?
   each side snipes down; desultory rifle-fire; shrapnel; my sense of equilibrium; a salient; a poetical figment; an R.E. officer; a show; a consolation prize.
5. What is the connection suggested between the death of Beaumont and the attack on the Germans when they "chucked all the bombs we had"? Was this attack especially vicious or heartless in any way?

6. Much of this passage illustrates the way in which men adapted themselves to the inhuman and extremely dangerous conditions of trench warfare.

(a) What evidence is there here that men had only very slight chances of surviving alive and unwounded?

(b) How did men react when "accustomed to death"?

(c) In what ways did men develop a discriminating sense of danger?

(d) What, apparently, was the usual attitude towards the wounded, or to the idea of being wounded?

(e) What disturbed even the most hardened men?

Where Have all the Flowers Gone?

Where have all the flowers gone?
Long time passing.
Where have all the flowers gone?
Long time ago.
Where have all the flowers gone?
Young girls picked them every one.
When will they ever learn?
When will they ever learn?

Where have all the young girls gone?
Long time passing.
Where have all the young girls gone?
Long time ago.
Where have all the young girls gone?
Gone to young men every one.
When will they ever learn?
When will they ever learn?

Where have all the young men gone?
Long time passing.
Where have all the young men gone?
Long time ago.
Where have all the young men gone?
Gone for soldiers every one.
When will they ever learn?
When will they ever learn?

Where have all the soldiers gone?
Long time passing.
Where have all the soldiers gone?
Long long time ago.
Where have all the soldiers gone?
Gone to graveyards every one.
When will they ever learn?
When will they ever learn?

Where have all the graveyards gone?
Long time passing.
Where have all the graveyards gone?
Long time ago.
Where have all the graveyards gone?
Gone to flowers every one.
When will they ever learn?
When will they ever learn?

PETE SEEGER

Discussing the Poem

1. What aspects of this poem suggest that it is indeed the words of a folk-song, and perhaps more effective sung than read?
2. How is repetition used (a) to reinforce and emphasize a common theme; and (b) to link each verse with the next. (c) What verse is the last verse linked with; i.e., what would you choose as a sixth verse?
3. What have "they" got to learn? Is this a lesson for us all?
4. Attempt to write the words of a "folk song" using a similar repetitive pattern of this kind.

2. ATOMIC WARFARE IN 1945

The Japanese city of Hiroshima was the target for the first atomic bomb which was dropped on 6th August, 1945, to force Japan to surrender in the Second World War. 60 000 men, women and children were killed and 100 000 injured—Kazuo M. was a fourteen-year-old boy.

Even at this distance, in the suburb of Furue, miles from the centre of the explosion, the gigantic force of the blast had been felt and within seconds had turned everything topsy-turvy that stood in its way. Never would Kazuo forget the flash of piercing light, which might have been reflected from the flat of some enormous, polished, naked sword, nor the dull reverberation far away. *Do . . . doo . . .* which as it drew close was transformed into a sharp, painful, and finally screeching *Ju . . . inn* that seemed to pierce through his eardrums, and which culminated in a sound like a thousand thunderclaps, *Gwann!*, that hurled him into a bottomless abyss. From this derives the Japanese word *Pikadon*, for *pika* means lightning and *don* thunder. . . .

Towards the end of August 1945, Kazuo M. noted in his diary: "Many rumours current in Hiroshima. For example, that the bomb contained poison. Anybody who breathed any of this in must die within one month. All grass and all flowers will wither away."

These rumours were almost universally believed, because many survivors who had been only slightly wounded by the *Pikadon*, or in many cases had not been hurt at all, became invalids on or about 20 August. Some of these rapidly developed the symptoms of what is today called "radiation sickness" (when the whole body had been subjected to a massive dose of radioactivity), and died. . . .

The M. family also began to show the painful symptoms that revealed the radiation sickness. Setsuo M. complained that his eyesight had suddenly deteriorated, his wife began to lose her hair, while little Hideko vomited several times a day. Kazuo sat for hours each day in front of the entrance that led down to the air-raid shelter and stared out over the vast field of rubble. Later he attempted to recapture his mood, as it had then been, in a poem that he sent me:

It rains and rains,
In the slanting rain I sit,
It drums upon my naked skull,
It drips across my singed eyebrows,
It runs into that bleeding hole, my mouth.

Rain on my wounded shoulders,
Rain in my lacerated heart.
Rain, rain, rain,
Wherefore do I live on?

An eyewitness, the poetess Yoko Ohta, has described this condition: "Each of us had for a time done everything possible, without knowing for sure what exactly it was that we were doing. Then we awoke, and now we wished to speak no more. Even the sheepdogs that roamed about ceased to bark. The trees, the plants, all that lived, seemed numb, without movement or colour. Hiroshima did not somehow resemble a city destroyed by war, but rather a fragment of a world that was ending. Mankind had destroyed itself, and the survivors now felt as though they were suicides who had failed. Thus the 'expression of wanting nothing more' came to be seen upon our faces."

(from *Children of the Ashes* by Robert Jungk)

Appreciation and Discussion

1. What would be the English translation of the Japanese word "Pikadon"?
2. What symptoms of radiation sickness (a) physical and (b) psychological, are described in this passage? (c) Discuss any other effects of overdoses of radioactivity that you have heard or read about.
3. Could the state of mind described in the second half of this passage have been caused by other aspects of the atomic explosion, even without the effects of radiation?
4. (a) Why did the inhabitants of Hiroshima have only rumours, rather than factual information, about what might happen after the explosion? (b) What grounds did they have for believing that some kind of "poison" had been released by the bomb?

5. Comment on Kazuo M.'s poem. What wounds or after-effects had he suffered? What effect does the emphasis on the rain have in this poem?

6. Contrast the kind of resignation described here—the "expression of wanting nothing more"—with the ways in which Graves and the Welsh miners adapted themselves to living with death in the trenches. How far are the attitudes of survivors the same and how far different?

7. Do you believe that "Mankind had destroyed itself" at Hiroshima? Was the dropping of the atom bomb an entirely new concept of warfare as compared with (a) the First World War and (b) the previous mass bombing raids on cities in Europe during the Second World War?

8. Was the dropping of the first atom bomb for any reason more justifiable than the use of hydrogen bombs in any future conflict could be?

The Responsibility

I am the man who gives the word,
If it should come, to use the Bomb.

I am the man who spreads the word
From him to them if it should come.

I am the man who gets the word
From him who spreads the word from him.

I am the man who drops the Bomb
If ordered by the one who's heard
From him who merely spreads the word
The first one gives if it should come.

I am the man who loads the Bomb
That he must drop should orders come
From him who gets the word passed on
By one who waits to hear from *him*.

I am the man who makes the Bomb
That he must load for him to drop
If told by one who gets the word
From one who passes it from *him*.

I am the man who fills the till,
Who pays the tax, who foots the bill
That guarantees the Bomb he makes
For him to load for him to drop
If orders come from one who gets
The word passed on to him by one
Who waits to hear it from the man
Who gives the word to use the Bomb.

I am the man behind it all;
I am the one responsible.

PETER APPLETON

Discussing the Poem

1. What nursery rhymes or traditional songs does this poem remind you of?
2. Does the poem use rhyme, or not? What is distinctive about its rhythm? Why do the verses become longer and longer, and then fall back to two lines at the end? Is it significant that there are only eight words of more than one syllable in the poem?
3. Who is responsible for what? Do you agree with the views expressed here?

Techniques

Exercise 1. The following passage is adapted from a radio talk, reprinted in *The Listener* in November, 1967, on *Chemical and Biological Warfare*. Read it carefully:

While the jargon of the nuclear age has become almost a part of everyday life—with its talk of megadeaths, nuclear equipoise and overkill—few people mention or probably even know the appalling fact that there is now enough nerve gas stockpiled to kill the world population many times over. Even fewer realise that the next major war—if it ever comes—is as likely to be fought with bacteria, viruses, LSD and "human insecticides" as it is with nuclear warheads. Indeed the insidious development of these weapons might well turn out to be as real a threat to the survival of man, other animals and even plants as any weapon ever devised. . . .

Chemical weapons have only been used on a massive scale in one war. Between 1915 and 1918, gas warfare—as it used to be called—caused more than a million casualties. . . .

Nerve gas has been described as the poor countries' answer to the highly expensive thermonuclear armoury. It's cheap to produce—as weapons go—and technically it's not very difficult. The chemical formulae and the means by which the chemicals can be made are freely available to anyone who cares to look them up in the scientific literature. In theory one B-52 bomber loaded with nerve gas could kill 30 per cent of the population in an area of 100 square miles—and that's roughly the immediate effective area of a 20-megaton thermonuclear device. . . .

There is worse to come. So far biological warfare—the deliberate spreading of infectious organisms that cause disease—has never been used. An American expert, General Rothschild, has claimed that an ounce of the material used to grow an organism that causes the lethal disease known as Q-fever is sufficient to kill no less than 28,000 million people. Other diseases, currently the focus of attention at a score or so of biological warfare centres throughout the world, are almost as potent; they include bubonic plague, anthrax, tulareamia, glanders, yellow fever and perhaps a dozen others. These research centres practise what has been aptly called public health in reverse. Their aim is to develop the organisms that cause disease, to make them more potent, longer-living and less susceptible to treatment with antibiotics or prevention with vaccines. . . . In 24 hours any one of these centres could produce enough infectious material, in theory, to eliminate the human population from the face of a continent.

Fortunately, there is reason to believe that this could not yet be done in practice. There are grave technical difficulties surrounding the development of biological weapons and they are still some way from a state of routine and reliable operation. And it is that fact, many scientists are now arguing, which makes the present time such a critical one. We have the chance, perhaps for the first time in history, to devise effective bans to prevent the use or further development of these weapons before they are actually perfected.

ROBIN CLARKE

Discuss the distinction Robin Clarke is making between chemical warfare and biological warfare. Is either more justifiable than the other? Is the use of such weapons morally worse than using atomic bombs or conventional weapons? Could drugs that temporarily remove the enemy's desire or capacity to fight be more easily justified, rather than substances that kill?

It is possible to summarize the argument of this extract in fewer than 150 words. Notice that much of the first paragraph is very general introduction, and that detailed examples in the fourth paragraph can be reduced to generalizations. Make sure that your written summary retains the essence of the author's warning conclusion.

Your summary should be in 120 to 150 words, avoiding the language of the article as far as is possible.

Exercise 2. (a) The passage in Exercise 1 refers to "the jargon of the nuclear age." What do you understand by *"jargon"*? Would you call the following words "jargon"? Give a definition for each of them:

1. from the extract from *Goodbye to All That*: sausage mortar-bomb; fire-step; sanitary-man; show.
2. from the extract from *Children of the Ashes*: pikadon; radiation sickness.

3. from the extract from Robin Clarke's article: megadeaths; nuclear equipoise; overkill; stock-piled; thermonuclear device.

(b) An up-to-date dictionary might include the following entry:

ăs'trōnaut, *n.* (f. Gk. *astron* star + *nautes* sailor). One who travels beyond the earth's atmosphere; expert on space travel.

astronautics, *n. pl.* science of space travel.

Try to make up full dictionary entries, or at least dictionary definitions, for the following recent additions to the English language:

admass	ergonomics	hitch-hike	pay-load
airlift	escalate (v.)	hovertrain	psychedelic
air pocket	fall-out	overdrive	teach-in
clearway	gerontology	overspill	thermoplastic
cybernetics	gimmick	owner-occupier	transistor

(c) The prefix mega- (used in the extract in Exercise 2 in "megadeaths") comes from the Greek "megas" = great. In a number of English words, this is its meaning:

megalith—large prehistoric stone;
megalomania—a passion for big things or one's own importance;
megaphone—an instrument for making a large sound;
megascope—a kind of magic lantern for enlarging a picture.

More recently, the prefix has been used to denote "a million times" in units of measurement:

megavolt—a million volts;
megohm—a million ohms;
megaton—a million tons (especially of T.N.T.);
megadeath—a million deaths;
megacycle—a million cycles (a measure of frequency).

Find and define a number of words using the following Latin or Greek prefixes, all of which have something to do with measurement:

bi-(L. twice)	hexa-(Gk. six)	poly-(Gk. many)
deca-(Gk. ten)	milli-(L. thousand)	quadri-(L. four)
demi-(L. half)	multi-(L. many)	semi-(L. half)
duo-(L. two)	octo-(L. eight)	tri-(Gk., L. three)
hemi-(Gk. half)	omni-(L. all)	uni-(L. one)

Exercise 3. (a) In the poem *The Responsibility* (on page 179) the numerous *adjective clauses* illustrate the fact that such clauses can have two slightly different functions in terms of their meaning.

In the sentence:

I am the man who gives the word.

the clause "who gives the word" is *definitive*, it is limiting "the man" to the one man who gives the command, and excluding all other men. It is the same with all, or nearly all, the adjective clauses in the poem.

On the other hand, in the extract from *Children of the Ashes* we find this sentence:

"Never would Kazuo forget the flash of piercing light, which might have been reflected from the flat of some enormous, polished, naked sword."

Here the adjective clause "which might have been reflected . . ." is simply *descriptive*. The comma before "which" emphasizes the more detached function of the adjective clause. Notice the difference in a case like this:

1. "The survivors who had been only slightly wounded or not hurt at all became invalids on or about 20 August."
2. "The survivors, who had been only slightly wounded, or not hurt at all, became invalids on or about 20 August."

Read the two sentences aloud, treating the commas in 2 almost as brackets.

Explain the difference in meaning between the two sentences in the following pairs:

1. (i) The parapet of a trench which we don't occupy is built up with ammunition boxes.
   (ii) The parapet of a trench, which we don't occupy, is built up with ammunition boxes.
2. (i) Today, at one part, which is only twenty yards away from an occupied German sap, I went along whistling to keep up my spirits.
   (ii) Today, at one part which is only twenty yards away from an occupied German sap, I went along whistling to keep up my spirits.
3. (i) In the war the men who did the fighting greatly outnumbered the women who did the nursing.
   (ii) In the war the men, who did the fighting, greatly outnumbered the women, who did the nursing.
4. (i) A scientist, whose research helps develop new and deadly weapons, is no more responsible than the taxpayer, who votes and pays for the country's arms policy.
   (ii) A scientist whose research helps develop new and deadly

weapons is no more responsible than the taxpayer who votes and pays for the country's arms policy.

(b) Analyse the following sentence, which forms the third verse of the poem *The Responsibility*, into clauses (there are seven clauses in all):

I am the man who drops the Bomb if (I am) ordered by the one who's heard from him who merely spreads the word the first one gives if it should come.

What verbs do the two "if" clauses modify?

(c) The following examples of *adverbs of degree* occur in the first passage and in the questions on it:

(i) I find that my reactions to danger are *extraordinarily* quick.
(ii) One can joke with a *badly* wounded man.
(iii) What was *even* worse about the trenches to the south?
(iv) The British were *less* well supplied with arms.
(v) Was this attack *especially* vicious?

You may remember that adverbs of degree usually modify adjectives or other adverbs, instead of modifying verbs, as in the following:

(vi) The other men took his death *badly*.

Here "badly" tells us *how* they "took his death"; whereas in example (ii), "badly" tells us *how far* the man was *wounded*, the degree to which he was hurt. Which of the adverbs in italics in the above examples modify adjectives, and which modify nouns?

ADVERB CLAUSES OF DEGREE have a similar function, and are normally introduced by "as............as" or "than". Study this sequence of examples:

(vii) The First World War was just as bloody *as the Second was*. (Modifies adjective "bloody".)
(viii) The servicemen who lost their lives in the First World War were usually younger *than the casualties in the Second World War* (*were*). (Modifies adjective "younger".)
(ix) Mobile forces were used more frequently in the Second World War *than they were in the first*. (Modifies adverbs "more frequently".)
(x) Civilians suffered as much in the Second World War *as the troops* (*did*). (Modifies adverb "much".)

Notice how the verbs (given in brackets) can often be omitted as "understood".

Now find the adverb clause of degree in each of the following sentences, and describe its function and relationship with the rest of the sentence:

1. Biological weapons are just as frightening as nuclear weapons are.
2. We taxpayers are really as responsible as the scientists.
3. Politicians can act as foolishly as generals.

4. The destruction of Hiroshima was more terrible than any of the mass bombing in Europe.
5. The British were less well supplied with arms at that time than the Germans were.
6. The next war is as likely to be fought with bacteria as it is with nuclear weapons.
7. Some people would rather destroy our civilization than let it be overrun.
8. He was more certain about his attitude to war than I.

Topics for Written Work

1. Write a discussion essay on the topic:

    Should Britain renounce the use of hydrogen and atomic weapons?

Here are six arguments for and against "banning the bomb"; these may help you to write a "balanced" essay. Even if you wish to express strong views on one side or the other, take account of the arguments on the opposite side, if only to refute them more convincingly:

(a) *For*

1. You cannot use the threat of H-bombs unless you are genuinely prepared to explode them and slaughter millions.
2. To use H-bombs would be more wicked and more foolish than to submit to Communism or any other enemy: you cannot fight evil with evil.
3. Both sides would lose any nuclear war and a small country like Britain would be utterly destroyed.
4. Continued atomic tests to develop weapons are themselves causing radiation that is becoming increasingly dangerous.
5. The more H-bombs there are, and the more widely they are distributed, the more likely it is that a war may start by accident.
6. By refusing to use H-bombs and turning neutral, Britain would earn international respect, and be able to mediate between the two sides in any future conflict.

(b) *Against*

1. Britain would be left at the mercy of her enemies if we gave up the H-bomb or left our defensive alliances with nuclear powers. These nuclear weapons deter our enemies.
2. It has only been because *both* Russia and America developed H-bombs that there has been peace between them.
3. The best way of getting international disarmament is for the West to remain strong (with nuclear armament) and united.

4. If an enemy were about to attack us, we should be right to resist with the most powerful weapons available.
5. Strict precautions are taken to prevent any accident with warning systems, etc., so an accidental nuclear war is impossible.
6. It would be better for us all to be destroyed in a war than for us to go on living as slaves to an enemy, perhaps under a Communist dictatorship.

2. After reading the passages in this chapter, perhaps with other extracts from *Goodbye to All That*, or Siegfried Sassoon's *Memoirs of an Infantry Officer*, or Edmund Blunden's *Undertones of War*, and reading some of the poetry of the First World War, particularly poems by Wilfred Owen and Siegfried Sassoon, write a poem or an imaginative description of your own, in which you try to capture something of the true atmosphere of trench warfare or an advance "over the top" and across "no man's land." Be as honest as you can—try to imagine what it would *really* be like, and to avoid an over-romantic picture of heroism and glory. In the poem opposite, by a fifth-former, he tries to recreate the horror of an attack made through a cloud of mustard gas.

Girls might perhaps prefer to imagine themselves as nurses in hospitals near the front, having to deal with the aftermath of battle as well as facing death themselves.

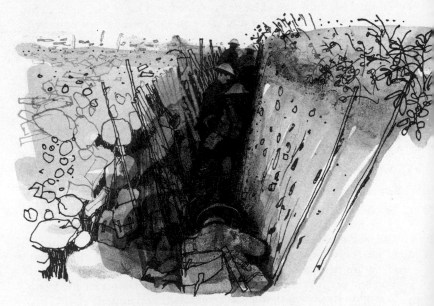

Assault

Gas;
faces turned
eyes scanned the sky,
hands feverishly ripped open canisters
and masks were soon covering faces.
A man choked
as the white cloud
swirling around him like fog caught him
unawares.
Then his body flopped over.
Shells floated across
as if suspended by hidden strings
and then tired
they sank earthwards.
A command
like a cold shower
to revive the mumbling shadows.
I fixed my bayonet
scrambled over the open trench
and struggled through
the thick pasty mud.
It was quiet
as we walked,
except for the sucking
groaning squelching sound
which came from the wet earth
as it tried
to creep into our stockings.
The wind cut me
with the skill of an executioner
as it came roaring down the ridge
towards which we were marching
over the wall.
Then a whistle:
"Good luck, mates."
Mind that hole! Through the wire,
over the top.
And kill.
"God. This is fun!"

ERNO

187

Oral Work

1. Discuss the picture of war given in books and films, with examples. Which of the following statements seems nearer the truth?

(a) "Nearly all books and films about war give a completely false picture. They glamorize violence; they present brutality as heroism; and they keep alive international hatred."

(b) "Most books and films about war provide a stirring record of courage. They give us examples of bravery and selflessness that we can look up to; they provide a warning of what can happen when evil men are allowed to gain power; they help us remember the sacrifices that our countrymen made for us."

Do some books and films about war come into one category and some into the other? Do some people read war books to get the same feeling of excitement that can be obtained from the sex-and-violence novelettes (see Chapter 9). Do you *enjoy* books and films about war? Refer to books that you have read, including this chapter's extracts; mention any films that you have seen, particularly "anti-war" films, and any plays you have seen or read, such as *The Long and the Short and the Tall*.

2. Prepare a tape-recording on the lines of the B.B.C.'s *Scrapbook* programmes, or of the theatre production *Oh What A Lovely War*, giving a picture of life in war-time, illustrated by songs, descriptions, statistics, poems and perhaps interviews with people who can still remember war-time incidents from their own experience. The B.B.C. *Scrapbook* Programmes for 1914 and 1940 (written and compiled by Leslie Baily) are both available on Fontana records (493 015 FDL and 493 014 FDL).

Activities and Research

1. There are many films dealing with many aspects of war in many different ways, but the following "anti-war" films are ones that are particularly worth seeing.

The War Game

This film was originally made for B.B.C. television but was never broadcast. It has been shown in some parts of the country by cinemas which do not belong to the major circuits. It demonstrates some of the probable effects of an atomic attack on this country.

On the Beach
This film does not deal with war itself, but with the plight of survivors in Australia after a world-wide nuclear war. There is no open propaganda in the film but, neverthelesss, it leaves one with an awful awareness of the dangers involved in nuclear weapons.

Paths of Glory
French troops in the First World War are ordered to attack an impregnable German position. They fail, and the incensed general demands scapegoats. Three men, picked at random, are accused of cowardice and executed, in spite of their commanding officer's attempts to save them.

King and Country
Although similar in setting and theme to *Paths of Glory*, this film makes a wider condemnation of war and its effect on individuals.

All Quiet on the Western Front
Made in 1930, this anti-war film, about a boy in the German army, was one of the first to explode the myth of martial heroics that was being established by the cinema.

2. The history of wars, weapons and warfare offers very wide scope for project work. Such topics as "The Charge of the Light Brigade" (see the Penguin Book *The Reason Why* by Cecil Woodham-Smith), the American Civil War (there is a Penguin book of that title by Bruce Catton) and the First World War (again the highly illustrated Penguin book by A. J. P. Taylor would be useful) are all suitable. Other groups of the class might tackle weapon development, or concentrate on tanks, or aircraft, or war at sea. Many museums contain much useful material and exhibits, above all the Imperial War Museum in London, where programmes of films can also be provided for school parties.

Further Reading

Goodbye to All That by ROBERT GRAVES (Cassell; Penguin) (928.2891)
Robert Graves wrote this autobiography, covering his life up to 1926, at the age of thirty-three. He gives a vivid account of the First World War, interesting sketches of his friends, and a candid self-portrait.

Sergeant Lamb of the Ninth by ROBERT GRAVES (Methuen; Penguin); *Proceed, Sergeant Lamb* (Methuen)
These two historical novels of the American War of Independence record the adventures of Roger Lamb, an Irish soldier in the British army. The second is a sequel to the first, but both books are self-contained stories. They evoke very effectively the spirit of the time.

Children of the Ashes by ROBERT JUNGK (Heinemann; Penguin) (952.197)
Interwoven with this report of a city's struggle against devastation, radiation sickness, fear, and hopelessness are a series of human stories which illustrate the appalling fate of many survivors.

Brighter than a Thousand Suns by ROBERT JUNGK (Penguin) (623.4543)
This is Robert Jungk's personal history of the atomic scientists.

On the Beach by NEVIL SHUTE (Heinemann; Pan)
In the vicinity of Melbourne, the last human survivors await death from the radio-active dust of cobalt bombs which has already destroyed life on the rest of the planet. It is a sombre and thought-provoking book.

Homage to Catalonia by GEORGE ORWELL (Secker & Warburg; Penguin) (946.081)
An extremely honest and vivid account of the Spanish Civil War by a man who was an idealist, deeply committed to the cause of freedom in Spain and angry at its betrayal, but above all a master-writer. The book includes an extremely vivid account of what is it like to be shot and quite seriously wounded, which would be worth reading (p. 177 onwards in the Penguin edition) before tackling Topics for Written Work, 2, (p. 186).

CHAPTER TWELVE

The Film World

In 1933 Christopher Isherwood was commissioned by "Imperial Bulldog Pictures" to write the script for a new musical film, "Prater Violet". It was his first excursion into the film world and he was intrigued by the organization and by the people who worked in it, such as the director, Bergmann, and Chatsworth, the producer.

In the meanwhile, whenever I got a chance, I went exploring. Imperial Bulldog had what was probably the oldest studio-site in London. It dated back to early silent days, when directors yelled through megaphones to make themselves heard above the carpenters' hammering; and great flocks of dazed, deafened, limping, hungry extras were driven hither and thither by aggressive young assistant directors, who barked at them like sheep-dogs. At the time of the panic, when Sound first came to England, and nobody's job was safe, Bulldog had carried through a hasty and rather hysterical reconstruction programme. The whole place was torn down and rebuilt at top speed, most of it as cheaply as possible. No one knew what was coming next: Taste perhaps, or Smell, or Stereoscopy, or some device that climbed right down out of the screen and ran around in the audience. Nothing seemed impossible. And, in the interim, it was unwise to spend much money on equipment which might be obsolete within a year.

The result of the rebuilding was a maze of crooked stairways, claustrophobic passages, abrupt dangerous ramps, and Alice in Wonderland doors. Most of the smaller rooms were overcrowded, under-ventilated, separated only by plywood partitions, and lit by naked bulbs hanging from wires. Everything was provisional, and liable to electrocute you, fall on your head, or come apart in your hand. "Our motto," said Lawrence Dwight, "is: 'If it breaks, it's Bulldog'."

Lawrence was the head cutter on our picture: a short, muscular, angry-looking young man of about my own age, whose face wore a frown of permanent disgust. . . .

"I don't know what the hell you imagine you're doing here,"

he said, a little later. "Selling your soul, I suppose? All you writers have such bloody romantic attitudes. You think you're too good for the movies. Don't you believe it. The movies are too good for you. We don't need any romantic nineteenth-century whores. We need technicians. Thank God I'm a cutter. I know my job. As a matter of fact I'm damned good at it. I don't treat film as if it were a bit of my intestine. It's all Chatsworth's fault. He's romantic, too. He *will* hire people like you. Thinks he's Lorenzo the Magnificent. . . . I bet you despise mathematics? Well, let me tell you something. The movies aren't drama, they aren't literature: they're pure mathematics. Of course, you'll never understand that as long as you live."

His deepest scorn was reserved for the Reading Department, officially known as Annexe G. . . .

There were the novels and plays which the Studio had bought to make into pictures. At any rate that was what they were supposed to be. Had Bulldog ever considered filming Bradshaw's Railway Timetable for 1911? Well, perhaps that had come originally from the Research Department. "But will you explain to me," said Lawrence, "why we have twenty-seven copies of *Half Hours with a Microscope*, one of them stolen from the Woking Public Library?"

Rather to my surprise, Lawrence approved of Bergmann and admired him. . . .

I was careful, however, not to inform Bergmann of Lawrence's political opinions. "All this fascist-communist nonsense," said Lawrence, "is so bloody old-fashioned. People rave about the workers. It makes me sick. The workers are just sheep. Always have been. Always will be. They choose to be that way, and why shouldn't they? It's their life. And they dodge a lot of headaches. Take the men at this place. What do they know or care about anything, except getting their pay-cheques? If any problem arises outside their immediate job they expect someone else to decide it for them. Quite right too, from their point of view. A country has to be run by a minority of some sort. The only thing is, we've got to get rid of these sentimental politicians. All politicians are amateurs. It's as if we'd handed over the Studio to the Publicity Department. The only people who really matter are the technicians. They know what they want."

"And what do they want?"

"They want efficiency."

"What's that?". . .

"Efficiency is doing a job for the sake of doing a job."

"But why should you do a job, anyway? What's the incentive?"

"The incentive is to fight anarchy. That's all Man lives for. Reclaiming life from its natural muddle. Making patterns."

"Patterns for what?"

"For the sake of patterns. To create meaning. What else is there?" ...

"Who's being old-fashioned now? That sounds like Art for Art's sake."

"I don't care what it sounds like ... technicians are the only real artists, anyway."

"It's all very well for you to make patterns with your cutting. But what's the use, when you have to work on pictures' like *Prater Violet*?"

"That's Chatsworth's worry, and Bergmann's, and yours. If you so-called artists would behave like technicians and get together, and stop playing at being democrats, you'd make the public take the kind of picture you wanted. This business about the box-office is just a sentimental democratic fiction. If you stuck together and refused to make anything but, say, abstract films, the public would have to go and see them, and like them ... still, it's no use talking. You'll never have the guts. You'd much rather whine about prostitution, and keep on making *Prater Violets*. And that's why the public despises you, in its heart. It knows damn well it's got you by the short hairs. Only, one thing: don't come to me with your artistic sorrows, because I'm not interested."

(from *Prater Violet* by Christopher Isherwood)

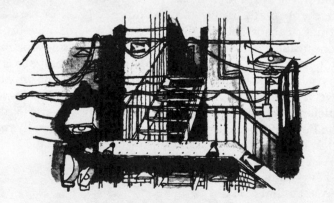

Appreciation and Discussion

1. What would prevent directors from yelling and carpenters banging during the shooting of sound films? What kind of changes would be necessary to adapt a studio to the demands of sound films?
2. Why was it considered "unwise to spend much money" when rebuilding the studios?
3. What further developments or "devices" have come to films since sound? Are any among those mentioned here?
4. Describe in your own words what is meant by "claustrophobic passages" and "Alice in Wonderland doors".
5. Give three examples of things we know Lawrence was disgusted by.
6. (a) What does the phrase "selling your soul" mean when Lawrence applied it to the author? (b) Who was Lorenzo the Magnificent, and why should Chatsworth (head of Imperial Bulldog films) think himself like him?
7. Bergmann was an Austrian Jew and the year was 1934. In view of those facts, why was the author careful not to tell Bergmann about Lawrence's political opinions?
8. "A country has to be run by a minority," said Lawrence. Which minority would he have wanted in power, ideally? Which minority would he have said was in power at the time do you think?
9. What does the author mean by "What's the incentive?" Do you agree with Lawrence's answer?
10. Discuss the philosophy of "Art for Art's sake". What other motive have artists for perfecting and carrying out their work? If Isherwood found this philosophy old-fashioned, what would his own idea be?
11. When he talks about "selling your soul", "romantic nineteenth-century whores" and "prostitution", what is Lawrence criticizing? What does he think is the reaction of the public at large to artists and their work, both "popular" and "artistic"?
12. How could the "cutting" of a film be reduced to "mathematics", as Lawrence suggests? Does this preclude "romance" and "sentiment", as Lawrence assumes?
13. What do the following mean, as used in this passage? aggressive; rather hysterical; in the interim; obsolete; intestine; anarchy; abstract films.

Techniques

Exercise 1. (a) Study the following passage and answer the questions below:

Who now goes to the cinema in Britain? The figures are all too clearly charted. From an exceptional 1,635 million admissions in 1946, to 1,396 million in 1950, to 515 million in 1960, to 415 million in 1962, the line goes steadily down. Just as in America the battle with television was intensified about 1951 when TV for the first time linked the entire United States, so in Britain the real slide in attendance figures dates from the mid fifties, when television sets were being bought at top speed by the working classes and also (coincidentally or not) when commercial television came into being. . . .

Statistics provide the background to the problems of the industry. It knows the audience it has; it tries, in devious and obvious ways, to keep them; and it knows the audience it has not got, the people who go to the cinema not at all, or so infrequently that their presence cannot be reckoned on the graphs; the people who turn out to make a *West Side Story* or a *Lawrence of Arabia* or a *Longest Day* one kind of success and a *Dolce Vita* another; the people every film producer is out to catch (indeed, *must* catch) when he invests a great deal of money in a movie.

In default of this audience, the cinema has turned, hopefully or desperately, to its teenagers. During the war, the film public could be taken to include pretty well everybody, which gave it a natural bias towards middle-age. . . .

But, as the age-level of the audience has fallen, so the films have gone out to meet it. We have had the rock films and the twist films and the hey-day of Elvis Presley; Hollywood has offered us *Hot Rod Girl, Dragstrip Girl, Reform School Girl, High School Confidential, School for Violence, Monster on the Campus,* and that ultimate fantasy *I Was a Teenage Werewolf;* the misunderstood adolescence theme is always with us, from Culver City to Tokyo. Efforts to cultivate the teenage audience have sent middle-aged film-makers out on forlorn expeditions into the hot-rod and Espresso territory; or have encouraged them to flirt naïvely with the censor, to put on displays of self-conscious daring intended to suggest that their really rather respectable wares are a sort of cinematic equivalent to reefer cigarettes. . . .

Now increasingly, in France and Italy and to some extent America we have the films which make hay with the conventions, the films conceived as personal statements, which we may watch with other people in a cinema or by ourselves in a viewing theatre, or on a television screen, the films which insist that *we* keep up with *them,* and which consequently are bound, by their density or their subtlety, their allusiveness or their technical unfamiliarity, to leave part of their audience behind. The gap has always been there: as wide between

Zero de Conduite and *It Happened One Night*, or *Les Dames du Bois de Boulogne* and *The Best Years of Our Lives*, as between *Marienbad* and *Lawrence of Arabia*. The difference is in two things: the number of people, all over the world, who now see what twenty or thirty years ago would have been thought of as defiant minority films; and the number of film-makers very consciously concerned with the language of the screen. We have a new public for something vaguely called a new cinema, spreading out from the specialized cinemas and the film societies, but also coming in from the Odeons and the Gaumonts. The movies have never found it easier to get an audience for work with genuine minority appeal or genuine mass appeal; and as long as that lasts, we may quite well be experiencing the decline of the cinema and, at the same time, the rise of the film.

(from The Contemporary Cinema by Penelope Houston)

1. Draw a graph to show the decline in cinema attendances, using these figures.
2. Where does the author place the chief blame for the declining figures?
3. Explain (a) why, and (b) in what ways the film-makers have turned to a teenage market.
4. Apart from films for young people, explain clearly and in your own words the *other* new direction in which film-making has been developing and finding a "new public".
5. What third kind of films (*not* mentioned in answers to questions 3 and 4) can *still* be box-office successes, according to this passage?
6. Explain the following words or phrases as used here: coincidentally; devious; the hot-rod and Espresso territory; allusiveness; defiant minority films.
7. Explain the contrast in: "The decline of the cinema and. . . . the rise of the film."

(b) The first *three* paragraphs discuss how the changing size and nature of the cinema audience turned film-makers towards the teenage market. Summarize this argument in not more than 120 of your own words. Do not quote actual figures or refer specifically to titles of films, but generalize from the information given. Do *not* include the argument in the fourth paragraph.

(c) Discuss the "new cinema" of "defiant minority films" as referred to in the last paragraph. What does it mean to say that films "make hay with the conventions" and that they are "conceived as personal statements"? What is "the language of the screen"? What kinds of films are shown in the "specialized cinemas and the film societies" as opposed to "the Odeons and the Gaumonts"?

In what various ways has television influenced the development of films of this kind? What films would you quote as examples of this development? What words and phrases in this fourth paragraph reveal the author's bias in favour of these films?

Exercise 2. In *Prater Violet,* Lawrence Dwight's conversation tends to be interspersed with short, forthright statements; what do they mean?

"If it breaks, it's Bulldog."

"Selling your soul . . ."

"The movies aren't drama, they aren't literature: they're pure mathematics."

"The workers are just sheep."

"All politicians are amateurs."

"Efficiency is doing a job for the sake of doing a job."

"Patterns . . . for the sake of patterns."

Consider the meanings of the following terms. Would any of the statements above serve as examples of these terms?

aphorism—a concise statement of a principle or rule of conduct, expressed briefly and forcefully.

epigram—a clever saying full of meaning, especially a short witty expression with an element of contrast or paradox in it.

maxim—a short saying expressing a general or scientific truth, rule or principle.

proverb—a concise sentence expressing a familiar piece of traditional wisdom often allegorically.

The four terms in fact overlap, so that one can say that an epigram is a proverb with a known author or that all epigrams are aphorisms. All four are concise, and in condensing their truths into a brief and memorable form, they often use *repetition* or *alliteration*; e.g.,

Don't kill the goose that lays the golden eggs.

He who laughs last laughs longest.

The proper study of mankind is man. (Pope.)

When a man is tired of London he is tired of life. (Johnson.)

Very often, too, such sayings are witty and contain elements of *paradox* (apparent contradiction) or *antithesis* (balanced contrast);

One man's meat is another man's poison.

The child is father to the man. (Wordsworth.)

There is only one thing in the world worse than being talked about, and that is not being talked about. (Wilde.)

Discuss and analyse all the following from these points of view: are they proverbs or epigrams? Do they contain repetition or alliteration? Is there an element of paradox or antithesis? What is the meaning of the saying, and is it metaphorically expressed?

(a) There's no fool like an old fool.
(b) Nothing venture, nothing gain.
(c) The spirit is willing but the flesh is weak. (The Bible.)
(d) Art lies in concealing art.
(e) All women become like their mothers. That is their tragedy. No man does. That's his. (Wilde.)
(f) The golden rule is that there are no golden rules. (Shaw.)
(g) Never do today what you can put off till tomorrow. (Punch.)
(h) To err is human, to forgive, divine. (Pope.)
(i) I find your work both good and original: unfortunately, what is good is not original and what is original is not good. (Dr. Johnson, on the work of an aspiring author.)
(j) You can take a horse to water but you can't make him drink.
(k) Fine feathers make fine birds.
(l) The only way to get rid of temptation is to yield to it. (Wilde.)

Exercise 3. (a) Lawrence Dwight's style of talking is brief, blunt and jerky. He talks in short emphatic sentences, and often cuts them back until they are grammatically incomplete:

"We need technicians. Thank God I'm a cutter. I know my job. As a matter of fact I'm damned good at it. I don't treat film as if it were a bit of my intestine. It's all Chatsworth's fault. He's a romantic too. He *will* hire people like you. Thinks he's Lorenzo the Magnificent . . ." (page 193).

Notice how the speaker's whole personality would change if he spoke in more complex and fuller prose:

"Since we need technicians, I thank God that I am a cutter, who knows his job; and, as a matter of fact, I'm damned good at it, so that I don't treat film as if it were a bit of my intestine. It is all Chatsworth's fault that he *will* hire people like you, because he, too, is a romantic, and he thinks he's another Lorenzo the Magnificent."

199

Rewrite part of Lawrence Dwight's next main speech in our extract (page 193), again altering the style to a more complex, fuller prose, without any incomplete sentences. Take the passage beginning:

"People rave about the workers. It makes me sick . . ." down to: ". . . They know what they want."

Alter the style without introducing any completely new ideas or radically altering the points Dwight is making.

(b) Lawrence Dwight's sentences:

"Reclaiming life from its natural muddle. Making patterns." are only meaningful and grammatically tolerable in the context of his conversation (on page 194). In formal written English, they would not be considered sentences at all—"reclaiming" and "making" are *not* finite verbs; they are presumably here *gerunds* (verbal nouns) and objects of the preposition "for", understood from the previous sentence:

"Man lives for reclaiming life from its natural muddle, and for making patterns."

Similarly, explain what, in formal written English, would be wrong with the following, and how they should be rewritten correctly:

1. It was six o'clock. Darkness creeping through the ill-lit streets. Lights twinkling in windows; a warm glow thrown on the glistening pavements; a few dark figures hurrying through the black curtain of dismal rain.
2. Tramping those lonely streets, the rain beat down and rebounded from the tarmac in a million tiny fountains, soaking the hero's shoes and the bottoms of his trousers.
3. After arriving at the cinema and leaving your coats in the cloak-room, the attendant will show you to your seats.
4. His parents objected to him working in a late-night cinema and returning in the small hours.
5. Millions of tiny insects flying, creeping crawling, hopping, jumping, climbing, fluttering, filling the whole auditorium, so that the seats seemed alive and the air thick with moving bodies.

(c) Each of the following sentences represents one other common error in colloquial English.

Discuss these errors, and the correct alternatives in formal written English:

1. These sort of questions are often asked by visitors looking round the film studios on their first visit.
2. The producer told the director that he hoped he would have his voice back in time for the shooting of the next scene.
3. The floor manager found the purse that had been left on the set after a special appeal to all the actresses to help.
4. The cinema today has had to find new audiences with the money, time and inclination to go out for their entertainment, and who will demand something different from the fare on television.
5. In the days of the silent film, most cinemas employed someone to provide suitable music on a piano which he usually had to make up himself as the film was shown.

Topics for Written Work

1. In writing about films or film extracts you have seen, it is often useful to have in mind certain categories into which films can (roughly) be divided. The Western, the gangster film, the spy story, crime films, war films, documentary or propaganda films, horror films, love-stories, teenage stories, animal stories, epics, historical films, film comedies, realistic films, surrealist or fantasy films, musicals, cartoons or animated films—all these are recognizable types, and it should be interesting to try to assign a particular film to one of these categories, and to compare it with others of that kind.

We have noted previously that constructive criticism avoids judging a book or film for not doing what it did not set out to do, although it is relevant to ask questions about a film's "values", about the attitude to life that such a work portrays and whether people should be influenced in this way. (For instance, is it important that a crime story should end with a triumph for the police?)

Try to go further than retelling the story of the film: consider the quality of acting, camera work, lighting, music, settings, costumes and effects, and the final editing. Ask yourself what attitudes to his story the director has, and why he chose to tell it in this particular way.

2. If possible, make written comparisons between *either* a film and the book from which the story was taken, *or* two films (or film extracts) on a similar theme, but in different styles. Do not necessarily try to praise one at the expense of the other, but rather note how differences in approach and in the medium lead to differences in the effect on the audience.

3. The extract from *Prater Violet* is rather like a record of the impressions of a visitor to the Imperial Bulldog Studios, who is being conducted through the buildings and talking to some of the people who work there. Write an account of any visit you have recently made (preferably with a school party) to a studio, factory, museum, theatre, zoo, or any place of historical, geographical or scientific interest. The report should be in a style suitable for publication in a school magazine. Notes made on the spot, or tape-recordings (especially if you could interview officials or people who work in the place) would obviously provide very useful material for your written account. Be careful not to spend too much space on unimportant detail about travel and refreshment, etc.

Oral Work

1. Discuss the clichés common in the publicity for films and film-stars, including both the posters and the short reviews in the newspapers. Here are some typical examples:

> The lover with a lust for blood.
> Finest stars of stage and screen.
> A film to shock the unshockable.
> Lonely, lost and damned.
> The Truth Laid Bare: the frankest love story ever screened.
> Five Academy Awards.
> Serious, searching, shocking: a film for the discerning public.
> Fall of Babylon: the film that cost four million.
> Music, mystery, moonlight and melody: you will be wafted away to the land of your dreams.
> He's mad, he's marvellous, he's the craziest man in town.
> Don't bring the children: if you're squeamish stay away yourself.
> The actress with everything.

What would you expect the films to be like? Is the publicity dishonest? What kind of public is each aimed at?

Collect other examples from posters, newspapers and magazines and analyse these.

2. Lawrence Dwight's remarks in the extract from *Prater Violet* are quite provocative on the subjects of art and technology in the modern world. Is he suggesting that artists (including poets, novelists, composers) have no place, or that their art has now to be subordinated to the demands of new techniques? The book *Prater Violet* was published in 1946; but was the author, through Dwight, looking forward to an age of electronic music and compositions put together by a computer, or to "kinetic art" or some aspects of today's "op art" or "pop art"? Traditionally, sculptors, painters and musicians have all been technically proficient craftsmen first, and creative, imaginative artists afterwards. Is this the age of the technician, the designer, the mathematician and the computer? In a world of specialist experts, is there any place now for an artist with a broad view of humanity and a "message" to his fellow men? Marshall MacLuhan gained much publicity in 1967 by asserting that "the medium is the message". Is it today more important to consider the technique of *how* you communicate (the skills of filming or advertising, for instance) rather that *what* you have to say?

Activities and Research

1. (a) Make a study of the history of the cinema, from the earliest machines for creating the illusion of movement in pictures (such as the zoetrope and praxinoscope), through the era of silent films, to the early sound pictures and the growth of Hollywood and the popular film star, down to the present day. Include a section on great actors and actresses: e.g., Buster Keaton, Charlie Chaplin, Rudolf Valentino, Mary Pickford, Douglas Fairbanks; and another on famous past directors: e.g., Eisenstein, Griffith, Pabst, King Vidor, René Clair. You could

also include sections on famous comedy teams (the Keystone Cops, Laurel and Hardy, the Marx Brothers), and on different types of film, such as musical comedy or screen epics, and the cinema in different countries. Wherever you can, illustrate your study with reference to particular films, and (where suitable) diagrams or photographs.

(b) Much of the jargon of film-making is the same as that of television (which we dealt with in Book Four), but find an explanation for the following technical terms: cross-cutting, dissolve, drumming, fade-out, flash-back, jump-cuts, montage, soft lighting, a take, wipe,

2. A group of the class might attempt making a short film with an 8-mm or 16-mm camera. Film-making can be very expensive unless the work is carefully planned to fit into (say) four minutes, and the shots scripted in detail so that they can be shot as far as possible in sequence to minimize editing. Be careful to choose subjects that do not require exotic locations or the services of actors you have not got, and to concentrate on stories that lend themselves to treatment in visual terms.

The most obvious subject for filming will be the short story sequence, preferably one in which the members of the group can themselves undertake most of the acting, and one in a local, contemporary setting. But groups might also like to consider other possibilities, such as the short documentary, in which a particular display, activity or visit is recorded, or in which you make a total study, perhaps of the rush-hour, or tourists and visitors at some local place of interest, or how people (children, elderly people, workers on a particular job, families) enjoy themselves or react to something or behave in a particular place (such as a waiting-room, a fun-fair, at a sporting event, etc.).

Another series of possibilities dispenses with human actors altogether. Simple animated films can be very effectively put together by using cut out figures against a painted or cut-out background. There is much room here for satire or comedy, and it is not necessary to draw thousands of individual shots—a few cut-out figures moved a fraction of an inch for each quick shot of the camera, on a large enough background, is quite sufficient. Finally, very striking visual effects can be obtained by begging lengths of old, developed and discarded film, bleaching these in any domestic bleach, and drawing, painting (felt-tipped pens are useful) or scratching patterns or even representational pictures directly on to the film.

204

Further Reading

Prater Violet by CHRISTOPHER ISHERWOOD (Methuen; Penguin)
This book is concerned not only with the film world but also with events in Europe which led up to the Second World War.

Mr Norris Changes Trains by CHRISTOPHER ISHERWOOD
 (Hogarth; Penguin)
The author originally set out to write a long novel about his experiences in Berlin before and during the rise of the Nazi party. Certain characters in this selection of adventures therefore overlap with the six pieces in *Goodbye to Berlin* (Penguin), which is also made up of diaries and sketches that were to be part of a much longer work. All three of these books are remarkable for the rich portrayal of cosmopolitan characters of that restless period in European history.

The Contemporary Cinema by PENELOPE HOUSTON (Penguin)
 (791.43)
This is an imaginative and interesting survey of the cinema after the Second World War up to 1963, showing how the industry adapted itself to changes in audiences and public tastes, and making clear the parts played by directors and promoters.

The Cinema as Art by RALPH STEPHENSON and J. R. DEBRIX
 (Penguin) (791.43)
With many and varied examples, this book shows in detail how directors have used the "language" of the screen to create works of art on film.

Cinema by THOMAS WISEMAN (Cassell) (791.43)
This very clear study of the cinema is beautifully illustrated with a wealth of photographs, mainly in colour.

CHAPTER THIRTEEN

Civilized Savages

After the outbreak of a third world war, a plane-load of boys from boarding-schools were marooned on a tropical island, without any adults, Ralph was elected leader, while Jack enjoyed organizing parties to hunt wild pig for meat. At first they discussed things, kept a signal fire going, and looked after the youngest children when they had nightmares about a dreadful "beast". But as they grew more afraid, so more of the boys turned to follow Jack and his hunters.

All the boys of the island, except Piggy, Ralph, Simon, and the two tending the pig, were grouped on the turf. They were laughing, singing, lying, squatting, or standing on the grass, holding food in their hands. But to judge by the greasy faces, the meat-eating was almost done; and some held coconut shells in their hands and were drinking from them. Before the party had started a great log had been dragged into the centre of the lawn and Jack, painted and garlanded, sat there like an idol. There were piles of meat on green leaves near him, and fruit and coconut shells full of drink.

Piggy and Ralph came to the edge of the grassy platform; and the boys, as they noticed them, fell silent one by one till only the boy next to Jack was talking. Then the silence intruded even there and Jack turned where he sat. For a time he looked at them and the crackle of the fire was the loudest noise over the bourdon of the reef. Ralph looked away; and Sam, thinking that Ralph had turned to him accusingly, put down his gnawed bone with a nervous giggle. Ralph took an uncertain step, pointed to a palm tree, and whispered something inaudible to Piggy; and they both giggled like Sam. Lifting his feet high out of the sand, Ralph started to stroll past. Piggy tried to whistle.

At this moment the boys who were cooking at the fire suddenly hauled off a great chunk of meat and ran with it towards the grass. They bumped Piggy who was burnt, and yelled and danced. Immediately, Ralph and the crowd of boys were united and relieved by a storm of laughter. Piggy once more was the centre of social derision so that everyone felt cheerful and normal.

Jack stood up and waved his spear.

"Take them some meat.". . .

The boys ranged themselves in rows on the grass before him but Ralph and Piggy stayed a foot lower, standing on the soft sand. Jack ignored them for a moment, turned his mask down to the seated boys and pointed at them with the spear.

"Who is going to join my tribe?"

Ralph made a sudden movement that became a stumble. Some of the boys turned towards him.

"I gave you food," said Jack, "and my hunters will protect you from the beast. Who will join my tribe?"

"I'm chief," said Ralph, "because you chose me. And we were going to keep the fire going. Now you run after food—"

"You ran yourself!" shouted Jack. "Look at that bone in your hands!"

Ralph went crimson.

"I said you were hunters. That was your job."

Jack ignored him again.

"Who'll join my tribe and have fun?"

"I'm chief," said Ralph tremulously. "And what about the fire? And I've got the conch—"

"You haven't got it with you," said Jack, sneering. "You left it behind. See, clever? And the conch doesn't count at this end of the island—"

All at once the thunder struck. Instead of the dull boom there was a point of impact in the explosion.

"The conch counts here too," said Ralph, "and all over the island."

"What are you going to do about it then?"

Ralph examined the ranks of boys. There was no help in them and he looked away, confused and sweating. . . .

There was a blink of bright light beyond the forest and the thunder exploded again so that a littlun started to whine. Big drops of rain fell among them making individual sounds when they struck.

"Going to be a storm," said Ralph, "and you'll have rain like when we dropped here. Who's clever now? Where are your shelters? What are you going to do about that?"

The hunters were looking uneasily at the sky, flinching from the stroke of the drops. A wave of restlessness set the boys swaying and moving aimlessly. The flickering light became brighter and the blows of the thunder were only just bearable. The littluns began to run about, screaming.

Jack leapt on to the sand.

"Do our dance! Come on! Dance!"

He ran stumbling through the thick sand to the open space of rock beyond the fire. Between the flashes of lightning the air was dark and terrible; and the boys followed him, clamorously. Roger became the pig, grunting and charging at Jack, who side-stepped. The hunters took their spears, the cooks took spits, and the rest clubs of firewood. A circling movement developed and a chant. While Roger mimed the terror of the pig, the littluns ran and jumped on the outside of the circle. Piggy and Ralph, under the threat of the sky, found themselves eager to take a place in this demented but partly secure society. They were glad to touch the brown backs of the fence that hemmed in the terror and made it governable.

"Kill the beast! Cut his throat! Spill his blood!"

The movement became regular while the chant lost its first superficial excitement and began to beat like a steady pulse. Roger ceased to be a pig and became a hunter, so that the centre of the ring yawned emptily. Some of the littluns started a ring of their own; and the complementary circles went round and round as though repetition would achieve safety of itself. There was the throb and stamp of a single organism.

The dark sky was shattered by a blue-white scar. An instant later the noise was on them like the blow of a gigantic whip. The chant rose a tone in agony.

"Kill the beast! Cut his throat! Spill his blood!"

Now out of the terror rose another desire, thick, urgent, blind.

"Kill the beast! Cut his throat! Spill his blood!"

Again the blue-white scar jagged above them and the sulphurous explosion beat down. The littluns screamed and blundered about, fleeing from the edge of the forest, and one of them broke the ring of biguns in his terror.

"Him! Him!"

The circle became a horseshoe. A thing was crawling out of the forest. It came darkly, uncertainly. The shrill screaming that rose before the beast was like a pain. The beast stumbled into the horseshoe.

"Kill the beast! Cut his throat! Spill his blood!"

The blue-white scar was constant, the noise unendurable. Simon was crying out something about a dead man on a hill.

"Kill the beast! Cut his throat! Spill his blood! Do him in!"

The sticks fell and the mouth of the new circle crunched and screamed. The beast was on its knees in the centre, its arms folded over its face. It was crying out against the abominable noise something about a body on the hill. The beast struggled forward, broke the ring, and fell over the steep edge of the rock to the sand by the water. At once the crowd surged after it, poured down the rock, leapt on to the beast, screamed, struck, bit, tore. There were no words, and no movements but the tearing of teeth and claws.

(from *Lord of the Flies* by William Golding)

Appreciation and Discussion

1. Why do you think the crowd fell silent as Ralph and Piggy approached the scene of the feast?
2. What evidence is there here that Sam (like his twin, Eric) had remained loyal to Ralph up till now?
3. What indications do Ralph and Piggy give that they are embarrassed and nervous at being faced with Jack's rival power?
4. What incident relieves the tension for Ralph as he faces Jack at the beginning of this sequence? Does it have an effect on Jack too?
5. What *three* advantages does Jack offer to the boys who follow him?
6. What advantages were there in following Ralph's leadership? What kind of organization did he stand for, and why didn't the boys respond to his call? (Why does he twice mention the fire as being important?)
7. The "conch" was a large shell that made a resounding horn-like sound when blown. What evidence is there here that it had become the symbol of order and authority for the boys?
8. What does Jack do to distract the younger boys from their fear of the tropical storm?
9. How do you think Jack and his hunters had come to develop (a) the idea of wearing "war-paint" (particularly Jack, with "his mask"); (b) their tribal dance; and (c) their chant (originally this had been: "Kill the pig . . .")?
10. What drew even Piggy and Ralph into the wild dance?
11. Who or what was the thing crawling out of the forest", "the beast", the voice "crying out something about a dead man on the hill"? If it was the boy, Simon (the only boy not present at the feast by that time), then why was he confused with "the beast" that they all feared?
12. Later, when discussing this incident more calmly with Ralph, Piggy's comment is:

    "It was an accident . . . coming in the dark—he hadn't no business crawling like that out of the dark. He was batty. He asked for it." He gesticulated widely again. "It was an accident."

    Do you agree? If it was murder or manslaughter, could any boy or boys be held responsible?

13. What would you expect to be the reaction of (a) Jack, (b) Ralph and (c) the other older boys when, later, they realized what they had done? Would the shock bring them to their senses? (Remember that they were still afraid of "the Beast"—Simon had been trying to tell them that it was no more than the corpse of an airman, with a parachute caught in the trees, that swayed and moaned in the wind; but of course they did not hear him.)

14. Piggy was wise and sensible, but he was also fat, asthmatic, short-sighted and an easy target for mockery. Where and how does he become a "scapegoat" (see page 62 for an explanation of this term) in this sequence?

15. What do the following words and phrases mean when used here?
garlanded; like an idol; the silence intruded even here; the bourdon of the reef; the centre of social derision; tremulously; this demented but partly secure society; the throb and stamp of a single organism; the mouth of the new circle crunched.

16. What part does the storm play in this sequence? Compare it with the tropical storm in the extract in Chapter One. Could the "accident" have happened without it?

17. Discuss the characters of Jack and Ralph respectively. Which would you have supported in this crisis, and why? Is it conceivable that a group of boys like this, all under 14 years old, would turn into a kind of savage tribe? Would boarding-school boys, from prosperous homes and with traditions of prefects and strict discipline, be *more* or *less* likely to follow a leader like Jack than would (say) ordinary boys from state day-schools?

I sit and look out upon all the sorrows of the world, and upon
    all oppression and shame,
I hear secret convulsive sobs from young men at anguish with
    themselves, remorseful after deeds done,
I see in low life the mother misused by her children, dying,
    neglected, gaunt, desperate,
I see the wife misused by her husband, I see the treacherous
    seducer of young women,
I mark the rankling of jealousy and unrequited love attempted
    to be hid, I see these sights on earth,
I see the workings of battle, pestilence, tyranny, I see martyrs
    and prisoners.
I observe a famine at sea, I observe the sailors casting lots who
    shall be killed to preserve the lives of the rest,
I observe the slights and degradations cast by arrogant persons
    upon labourers, the poor, and upon Negroes, and the like;
All these—all the meanness and agony without end I sitting
    look out upon,
See, hear, and am silent.

                             WALT WHITMAN

Discussing the Poem

1. Which parts of this catalogue would you list as "sorrows",
   which as "oppression" and which as "shame"?
2. Discuss what each of the following words or phrases imply?
   convulsive; remorseful; gaunt; ranklings; unrequited love;
   pestilence; casting lots; slights and degradations.
3. What repetition is there in this poem, and what effect does it
   have?
4. Who is the "I" of this poem? Consider the emphasis on: "I
   sit and look out"—"I sitting look out", and the remark
   "I see these sights on earth," and the last, short line.

Techniques

Exercise 1. The following passage is part of a preface written by Margaret Mead, the anthropologist, to her book *Coming of Age in Samoa*. Using the information given here, write *two* summaries. The *first* is to show what anthropologists like Margaret Mead are trying to do, and how they set about it. The *second* should show what Margaret Mead herself aimed to achieve by studying the lives of these adolescent girls in Samoa. Your *two* summaries *together* should *not be more than 200 words* long: they should be in clear, concise English, mainly in your own words. You are *not* expected to summarise the whole passage from the beginning through to the end.

What method, then, is open to us who wish to conduct a human experiment but who lack the power either to construct the experimental conditions or to find controlled examples of those conditions here and there throughout our own civilization? The only method is that of the anthropologist, to go to a different civilization and make a study of human beings under different cultural conditions in some other part of the world. For such studies the anthropologist chooses quite simple peoples, primitive peoples, whose society has never attained the complexity of our own. In this choice of primitive people like the Eskimo, the Australian, the South Sea islander, or the Pueblo Indian, the anthropologist is guided by the knowledge that the analysis of a simpler civilization is more possible of attainment....

So, in order to investigate the particular problem, I chose to go not to Germany or to Russia, but to Samoa, a South Sea island about thirteen degrees from the Equator, inhabited by a brown Polynesian people. . . . I concentrated upon the girls of the community. I spent the greater part of my time with them. I studied most closely the households in which adolescent girls lived. . . .

In the following chapters I have described the lives of these girls, the lives of their younger sisters who will soon be adolescent, of their brothers with whom a strict taboo forbids them to speak, of their older sisters who have left puberty behind them, of their elders, the mothers and fathers whose attitudes towards life determine the attitudes of their children. And through this description I have tried to answer the question which sent me to Samoa: Are the disturbances which vex our adolescents due to the nature of adolescence itself or to the civilization? Under different conditions does adolescence present a different picture?. . . .

Each primitive people have selected one set of human gifts, one set of human values, and fashioned for themselves an art, a social organization, a religion, which is their unique contribution to the history of the human spirit. Samoa is only one of these diverse and gracious patterns, but as the traveller who has been once away from home is wiser than he who has never left his own doorstep, so a knowledge of one other culture should sharpen our ability to scrutinize more steadily, to appreciate more lovingly, our own.

And because of the particular problem which we set out to answer, this tale of another way of life is mainly concerned with education, with the process by which the baby, arrived cultureless upon the human scene, becomes a full-fledged adult member of his or her society. The strongest light will fall upon the ways in which Samoan education, in its broadest sense, differs from our own. And from this contrast we may be able to turn, made newly and vividly self-conscious and self-critical, to judge anew and perhaps fashion differently the education we give our children.

Exercise 2. (a) The passage from *Lord of the Flies* contains examples of sentences in which slight alterations to punctuation may alter meaning substantially. Consider:

    (i) They bumped Piggy, who was burnt and yelled and danced.

    (ii) They bumped Piggy who was burnt, and yelled and danced.

    (iii) They bumped Piggy, who was burnt, and yelled and danced.

    (iv) They bumped Piggy, who was burnt and yelled, and danced.

Compare each of the following with the punctuation as printed in the passage on pages 206, 208 and 209.

1. At this moment the boys, who were cooking at the fire, suddenly hauled off a great chunk of meat and ran, with it towards the grass. They bumped Piggy who was burnt, and yelled and danced immediately. Ralph and the crowd of boys were united. And, relieved by a storm of laughter, Piggy once more was the centre of social derision, so that everyone felt cheerful and normal.
2. Now, out of the terror rose another: desire, thick, urgent, blind.
3. At once the crowd surged, after it poured down the rock, leapt on to the beast, screamed, struck, bit, tore.

The following are differently punctuated versions of sentences from the passage in Exercise 1. Explain the difference as compared with the originals on pages 213 and 214.

4. I studied most closely the households, in which the adolescent girls lived.
5. Are the disturbances, which vex our adolescents, due to the nature of adolescence itself or to the civilization?
6. The traveller, who has been away from home, is wiser than he, who has never left his doorstep.

(b) In many English sentences it is the word order itself that leads to ambiguity; by altering the position of an adverb, or an adverb or adjective phrase or clause, one can substantially alter the meaning:

e.g.   (i) Mr. Merridew had only one son called Jack.
     (ii) Mr. Merridew had one only son called Jack.
    (iii) Mr. Merridew had one son only called Jack.
    (iv) Mr. Merridew had one son called Jack only.

Rewrite the following to modify the meaning by altering the position of the word, phrase or clause in italics:

1. Simon *alone* climbed the mountain.
2. *On the mountain* the beast seemed very real.
3. The boys really needed a good wash *for a very long time.*
4. Anthropologists try to study primitive people *without preconceptions or prejudices.*
5. *In Samoa* Margaret Mead kept notes on all the girls she was studying.
6. The social scientists were studying the behaviour of the students *with the closed circuit television apparatus.*
7. Ralph failed *completely* to convince the other boys that he was right.
8. The boys believed they had seen the beast *from the top of the mountain.*
9. Had they really killed the body *there on the sand?*
10. Ralph was a friend of Simon *who was despised by Jack.*

Exercise 3. (a) In Book Four we considered *non-finite parts of the verb :*

Present participle—always adjectival: ends in -ing.
Past participle—always adjectival: usually ends in -ed, -t.
Infinitive—usually a noun, but can be adjective or adverb: usually preceded by "to".
Gerund—always a noun: ends in -ing.

What non-finite part of a verb is each of the words in italics, from the extract from *Lord of the Flies*?

1. Jack, *painted* and *garlanded*, sat there like an idol.
2. And Sam, *thinking* that Ralph had turned to him accusingly, put down his *gnawed* bone with a nervous giggle.
3. *Lifting* his feet high out of the sand, Ralph started *to stroll* past.
4. Ralph looked away, *confused* and sweating.
5. The thunder exploded again so that a littlun started *to whine*. Big drops of rain fell among them *making* individual sounds when they struck.
6. The littluns began *to run* about, *screaming*.
7. The shrill *screaming* that rose before the beast was like a pain.
8. There were no words, and no movements but the *tearing* of teeth and claws.
9. The beast was on its knees in the centre, its arms *folded* over its face.

(b) There is one other non-finite part of the verb, the GERUN-DIAL ADJECTIVE. When we say that these boys (in *Lord of the Flies*) were from "*boarding* schools", this is not quite the same kind of word as in "*flourishing* schools": the schools were not themselves boarding, although they were themselves flourishing. Similarly a "swimming pool" does not swim (but a "swimming child" does), a walking stick cannot walk, a running track cannot run, a dining room does not eat. They are places *for* boarding, swimming, running, dining; the gerund (with its noun function) has been extended to make an adjective.

Distinguish present participles, gerunds and gerundial adjectives in the following passage:

When Jonathan arrived, most of the other competitors in the swimming gala had finished undressing in the changing rooms. Throwing his trousers untidily into the hanging cupboard, he pulled on his bathing trunks and walked down to the pool. The beating of his heart sounded like a drum as he dived into the cooling water and floated, panting for breath, on the shimmering surface.

*(c) Since participles, infinitives, and gerunds are non-finite parts of *verbs,* they retain certain verbal characteristics, even while acting as nouns, adjectives or adverbs. Thus, for instance, a present participle can retain an object:

(i) Lifting *his feet* high out of the sand, Ralph . . .
An infinitive can be modified by an adverb:
(ii) The littluns began to run *about,* . . .
A past participle can be modified by an adverb phrase:
(iii) . . . its arms folded *over its face.*
A present participle can have a noun clause as its object:
(iv) Sam, thinking *that Ralph had turned to him accusingly* . . .
And a gerund, since it is a noun, can also be described by an adjective clause:
(v) The shrill screaming *that rose before the beast* was like a pain.

This means that, in clause analysis, we may often meet clauses that are attached, not to verbs or nouns in the rest of the sentence, but to non-finite parts of verbs.

Pick out the subordinate clauses in the following sentences, and state their function, and relationship to the rest of the sentence:

1. William Golding, writing what he believed to be the truth about boys, reached rather depressing conclusions.
2. In the end we find Ralph crying because his wise friend Piggy is killed.
3. Studying how people in different cultures behave can be fascinating.
4. An anthropologist likes to work where people have preserved a way of life utterly different from ours.
5. It is not accurate to think of savages as doing whatever they feel like doing.

Complete the following with an appropriate clause (remember that this means a finite verb), and then analyse the sentence you have completed.

6. Wrecked where........................, we had little hope of immediate rescue.
7. We just had to hope that....................
8. Dreaming that.................could be very depressing.
9. There we were, building what..................., when the storm overtook us.
10. Drying our clothes so that..................seemed a good idea at the time.

217

Topics for Written Work

1. Whether you have read the whole of *Lord of the Flies* (or seen the film), or not, it is interesting to imagine yourself as one of the twelve- or thirteen-year-old boys wrecked on the island and try to decide whether you would support Ralph or Jack.

You will probably have discussed the different attitudes that the two represent, and the way in which their fears of something evil threatening them have driven them towards hysteria and the protection that Jack seems to offer. "Which is better?" Piggy shouts later, when Jack's followers have cruelly stolen his glasses to start their own fire, and Ralph and Piggy try to reason with Jack's tribe:

"Which is better—to be a pack of painted niggers like you are, or to be sensible like Ralph is?"

"Which is better—to have rules and agree, or to hunt and kill?"

"Which is better, law and rescue, or hunting and breaking things up?"

On the other hand, Jack is a successful hunter, he does have authority, he does offer fun, and he does say that he and his hunters will defend everyone from the beast they are all afraid of.

Finally, particularly if you are a girl, consider what difference there might have been in the course of events on the island if girls of the same age had been there as well.

2. Imagine yourself marooned on a tropical (or at least a habitable) island, either alone or with a few others of your own age, and describe what you would feel, what you would do and what experiences you would expect to have. This could be in the form of a story or a diary.

3. On page 219 there is a map (using mainly Ordnance Survey symbols) of a small island. Study it very carefully and, using all the information and supplementing this from your imagination, write a full description of the island in words.

Scale = 1 cm to 1 km

Oral Work

Below, you are given several triple choices: in each case select one and prepare a short speech to justify your choice as against the other two, and be ready to take part in a general discussion on each choice.

1. Which leader would you choose if you were among the boys on the island in *Lord of the Flies*?

(a) Jack—he is one of the oldest boys, tall, strong, confident, has experience as head boy of his prep. school, is clever, fearless, fond of enjoying himself, a good hunter, but likes to have power and order others about.

(b) Piggy—he is very clever and level-headed, with imagination, initiative and a methodical approach to problems. He is rather fat, asthmatic and short-sighted, and speaks less well than the others, but in many ways he is the wisest and most mature of the older boys.

(c) Ralph—he is one of the oldest boys, well-built, quite tough, a good talker, clever and willing to take responsibility. He is anxious to keep a sense of order in which every boy is respected, the older look after the younger, and they work together towards the goal of being rescued; but he finds it difficult to convince the others of the need for this.

2. Which holiday would you choose if the following were offered you?

(a) A cruise round the Baltic, arranged for a party from your school. Much of the time would be spent on board ship with boys and girls in your party and other similar school parties from Britain. You would pay visits to ports in Norway, Denmark, Sweden, Germany, Finland and Russia. It might not be warm enough for swimming or sun-bathing.

(b) Youth hostelling in Europe with a friend who has a motor-scooter. Neither of you has travelled abroad alone before and you have not enough money to go with an organized tour. You would be free to travel where you like, but very much responsible for looking after yourselves.

(c) A holiday camp in Britain. You would have plenty of spending money and full board and lodging. The camp is big, well-equipped, with a full programme of entertainment including indoor swimming, and there will be plenty of young people there. You have to take a chance on the weather, the company, and the food.

3. Which girl would you choose as a friend?

(a) She is well-read, clever, talks interestingly and dresses well, but she is not exceptional in her looks, with straight brown hair and no make-up. She likes tennis, sailing and going to the theatre and concerts.

(b) She is always active, talks all the time, wears very striking clothes and takes a lot of care over her appearance, which is attractive. She has long red hair. She likes to be driven fast and be taken out to dances, films and restaurants, but is not very interested in sports.

(c) She is very sympathetic, interested in other people and a good listener. She dresses rather conventionally and wears make-up for special occasions. She works hard, and likes to swim, travel, meet people and do things for others. She has a charming smile and a generous nature.

4. Which boy would you choose as a friend?

(a) He has travelled a lot and seems to be able to talk about anything with confidence. He is very sure of himself and argues forcefully. He is smart and fairly active, having tried most games and hobbies, without being keen on any one. He gets on well with people, drinks, smokes and has many acquaintants.

(b) He is shy but very clever. He spends a lot of his time studying, but can talk fascinatingly on a subject he knows about. He doesn't play games, or go out much, but has a number of very successful hobbies, so that he seems to be able to make or mend almost anything. He has few friends but they are close ones.

(c) He is handsome and athletic. He can swim, ski, drive, play tennis, rugby, cricket, badminton and other games with equal skill. He would rather be active than talk, but his physique gives him confidence. He dresses well and enjoys modern music and dancing, but he won't smoke or allow anything to interfere with his athletic training programme.

5. Make up other choices (e.g. of careers or places to live) for yourselves.

Activities and Research

1. Find out about the work done by the following social scientists and the differences between their approaches to human problems: anthropologists; economists; historians; human geographers; psychiatrists; psychologists; social anthropologists; social historians; social psychologists; sociologists.

2. (a) The novel *Lord of the Flies* was written partly as a conscious contrast to the nineteenth-century story *Coral Island*. Read both books and notice the parallels in background and circumstances and between the three main characters in each book. Which book, in your opinion, gives a more "realistic" picture of what might happen to boys on a deserted tropical island? Which book is more enjoyable? Why does Golding deliberately refer to *Coral Island* in *Lord of the Flies*?

(b) If possible, see Peter Brook's film of *Lord of the Flies* and compare this with the novel. Find out what you can about the way in which Brook selected his boy actors and "trained" them to re-enact the story—he wrote an article about filming *Lord of the Flies* for *The Observer Weekend Review* on 26th July, 1964. How faithful is the film to the book, and which made the bigger impression upon you?

Compare this with other instances of reinterpreting books in "film language".

Further Reading

Lord of the Flies by WILLIAM GOLDING (Faber; Penguin)
This novel is at once a gripping story, a profound fable for our time that rings disturbingly true, and a sensitively written piece of literature. As we have suggested, it is particularly interesting to contrast it with *Coral Island*, the schoolboy classic of the nineteenth century, by R. M. Ballantyne, in which right always triumphs over evil.

The Inheritors by WILLIAM GOLDING (Faber)
Lok and his family group are ape-men, who are gradually exterminated by the "true" men of the Stone Age. Most of the events are seen through the eyes of Lok, who thinks in pictures rather than words, but near the end of the book we enter the mind of Tuami, one of the true men. This again is a novel that can be enjoyed as a story, but is interesting also on a deeper level.

Free Fall by WILLIAM GOLDING (Faber; Penguin)
This novel traces the life of Sammy Mountjoy from his neglected childhood to middle age.

Coming of Age in Samoa by MARGARET MEAD (Penguin) (159.92279)
This book records a famous anthropologist's study of the girls in a primitive community. It is also a fascinating and very readable account of life in a remote part of the world, very different from our own, and it has remained a best seller since its publication in 1928.

Growing Up in New Guinea by MARGARET MEAD (Penguin) (159.92279)
There are some clearly marked differences between the rather permissive society that the author found in Samoa and the more rigid and puritanical organization of life among the Manus tribe in New Guinea. Again, the account of these people is interesting in itself, and doubly so as a comment on problems in our own more complex and "advanced" community.

CHAPTER FOURTEEN

A Last Look at School

The narrator is a young man just starting his teaching career. His first school, Stonehill Street, is set in a rough district and filled with rough, noisy boys — not the most comfortable place for an inexperienced and uncertain teacher.

"You'll have to keep Class 2 under your thumb," said the headmaster. To make this clear, he showed me his own thumb; a huge thing, like a pocket cudgel. I felt very pale. I had reason enough to distrust my thumb.

Class 2. They were top-year boys. Their own teacher had been sick for a long time; a succession of startled substitutes had stood before them, ducked, winced and fled. I was the seventh that term. No one quite knew where the class had got to in any subject. It was plain that the headmaster thought they had got nowhere. But I was to take them for nearly everything; and first, that awful afternoon, for history.

I trembled down to Room H. In the hall I was nearly knocked over by a boy illegally running. I should have told him off, instead, I apologized. It was all wrong; my mood was all placatory; I was, inwardly, all white flag.

The room was easily traced by the noise that was coming from it. It didn't sound a studious noise. I crept through the door. Enormous boys were everywhere, doing indefensible things. I can't recall much in particular that they were doing; indeed, that was the worst of it — that these improprieties couldn't be nailed down.

I managed to make out that mixed up with these young giants was a certain amount of furniture. This consisted, I found, of individual desks; doll's-house things that rested on mountainous knees and swayed from side to side. Too negligently or maliciously treated, one would, from time to time, crash to the floor. There were certainly fights going on; and I believe one desk was chasing another. The air was full of pieces of chalk, a strange rain of it.

Feeling invisible, I walked towards the teacher's desk. Not

223

an eye was turned in my direction. I just stood there and looked at them and the awful pointless indignation mounted in me. Was I not a teacher! Had I not been approved by the Ministry itself! Was I really so puny, so ineffective?

"Now, shut up," I shouted. There was a fatal note of pleading in my voice. They took no notice, so I shouted again.

And then I said, "If you don't shut up, I'll . . ." Now they heard me and an awful silence came, not an obedient silence but a sceptical one. My voice trailed away. If they didn't shut up, I would—what? I was toying inwardly with ideas of thunderbolts, earthquakes, mass executions. But in cold blood I could think of no practicable substitute for these dramatic punishments.

A boy leaned back in his desk, indolently far back, and said, "Are you going to try to teach us?" He looked round and laughed. There was a murmur from the back of the room and another laugh.

I was shocked to the core. Shocked, stung and frightened. "Yes, I am," I shouted. "And you—you had better shut up."

They all laughed. Then they turned to one another and discussed the matter. A fight began at the back. But what hurt me most was that in the middle of the room sat a very studious-looking boy reading a book. He looked up, raised a wry eyebrow, looked at me, raised his eyebrow higher, and shrugged himself back into his book.

I shouted for a while, but it was beyond me. I hadn't the manner, was a plain impostor. My blushing and bawling were a joy to them. There was, for a time, pandemonium, like the big scene in an opera being played backwards on a gramophone.

Then, since there had to be some resemblance between this and what I understood to be a lesson, I fumbled for a theme. I had dimly planned, coming down, to ask them where they had got to in history. I could guess now at the answers I might get. Feeling like a cornered film brigand who tries to keep a crowd at bay with a single pistol, I edged towards a cupboard, keeping my face turned to the class. Out of the corner of an eye I saw the cupboard was, except for crumpled paper, bare. What was I to do?

It struck me that I had in my brief-case a book on Chaucer. It contained a large number of documents of the period. Accounts of street brawls. It seemed apposite. I felt in the case and brought out the book.

It was, alas, very big and looked very academic. "Cor, the Bible," said a voice. "Read any good books lately?" said another. "You hit me with that and I'll tell my dad." "He can *read*!" And, in falsetto, "Tell us a fairy story!"

"Shut up," I shouted, and desperately turned the leaves. The street brawls eluded me. But here was a bit about four-teenth-century trading regulations "A long time ago . . ." I roared.

By accident there was silence at this moment. So the voice that shouted, "Tell me the old, old story," was very clear indeed. And the shouter was very easy to identify. My nerves gave a twitch and I shouted back. "What's your name, you . . . I'll . . . Come on, what's your name?"

I had much to learn about this sort of inquisition. "Chumley," he shouted. "Lord Chumley." "Of Chumley Manor," came another voice. My own accent came at me, insolently—and, indeed, most skilfully—exaggerated.

"You'll have to come with me to the headmaster," I howled. To my mind, or rather to the hot whirling chaos that had been my mind, this was a terrible threat. I expected instant capitu-lation. Instead, the boy chose to consider himself insulted. "You can't prove nothing," he shouted. "I ain't done nothing. You ain't going to get me in trouble."

It sounded, in the way he said it, as though I'd threatened him with improper assault. And he did it so well that I felt guilty as well as fury.

"You mean to sit there and . . ." I bawled.

But he did mean to sit there and . . . They all did. I lost every round, that awful afternoon. In the end, hot, incredulous and delirious, I went under. I dodged the chalk and longed for the bell.

When a cupboard went over, spilling out a many-volumed encyclopedia and a jug of ink, I made one last effort at coer-cion. "Right," I shrieked. "You'll all stay in at half past four."

"Going to the pictures," said a menacing voice.

"Paper round."

"You'd better not."

"Against the law."

"Bring my dad up."

I didn't keep them in. And when the bell went at last, I tried not to run away. I ordered them to put their chairs on their desks, a practice that made life easier for the cleaners.

With a sound like a furniture-lorry overturning, they did so. Then the gas went out. "Ooh, I'm frightened," came a voice. Then someone at the back pushed his chair. It fell, knocking down the chair in front. At this, every chair in the room fell down. Howls of simulated terror came from the darkness.

I fled.

(from Roaring Boys by Edward Blishen)

Appreciation and Discussion

1. (a) What indications are there that the author was a "supply teacher", sent in to a school to fill a temporary vacancy on the staff?

    (b) Write out the sentence that indicates that he was nevertheless a fully qualified teacher.

    (c) In what ways did he obviously lack experience?

2. Write at least five statements from this passage that indicate that the author was nervous.

3. (a) What was the author indignant about, in the sixth paragraph?

    (b) Why was this "awful, pointless" indignation?

4. Why did "accounts of street brawls" in the time of Chaucer seem "apposite"?

5. What is a "falsetto", and why do you think the boy adopted this tone for his remark "Tell us a fairy story!"?

6. When the author says: "My own accent came at me insolently . . . exaggerated", what kind of accent do you think he had and how does his way of speaking contrast with that of the pupils in the examples here?

7. What details in this extract suggest that the school buildings were rather old-fashioned and unsuitably furnished?

8. What do the following words or phrases mean, as used in this passage?

    a cudgel; placatory; improprieties; negligently or maliciously treated; a sceptical (silence); pandemonium; eluded me; inquisition; capitulation; coercion; simulated terror.

9. Discuss the similes and metaphors used here, for instance:

a huge (thumb) like a pocket cudgel;
I was, inwardly, all white flag;
one desk was chasing another;
there was, for a time, pandemonium, like the big scene
in an opera being played backwards on a gramophone;
feeling like a cornered film brigand who tries to keep a
crowd at bay with a single pistol;
the hot whirling chaos that had been my mind;
it sounded . . . as though I'd threatened him with
improper assault;
with a sound like a furniture-lorry overturning.

10. The author's diction (his choice of words) is interesting.
Discuss the following:

a succession of startled substitutes;
I trembled down to Room H;
It didn't sound a studious noise;
doll's-house things that rested on mountainous knees;
a strange rain of (chalk);
a fatal note of pleading;
a boy leaned . . . indolently far back;
shocked, stung and frightened;
raised a wry eyebrow;
shrugged himself back into his book;
I fumbled for a theme;
hot, incredulous and delirious.

11. Why do you think the teacher was so hurt by the attitude
of the one studious-looking boy?

12. He says he had much to learn about this "sort of inquisition" when disciplining an individual boy. What did he do
wrong, and how should he have gone about it?

13. Sum up the various kinds of indiscipline the boys were
guilty of. What basic principles of keeping order did the
author apply (for instance, did he avoid turning his back on
the class?) What went wrong? How do you think an
experienced and competent schoolmaster would have dealt
with this class?

14. Draw on your own experience of different teachers over
some ten years of your schooling to comment on the *realism*
of this passage. How do the weakest teachers you have ever
encountered compare with this man? Are the class in this
extract impossibly bad, in your opinion?

Last Lesson of the Afternoon

When will the bell ring, and end this weariness?
How long have they tugged the leash, and strained apart,
My pack of unruly hounds! I cannot start
Them again on a quarry of knowledge they hate to hunt,
I can haul them and urge them no more.

No longer now can I endure the brunt
Of the books that lie out on the desks; a full threescore
Of several insults of blotted pages, and scrawl
Of slovenly work that they have offered me.
I am sick, and what on earth is the good of it all?
What good to them or me, I cannot see!

                        So, shall I take
My last dear fuel of life to heap on my soul
And kindle my will to a flame that shall consume
Their dross of indifference; and take the toll
Of their insults in punishment?—I will not!—

I will not waste my soul and my strength for this.
What do I care for all they do amiss!
What is the point of this teaching of mine, and of this
Learning of theirs? It all goes down the same abyss.

What does it matter to me, if they can write
A description of a dog, or if they can't?
What is the point? To us both, it is all my aunt!
And yet I'm supposed to care, with all my might.

I do not, and will not; they won't and they don't; and that's all!
I shall keep my strength for myself; they can keep theirs as well.
Why should we beat our heads against the wall
Of each other? I shall sit and wait for the bell.

D. H. LAWRENCE

Discussing the Poem

1. What facts can we deduce about the size of the class and the kind of work they were supposed to be doing that afternoon? Is there anything about these conditions to suggest that they are now more than fifty years out of date?
2. Analyse the metaphors (or "images") used in the first and third verses. Do these seem particularly appropriate?
3. Is the personal and conversational style of the poem effective? Notice how, although divided into stanzas and rhyming, the poem has no rigid structure. Does it sound better read with the Midland accent that D. H. Lawrence himself had as a young teacher?
4. Has the teacher got a good case for refusing to teach the children any more? Does it really go "down the same abyss"? What is wrong—the teacher, the pupils, the kind of work he expects or the whole idea of conventional education?

Techniques

Exercise 1. Study and discuss the following passage, which is another extract from one of the 1967 *Reith Lectures* by Edmund Leach, in which he discusses the way our class-conscious society uses competitive examinations, and suggests that we shall in future need a more positive approach to education.

Even if it were true, which it isn't, that success at school and university guaranteed success in adult life, the rat race is conducted at terrible cost. Over the past 50 years we in England have partly replaced the old system of class stratification based
5   on hereditary wealth by a new class system based on achieved status. Simultaneously our educational system has developed into an entirely ruthless machine for the elimination of the unworthy. Suicide and mental breakdown are now so common in student populations that they are almost taken for granted.
10   We instil competitive values into our children from entirely dishonest motives. Few of us have any deep concern about whether our offspring become civilized human beings: we are only worried about social class. We are hag-ridden by the fear and envy endemic to a society which combines class stratificaton
15   with the possibility of social mobility. Those who are high up in the existing order are driven to compete by fear and contempt for those below; those lower down are driven by envy of those above. . . .

It seems probable that everyone, including those who are

20 now most successful, would feel much more comfortable in a less competitive world, and, if we are looking towards the future this should be one of our long-term objectives. It won't be easy to achieve but this much is quite plain. In order to arrive at a system in which less value is placed on the *relative* merit of indi-
25 viduals we shall need to make quite basic changes to the over-all structure of formal school education. . . .

The people who are going to be able to cope with our rapidly changing future are those who are temperamentally unortho-dox—the curious, the sceptical, the ones who don't care a fig for
30 established opinion, people like Charles Darwin, who said of himself: "I have steadily endeavoured to keep my mind free so as to give up any hypothesis, however much beloved, as soon as facts are shown to be opposed to it."

If all this is true, the implications for education should be
35 fairly obvious. We should be looking for people with divergent unorthodox kinds of intelligence, not conformist orthodox types. But since all methods of selection by competitive examination can only be based on established orthodoxies, we must try to get rid of competitive examinations altogether. The aim must be to
40 maximize variation. We need to give all children equal oppor-tunity to learn how to learn, but after that they should be en-couraged to follow their own special interests instead of the text-book conventions of examination syndicates.

(from *The Listener*, Dec. 1967)

(a) (i) Each of the following statements is, according to the evidence of this passage, TRUE, FALSE or UNKNOWN. For instance, the statement:

We are to some extent honest when we bring up our child-ren to be competitive.

is a FALSE statement, according to the author's opinion in lines 10–11.

Label each of the following TRUE, FALSE or UNKNOWN, and be prepared to justify your opinion.

1. The author believes that success at school brings success in one's career.
2. Fifty years ago English society was divided into classes based on inherited wealth.
3. Our educational system first became competitive and subsequently our class system changed.
4. Although we have not abolished social classes, it is now

231

much more possible for people to move from one class to another.

5. The only motives for competition between classes are fear, contempt and envy.

6. The author is certain that even the most successful people would prefer to live in less fierce competition with others.

7. Changes in our educational methods will be essential to create a less competitive society.

8. Rebels, outsiders and eccentrics are the kind of people who (according to the author) will best adapt to the needs of the future.

9. The value of unorthodox intellectuals will be established by a new kind of competitive examination.

10. The writer is arguing that all kinds of children, orthodox or unorthodox, are equal in ability, even if otherwise different.

(ii) Three alternative meanings are given for each of the following words from the passage. Choose the correct one in each case, to suit the context in this passage, e.g.

Simultaneously (line 6)—in the same way, at the same time, with great ease.
"at the same time" is the correct meaning.

1. stratification (line 4)—levelling off, narrowing down, maintenance of levels.

2. hereditary (line 5)—essentially belonging to, passed on by inheritance, irreligious.

3. instil (line 10)—gradually but definitely teach, place in a particular position, stir up.

4. endemic (line 14)—penetrating through the skin of, prevalent in, rapidly spreading (like a disease) among.

5. temperamentally (line 28)—in an irritable way, moderately and without excess, according to their basic character and disposition.

6. sceptical (line 29)—people who require proof for their beliefs, a container for biological specimens, those with poisoned minds.

7. hypothesis (line 32)—insincere idea, unproved theory or explanation, a syringe used by biologists.

8. orthodoxies (line 38)—opinions approved as correct, committees of leaders of learning, previous years' results.

9. maximize (line 40)—make as small as possible, base on traditional principles, make as large as possible.

232

10. syndicates (line 43)—commercial companies, university councils, those working at the same time.

(b) Make a summary of this passage in between 150 and 170 words. Avoid the language of the passage as far as possible. State at the end of the summary the number of words you have used. The passage contains about 470 words.

Exercise 2. The following conversation is from Dickens' novel *Nicholas Nickleby*. Squeers runs a private boarding school, and is showing his new assistant, Nicholas, round.
(a) Rewrite the conversation, inserting all the inverted commas, commas, full stops, question marks or semi-colons, and apostrophes, that are necessary to complete the direct speech punctuation.
(b) Rewrite the conversation as reported (or indirect) speech.

This is the first class in English spelling and philosophy Nickleby said Squeers beckoning Nicholas to stand beside him Well get up a Latin one and hand that over to you Now then wheres the first boy

Please sir hes cleaning the back parlour window said the temporary head of the philosophical class.

So he is to be sure rejoined Squeers We go upon the practical mode of teaching Nickleby the regular education system C-l-e-a-n clean verb active to make bright to scour W-i-n-win d-e-r winder a casement When the boy knows this out of the book he goes and does it Its just the same principle as the use of the globes Wheres the second boy

Please sir hes weeding the garden replied a small voice

To be sure said Squeers by no means disconcerted So he is B-o-t bot t-i-n tin bottin n-e-y ney bottinney noun substantive a knowledge of plants When he has learned that bottinney means a knowledge of plants he goes and knows em Thats our system Nickleby what do you think of it

Its a very useful one at any rate answered Nicholas

(c) Reported speech can be the source of certain ambiguities. The rule about questions, for instance, is that they become statements in reported speech; the only exception to this is when the report itself is a question. Study the following examples:

(i) He asked her, "How do you do it?"
(ii) Did he ask her, "How do you do it?"?

233

(iii) He asked her how she did it.

(iv) Did he ask her how she did it?

Bearing this in mind, turn into reported speech the *three* paragraphs in the extract from *Roaring Boys*, beginning:

"Feeling invisible, I walked towards the teacher's desk . . .".

Begin your reported version like this:

Edward Blishen recalls that he walked towards the teacher's desk feeling invisible, since not an eye was turned in his direction. He just stood there and looked at the boys and the awful pointless indignation mounted in him. He reminded himself that he was a teacher . . .

(d) Apart from ambiguities with pronouns (which we referred to in Book Four), adverb phrases and clauses are often a source of confusion. Explain the two meanings in each of the following sentences in reported speech by rewording each in at least two clear and unambiguous ways:

1. The new teacher asked where he was to teach when he arrived.
2. He had told the headmaster how he might help with drama when he first came to the school.
3. She said after morning break he could take an extra lesson.
4. The headmaster told the boys that they could take off their ties in the assembly.
5. Their form-master announced that there would be a form party at the end of term in the form period.

Exercise 3. Many of the terms used in schools have specialist meanings, and would be unfamiliar to an English-speaking person (an American, for example) from another country. Write a short explanation of the terms given below. Begin with a *definition*, in one sentence, then reinforce this with two or three sentences of explanation or illustration.

For example, "working at home" would be a poor explanation of "homework"; would the following be adequate?

Homework is work set to be done by a pupil after school hours. It usually takes the form of preparation for a lesson — reading or learning information — or practising and applying what has been taught, by doing exercises, writing up notes, or writing one's own compositions. Many schools expect pupils

234

to spend between one and three hours of their own time each
day on this work.

assembly	form-master/mistress	set
aural aids	grammar school	stream
break	house	student teacher
comprehensive school	ordinary level	supply teacher
detentions	prefect	technical school
film-loop	public school	visual aids
film-strip	reports	

Add other terms in use in your own area or school if they are
not covered here.

Topics for Written Work

1. Choose *one* of the following topics for a discussion essay:

(a) "All secondary schools should be boarding schools."

(b) "All schools should be coeducational."

(c) "Practical subjects are a necessary part of education."

(d) "Competitive public examinations are an inefficient
method of selecting the people who are of least use in a
changing society."

(e) "Games have always played too large a part in English
education."

(f) "The prefect system is harmful to those who are given
authority and to those who are forced to submit to it."

(g) "There is no place for punishment in schools—education
should be a matter of catching a pupil's interest and reward-
ing his progress."

(h) "In schools of the future we shall not need teachers, only
librarians and technicians to make the appropriate information available for individual study."

(i) "The most valuable part of a school's work is not what
happens in the class-room, but the personal contact
between teacher and pupils in clubs and societies and out
of school."

(j) "Selection in education, segregating the brighter pupils so
that they can be taught separately, leads to a disastrous
situation in which the majority of pupils regard themselves
as inferior failures."

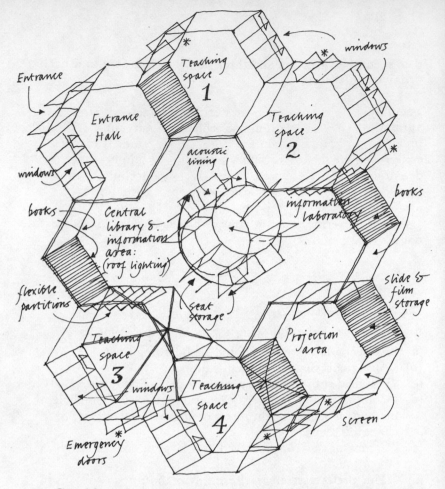

Entrance

Entrance
Hall

windows

books

Central
library &
information
area:
(roof lighting)

flexible
partitions

Teaching
space
1

acoustic
lining

Teaching
space
2

windows

windows

information
laboratory

books

slide &
film
storage

seat
storage

Teaching
space
3

windows

Teaching
space
4

Projection
area

Emergency
doors

screen

2. Consider what you would regard as an ideal school for the
future. Look back on your own education and the buildings,
staff and equipment that were available to you. What short-
comings can you specify? How could your own talents have
been better fostered? What subjects or areas of information
were omitted? Then list the kinds of equipment and methods
that might be made available when new schools are planned and
built in, say, the next twenty years. How might their methods
alter the design of buildings? (For instance, might computers
and audio-visual aids revolutionize the school library?) Include
sections on the planning of the buildings (illustrated with
suitable diagrams), on the provision of equipment, on staffing
and curriculum (would individual learning take over from
class teaching, for instance?), and on the subject-matter that
would form the basis of the timetable.

3. The poem *Last Lesson of the Afternoon* gives the schoolmaster's view of one aspect of school. Look at his poem *The Best of School* for D. H. Lawrence's feelings about the more attractive side of teaching—perhaps almost too rosy a picture? Look also at accounts of schools in novels, etc., some of which are referred to in the *Activities and Research* section below, and at Yevgeny Yevtushenko's poem *Schoolmaster* as translated in the Penguin Poets volume.

Look back over your own school career, the staff who have taught you, the pleasant and unpleasant incidents, the atmosphere in various lessons. Choose one subject, or aspect of school life, and write a free verse comment on this. Here is one such piece by a fifth former:

> Room hot and stuffy,
> So is the master.
> Lesson lasts for ever.
> The voice drawls on:
> "The liberation of CO_2 is due to . . ."
> Who cares what it's due to?
> Rugger match tomorrow,
> Bound to be wet and muddy:
> Might be cancelled.
> "The gas jar is filled with . . ."
> Windows wet and steamed up,
> Heaters far too hot,
> Trousers damp and clinging.
> Got a lot of homework.
> Can't do maths.
> "For homework tonight
> You will write up your notes."
> What notes?
> What experiment?
> Oh . . . copy off Chris tomorrow.

IAN

Oral Work

1. Be prepared to give your views on:

(a) Rewards and punishments in schools—how attitudes have changed over the years and what you think are the right ways to treat children of different ages and temperaments in schools today. Is there a place for corporal punishment? What would happen in a school where there was no authority imposed at all? What were A. S. Neil's theories on how to deal

237

with difficult children? Remembering *Lord of the Flies*, would you say that children *want* rules and discipline?

(b) The virtues of a prefectional system — why do many schools have a system of prefects with privileges and responsibilities? Is it good for senior pupils that they should have some experience of wielding authority? Should some pupils have power to order other pupils about? What punishments (if any) should prefects be able to impose and what privileges should they enjoy?

(c) The school curriculum — attack those subjects you would like to see dropped, defend any new ones that should be taught (how to drive a car, for instance), and give your views on the balance you would like to see between subjects on the timetable, and on the principles upon which a curriculum should be based.

(d) The place of examinations and selection — would you wish examinations to be maintained, abolished, or changed in their form and purpose? Do we need to select people (for instance, for university or specialized training and work), and if so, how could this be done most efficiently?

(e) Young people and students today — should the under-21s have more say in the management and development of the world they will grow up in? What age would you set for (i) voting; (ii) marrying; (iii) being financially responsible; (iv) driving a car; (v) being responsible in law for any crime one commits — and why? How much influence should students have on the teaching and government of their universities, or sixth-formers on the policy of their schools?

2. Act, tape-record or film the scene described in the extract from *Roaring Boys*. Adapt it if necessary to suit a cast of girls.

Activities and Research

1. Collect an anthology of extracts from books, plays and poems that describe schools or school-teachers, past and present. Here are a few suggestions for sources for passages:

> *Life in Shakespeare's England* (by J. Dover Wilson) (Penguin) —the "Grammar School" section of part IV, "Education".
> *David Copperfield* (by Charles Dickens) — chapter 7 on Salem House; also descriptions of Dotheboys Hall in *Nicholas Nickleby* and Mr Gradgrind's school in *Hard Times*.
> *Christ's Hospital Five and Thirty Years Ago*, an essay by Charles Lamb.

Portrait of the Artist as a Young Man (by James Joyce)—the last part of chapter 1.
The Rainbow (by D. H. Lawrence)—parts of chapter 13.
The Blackboard Jungle (by Evan Hunter).
To Sir, With Love (by E. R. Braithwaite).

2. Write a short history, either of your own school, or of a particular well-known school, or of one type of school (such as the grammar school or elementary schools or church schools or "progressive" schools).

Further Reading

Roaring Boys by EDWARD BLISHEN (C. Chivers)
This is not a straight autobiography, although it is based firmly on the author's own experience. As he says in his Author's Note: "I know, with considerable intimacy, a teacher whose initiation was not unlike the one I have described." Funny, sympathetic, and very readable, this book will also give you an insight into some of the problems that a teacher has to face.

Blackboard Jungle by EVAN HUNTER (Constable)
This novel also deals with teaching in a rough district, but the treatment of the theme is quite different from that in *Roaring Boys*. A comparison of the two books is therefore interesting.

Nicholas Nickleby by CHARLES DICKENS (various publishers)
Behind all Nicholas's various adventures there always lurks the sinister figure of his miserly uncle, Ralph Nickleby. As a high-spirited and generous young man, he tries his hand at teaching, acting, and work in the service of the benevolent Cheeryble brothers. But the best remembered of his adventures are those at the notorious school run by Wackford Squeers, who starves and maltreats forty urchins whom he is supposed to be educating.

The Rainbow by D. H. LAWRENCE (Heinemann; Penguin)
This is not the shortest or easiest of D. H. Lawrence's stories but is one of his finest novels, tracing the fortunes of a remarkable Nottinghamshire family through three generations, and probing all the time into their emotional relationships. Towards the end the grand-daughter, Ursula, in rebellion against her family, forces herself to take up work as a teacher in the overcrowded, grim class-rooms of an elementary school in urban Nottingham before the First World War.

CHAPTER FIFTEEN

Love—and Marriage?

Bathsheba, mistress of a farm inherited from her uncle, was dazzled by the handsome young Sergeant Frank Troy. Once they were married, he showed himself irresponsible as a farmer and extravagant with his wife's money. Gradually, Bathsheba came to suspect him of a previous affair with her former servant-girl, Fanny Robin, who then returned to the village to die in childbirth. Her coffin lay overnight at Bathsheba's farm.

She paused in the hall, looking at the door of the room wherein Fanny lay. She locked her fingers, threw back her head, and strained her hot hands rigidly across her forehead, saying, with a hysterical sob, "Would to God you would speak and tell me your secret, Fanny! ... O, I hope, hope it is not true that there are two of you! ... If I could only look upon you for one little minute, I should know all!"

A few moments passed, and she added, slowly, *"And I will."*

Bathsheba in after times could never gauge the mood which carried her through the actions following this murmured resolution on this memorable evening of her life. She went to the lumber-closet for a screw-driver. At the end of a short though undefined time she found herself in the small room, quivering with emotion, a mist before her eyes, and an excruciating pulsation in her brain, standing beside the uncovered coffin of the girl whose conjectured end had so entirely engrossed her, and saying to herself in a husky voice as she gazed within—

"It was best to know the worst, and I know it now!" ...

Her tears fell fast beside the unconscious pair in the coffin; tears of a complicated origin, of a nature indescribable, almost indefinable except as other than those of simple sorrow. Assuredly their wonted fires must have lived in Fanny's ashes when events were so shaped as to chariot her hither in this natural, unobtrusive, yet effectual manner. The one feat alone—that of dying—by which a mean condition could be resolved into a grand one, Fanny had achieved. And to that had destiny subjoined this rencounter to-night, which had, in Bathsheba's wild imagining, turned her companion's failure to success, her humiliation to triumph, her lucklessness to ascendency; it had thrown over herself a garish light of mockery, and set upon all things about her an ironical smile. . . .

She knelt beside the coffin, covered her face with her hands, and for a time the room was silent as a tomb. Whether from a purely mechanical, or from any other cause, when Bathsheba arose it was with a quieted spirit, and a regret for the antagonistic instincts which had seized upon her just before.

In her desire to make atonement she took flowers from a vase by the window, and began lying them around the dead girl's head. Bathsheba knew no other way of showing kindness to persons departed than by giving them flowers. She knew not how long she remained engaged thus. She forgot time, life, where she was, what she was doing. A slamming together of the coach-house doors in the yard brought her to herself again. An instant after, the front door opened and closed, steps crossed the hall, and her husband appeared at the entrance to the room, looking in upon her.

He beheld it all by degrees, stared in stupefaction at the scene, as if he thought it an illusion raised by some fiendish incantation. Bathsheba, pallid as a corpse on end, gazed back at him in the same wild way. . . .

The candle was standing on a bureau close by them, and the light slanted down, distinctly enkindling the cold features of both mother and babe. Troy looked in, dropped his wife's hand, knowledge of it all came over him in a lurid sheen, and he stood still.

So still he remained that he could be imagined to have left in him no motive power whatever. The clashes of feeling in all directions confounded one another, produced a neutrality, and there was motion in none.

"Do you know her?" said Bathsheba, in a small enclosed echo, as from the interior of a cell.

"I do," said Troy.

"Is it she?"

"It is."

He had originally stood perfectly erect. And now, in the wellnigh congealed immobility of his frame could be discerned an incipient movement, as in the darkest night may be discerned light after a while. He was gradually sinking forwards. The lines of his features softened, and dismay modulated to illimitable sadness. Bathsheba was regarding him from the other side, still with parted lips and distracted eyes. Capacity for intense feeling is proportionate to the general intensity of the nature, and perhaps in all Fanny's sufferings, much greater relatively to her strength, there never was a time when she suffered in an absolute sense what Bathsheba suffered now.

What Troy did was to sink upon his knees with an indefinable union of remorse and reverence upon his face, and, bending over Fanny Robin, gently kissed her, as one would kiss an infant asleep to avoid awakening it.

At the sight and sound of that, to her, unendurable act, Bathsheba sprang towards him. All the strong feelings which had been scattered over her existence since she knew what feeling was, seemed gathered together into one pulsation now. The revulsion from her indignant mood a little earlier, when she had meditated upon compromised honour, forestalment, eclipse in maternity by another, was violent and entire. All that was forgotten in the simple and still strong attachment of wife to husband. She had sighed for her self-completeness then, and now she cried aloud against the severance of the union she had deplored. She flung her arms round Troy's neck, exclaiming wildly from the deepest deep of her heart—

"Don't—don't kiss them! O, Frank, I can't bear it—I can't! I love you better than she did: kiss me too, Frank— kiss me! *You will, Frank, kiss me too!*"

There was something so abnormal and startling in the child-like pain and simplicity of this appeal from a woman of Bathsheba's calibre and independence, that Troy, loosening her tightly clasped arms from his neck, looked at her in bewilderment. It was such an unexpected revelation of all women being alike at heart, even those so different in their accessories as Fanny and this one beside him, that Troy could hardly seem to believe her to be his proud wife Bathsheba. Fanny's own spirit seemed to be animating her frame. But this was the mood of a few instants only. When the momentary surprise had passed, his expression changed to a silencing imperious gaze.

"I will not kiss you!" he said, pushing her away. . . .

"You are nothing to me—nothing," said Troy, heartlessly. "A ceremony before a priest doesn't make a marriage. I am not morally yours."

A vehement impulse to flee from him, to run from this place

hide, and escape his words at any price, not stopping short of death itself, mastered Bathsheba now. She waited not an instant, but turned to the door and ran out.

(from *Far From the Madding Crowd* by Thomas Hardy)

Appreciation and Discussion

1. Why does Bathsheba want to look at Fanny inside the coffin?
2. There are *two* facts about the circumstances of Fanny's death that Bathsheba does not know at the beginning of this extract, but learns when she unscrews the coffin. What are these two facts?
3. Bathsheba believes she knows "the worst" when she has opened the coffin. (a) What is so humiliating about it? (b) Do you think that she has any worse shocks to come before the end of this extract?
4. State in your own words what Bathsheba's feelings were immediately after looking at Fanny. How does she show them?
5. What effect did praying have upon Bathsheba? How does she show a changed attitude?
6. What was Troy's immediate reaction to seeing the inside of the coffin and Bathsheba beside it?
7. What is the significance of Bathsheba's question, "Is it she?"?
8. Bathsheba's violent outburst when Troy knelt and kissed Fanny is described as "a revulsion from her indignant mood". (a) Why had she been angry with Troy earlier? (b) Why was she passionate and hysterical, now?
9. (a) What shocked and bewildered Troy about Bathsheba's appeal to him to kiss her? (b) This paragraph, about his bewilderment, tells us much about the contrasts between Fanny and Bathsheba—sum these up in your own words.
10. Does Troy really appear "heartless" in his final reaction to Bathsheba's appeal?
11. What do the following mean?

gauge; an excruciating pulsation; conjectured end; unobtrusive; ascendency; a garish light; to make atonement; stared in stupefaction; pallid; enkindling; a lurid sheen; an indefinable union of remorse and reverence; calibre; a vehement impulse.

12. Discuss the meaning and implications of the following extracts from the passage:

(a) Assuredly their wonted fires must have lived in Fanny's ashes when events were so shaped as to chariot her hither in this natural, unobtrusive, yet effectual manner.

(b) And to that had destiny subjoined this rencounter to-night, which had, in Bathsheba's wild imagining, turned her companion's failure to success, her humiliation to triumph, her lucklessness to ascendency; it had thrown over herself a garish light of mockery, and set upon all things about her an ironical smile.

(c) He . . . stared in stupefaction at the scene as if he thought it an illusion raised by some fiendish incantation.

(d) The clashes of feeling in all directions confounded one another, produced a neutrality, and there was motion in none.

(e) And now, in the wellnigh congealed immobility of his frame could be discerned an incipient movement. . . .

13. Discuss the attitudes of the author to Fanny and to Bathsheba. What is implied by saying that Fanny had "resolved a mean condition into a grand one" by dying in this way? Discuss what the author says about Bathsheba's sufferings compared with those of Fanny (who died deserted, exhausted and poverty-stricken, in the workhouse, and in the pangs of childbirth), when she watches Troy kiss Fanny's body. Consider also Troy's reaction to Bathsheba's appeal to him at the end of this extract, and Bathsheba's mood when she finally runs out of the house.

14. Does this extract leave you with the impression that Troy's behaviour had been (or was) selfish, cruel and lacking in any sympathy and understanding? What defence can one make of Troy on the evidence in this passage?

15. Discuss Troy's assertions that a marriage needs more than a religious ceremony to make it binding, and that he is "morally" Fanny's rather than Bathsheba's. What words in this extract suggest that he and Bathsheba had had no children? Does this fact alter his responsibilities to the two women?

If You'll Give Me a Kiss and Be My Girl

If you'll give me a kiss and be my girl
Jump on my bike, we'll do a ton.
We'll explode from the city in a cloud of dust
And roar due west to the setting sun.

We'll bounce the days all over the beach
Pop 'em like seaweed and scatter ourselves
Careless as kids with candyfloss
Into all of the shapes of all of the shells.

We'll go as giddy as merry-go-rounds
Bump with a crash like dodgem cars
Float in a basket of coloured balloons
Or jump in a rocket and whizz for Mars.

If you love to be blown by a roar of wind
If you love to twist and spin and twirl
If you love to crash on the shore like waves
Then give me a kiss and be my girl.

I love to be blown by a roar of wind
But I love to watch the sea asleep
And breathe in salt and fresh-caught shrimps
As we wind our way through snoring streets.

I'll rave in a cellar till the band drops dead
But I want you to sing on your own guitar
For no one but me and a moonlight oak
Then dive in the silent lake for a star.

I love to spin the night away
But I love to hold you dark and still.
I love your kick that drives us miles
But I love the view from the top of a hill.

But if you give me the crashing waves
And sing me the blues of the sea as well,
Then, whether there's candyfloss or not,
I'll give you a kiss and be your girl.

LEO AYLEN

Discussing the Poem

1. Examine generally the difference between what the boy offers and what the girl wants. Do these represent a common difference of attitude between the sexes?

2. Discuss the structure and images of the poem: what ideas from the first four verses are reflected in the second half? Some of the vocabulary is used by today's teenagers ("do a ton", "rave")—what kind of place are they going to visit? Where might they "jump in a rocket and whizz for Mars"?

3. Look back to pages 141–2, at the last three paragraphs of the extract from "Uses of Literacy"; is there a similar kind of "escapism" in the boy's idea of enjoying himself in this poem? Does the girl really reject his "candyfloss world" as false or unimportant?

Techniques

Exercise 1. The following passage is adapted from an article in *The Guardian* in January, 1968. It appeared on the women's page and was addressed to British readers, suggesting that the problems of world over-population should affect our own way of life in this country.

The most serious threat now facing the human race is not the much-publicized Bomb, nor war, nor racial strife as such, nor militant communism, nor fascism, nor any of the other acknowledged ills, but something much more fundamental which a great many people do not even see as an evil because in their own society it isn't—yet. I mean the world population growth. It was ironic that well-intentioned demonstrators adopted as a piece of innocent love-morality the pernicious slogan "Make love, not war" when it is the short-sightedness of human love and desire that is the real threat to human life itself.

The figures are not, of course, new, but it seems they need to be continually restated if they are to become part of even the intelligent reader's consciousness. The number of people on earth is increasing hourly in geometric progression. It took 200,000 years for us to reach the present figure of about 3,400 million, but that total is likely to be doubled by the end of the century. *Nor is this problem confined to Asian countries.* It is reckoned that, if present birth rates continue, the population of the USA will reach one billion in under 100 years from now. (In 800 years there would be one person per square foot, but obviously, long before this stage could be reached total war and famine would—.will?—destroy humanity as we know it.) The prediction for Europe is similar, and in practical terms rather worse, in that most of Europe is already highly industrialized with little room for expansion.

Some people take the view that Great Britain is already, today, about twenty million people overpopulated. Unlike France, she has been unable to live on her own natural resources since the mid-nineteenth century, she is entirely dependent on raw materials that come from underdeveloped countries—that will come for how long? . . .

In terms of amenities and social services we are constantly running in order to keep in the same place. Our present population growth of 0.7 per cent per annum may sound small, but we cannot really afford *any increase*. Even though we are probably only averaging half a child too much per couple, those "half children" will, by the year 2000, have added up alarmingly. . . .

The message is clear, and it is a message for *us*. But many enlightened people who are all in favour of Indian village women having contraceptives do not seem to apply the moral nearer home at all. The nineteenth-century idea that a big family is something to be proud of, and that the country "needs" more and more children, survives and is refurnished. The false logic that runs "Two babies—good; four babies—twice as good" is, in the long run, calamitous, but it is considered socially bad form to say so—as if one were saying one hated the baby as an individual, or enjoyed arranging abortions.

GILLIAN TINDALL

Make a summary of the author's views in not more than 160 of your own words. Generalize from the statistics given. State at the end the number of words you use, and give your summary a *suitable short title*.

Exercise 2. (a) The extract from *Far From the Madding Crowd* contains a number of words which now have a more common, more modern meaning than that intended in the context of the extract. Write a sentence using each of the words in italics in a different and more modern sensè, and be prepared to explain the difference in meaning:

1. The one feat . . . by which a *mean* condition could be *resolved* into a grand one.

2. From a purely *mechanical* . . . cause, Bathsheba arose . . . with a quieted *spirit*.

3. Bathsheba was regarding him . . . with parted lips and *distracted* eyes.

4. She had meditated upon *compromised* honour.

5. . . . this appeal from a woman of Bathsheba's *calibre* and independence.

6. . . . . all women being alike even those so different in their *accessories* as Fanny and this one beside him.

(b) The extract also contains a number of words that are often confused with others of similar sound. Find the first word of each of the following pairs in the passage, and note its meaning in the context there, and then make up a sentence to illustrate the distinct meaning of the second word in the pair:

    minute (n.) — minute (adj.)
    gauge (v.) — gorge (n.)
    wonted (adj.) — wanted (v.)
    effectual (adj.) — affected (adj.)
    garish (adj.) — ghoulish (adj.)
    entrance (n.) — entrance (v.)
    stupefaction (n.) — stupidity (n.)
    illusion (n.) — allusion (n.)
    congealed (adj.) — concealed (adj.)
    incipient (adj.) — insipid (adj.)
    revulsion (n.) — revelation (n.)
    eclipse (n.) — ellipse (n.)
    severance (n.) — severity (n.)
    momentary (adj.) — momentous (adj.)
    imperious (adj.) — imperial (adj.)

(c) The following words appear in the passage *with* a *negative prefix*, in-, un-, il-, ir-, dis-, im-, or ab-. Find them and write them out as pairs, e.g., defined — undefined

    covered; conscious; describable; definable; obtrusive; mobility; limitable; endurable; normal; expected.

(d) Paraphrase the following passage of sixteenth-century English without altering its ideas in any way:

A FOREIGN VIEW OF ENGLISH WOMEN

But although the women there (in England) are entirely in the power of their husbands, except for their lives, yet they are not kept so strictly as they are in Spain or elsewhere. Nor are they shut up: but they have the free management of the house or housekeeping after the fashion of those of the Netherlands, or others their neighbours. They go to market to buy what they like best to eat. They are well dressed, fond of taking it easy, and commonly leave the care of household matters and drudgery to their servants. They sit before their doors, decked out in fine clothes; in order to see and be seen by the passers-by. In all banquets and feasts they are shown the greatest honour; they are placed at the upper end of the table, where they are first served; at the lower end they help the men. All the rest of their time they employ in walking and riding, in playing at cards or otherwise, in visiting their friends and keeping company, conversing with their equals (whom they term gossips) and their neighbours, and making merry with them at childbirths, christenings, churchings, and funerals; and all this with the permission and knowledge of their husbands, as such is the custom. Although the husbands often recommend to them the pains, industry and care of the German or Dutch women, who do what the men ought to do both in the house and in the shops, for which services in England men are employed, nevertheless the women usually persist in retaining their customs. This is why England is called the Paradise of married women. The girls who are not yet married are kept much more rigorously and strictly than in the Low Countries.

The women are beautiful, fair, well-dressed and modest, which is seen there more than elsewhere, as they go about the streets without any covering either of huke or mantle, hood, veil, or the like. Married women only wear a hat both in the street and in the house; those unmarried go without a hat, although ladies of distinction have lately learnt to cover their faces with silken masks or vizards, and feathers—for indeed they change very easily, and that every year, to the astonishment of many.

(from: Van Meteren's *Nederlandtsche Historie*, 1575)

(A "huke" is a hooded cloak or cape.)

Exercise 3. (a) Longer and more complex sentences are characteristic of older writers of English. Many of Thomas Hardy's sentences are complex in their use of parallel phrases; the last sentence of our extract is an example:

A vehement impulse to flee from him, to run from this place, hide and escape his words at any price, not stopping short of death itself, mastered Bathsheba now.

This sentence has only one finite verb—"mastered"—and is therefore all one main clause.

Other long constructions in the extract are *compound*, rather than complex, and consist of several main clauses paralleled:

An instant after, the front door opened and closed, steps crossed the hall, and her husband appeared at the entrance to the room, looking in upon her.

This has four main verbs—"opened", "closed", "crossed", "appeared"—and therefore four main clauses, all *coordinate*.

Often Hardy uses several subordinate clauses paralleled—in this sentence, the main verb "forgot" has four objects, two of them noun clauses:

She forgot time, life, where she was, what she was doing.

In the following sentences from the extract the division into clauses has been marked by strokes. Explain the kind, function and relationship of each clause:

1. When Bathsheba arose | it was with a quieted spirit and regret for the antagonistic instincts | which had seized upon her just before.
2. He beheld it all by degrees, | (he) stared in stupefaction at the scene, | as (he would) | if he thought it an illusion raised by some fiendish incantation.
3. So still he remained | that he could be imagined to have left in him no motive power whatever.
4. Perhaps in all Fanny's sufferings, much greater relatively to her strength, there never was a time | when she suffered in an absolute sense | what Bathsheba suffered now.
5. What Troy did | was to sink upon his knees with an indefinable union of remorse and reverence upon his face, | and, bending over Fanny Robin, (he) gently kissed her, | as one would kiss an infant asleep to avoid awakening it.
6. All the strong feelings | which had been scattered over her existence | since she knew what feeling was, | seemed gathered into one pulsation now.
7. It was such an unexpected revelation of all women being alike at heart, even those so different in their accessories | as Fanny and

this one beside him (were), | that Troy could hardly seem to believe her to be his proud wife Bathsheba.

(b) Compose complex sentences from clauses as indicated by the following instructions—one main clause is given as a basis in each case.

e.g. Bathsheba was a woman + (adjective clause) + (adverb clause of time).

Bathsheba was a woman who would not easily accept defeat when she was thwarted.

1. (Adverb clause of time) + Bathsheba asked herself + (noun clause object).
2. Bathsheba was better educated and richer + (adverb clause of degree) + (adjective clause).
3. Yet Fanny Robin was as attractive to Troy + (adverb clause of degree) + (adverb clause of time).
4. (Adverb clause of concession) + (another adverb clause of concession) + Bathsheba persuaded herself + (noun clause object) + (adjective clause).
5. Troy was Bathsheba's husband + (another main clause) + (adjective clause) + (adverb clause of place).
6. Bathsheba was in such an emotional state + (adverb clause of result) + (adverb clause of condition) + (noun clause).

Work out a full clause analysis of each of your sentences.

Topics for Written Work

1. Write a short story in which you describe a real or imaginary experience of taking a girl-friend or boy-friend out or taking them home to meet your parents for the *first* time.

2. (a) Study the following discussion, and make brief notes on the main arguments put forward by A and B:

A. I believe that chastity is basically self-restraint, practised for the sake of other people, and that promiscuity is essentially a kind of selfishness. If we respect other people, their privacy, their feelings and their rights, then we shall not want to exploit them for our own pleasure or the satisfaction of our own desires.

B. Your argument is based on an outdated view of sexual relationships. Why should you assume that this is just a matter of a man exploiting a woman for his own pleasure? If two people are physically attracted by each other, then the pleasure will be mutual, and what they decide to do is no one else's business.

A. You are underestimating the depth of a sexual relationship. Loyalty between partners is right, for the simple reason that if either leaves the other, then he or she will cause great pain and humiliation. Our sexual drives are strong, and sexual jealousy is a very real emotion. In this world we are not all equally attractive, nor do we remain careless and young. I think that a man has a deep responsibility to any woman who loves him and gives herself to him. That is what I mean by chastity.

B. When you use a phrase like "give herself to him", you show how little you understand the relationship between men and women today. Young men and women now feel equally free, because of reasonably safe methods of contraception, to explore the whole range of human experience. They do not want to grow up having known only one member of the opposite sex intimately. They want to be liberated from a convention that restricts them to spending the rest of their lives with the first man or woman that they happen to find sexually attractive. Remember, too, that many people have in the past found out too late that they were sexually incompatible with the partner they married.

A. These are typically male arguments. Human experience has shown again and again that a love relationship deepens and grows as the two people become more intimate. This stable union—two people growing together—is the finest basis for bringing up a family that our civilization has been able to devise. Psychologists and social workers are all agreed about the incalculable harm that is done to the children of broken homes, where there is no real trust or love between the parents.

B. Yet surely equal harm is done by legally uniting two people who then find they are not able to live together? Why should society put moral pressure upon such people to be nominally faithful, whether they have children or not?

A. I can hardly deny that some marriages do not work. But I cannot see why encouraging young people to take a more casual attitude to sexual relations will make it any easier for couples to settle down to a steady and growing love relationship. Society should do all it can to encourage stable unions based on love and loyalty, and to me that implies chastity, in and before marriage.

253

(b) Consider and discuss the following points:

(i) A accuses B of putting forward "typically male arguments". Do you agree that A's views are more likely to be held by girls or women, and B's by men? If so can you suggest why there should be any marked difference in attitude?

(ii) B suggests that A is being old-fashioned. Is it true that A's arguments are typical of older, or more conventional, or more religious people? Have new developments (such as the contraceptive pill, or the better education of women to have independent careers of their own) really altered our attitude to sexual relations or marriage?

(c) Continue this discussion for at least six more speeches. If you wish, you may introduce a new character, called C, to put any point of view that you feel neither A nor B would support.

3. What, in your opinion, are the necessary conditions for a lasting and happy marriage? Consider such questions as the ages of the partners, their comparative education, religion, temperament, family background and wealth; what conditions they set up home in, how many children they have and how soon; how far they should have had experience of other partners; how much they need to have in common, and whether the wife should have a career or interests of her own.

Oral Work

1. Discuss differents kinds of love—love of God, your neighbours, your country, parents and children, first love, sexual love, true love, married love, love of money, power or oneself. Do we need different words, or have they all a basis in the same emotion?

Reread the famous passage from 1 Corinthians, chapter 13 (try the New English Bible version, and compare it with the Authorized version). Examine these quotations and add others of your own choosing:

(a) Men have died from time to time, and worms have eaten them, but not for love. (*As You Like It*, IV, ii, 110)
(b) Love sought is good, but given unsought is better. (*Twelfth Night*, III, i, 170)
(c) Who ever loved, that loved not at first sight? (Marlowe's *Hero and Leander*)

(d) Greater love hath no man than this, that a man lay down his life for his friends. (St. John, xv, 13)

(e) Next to being married, a girl likes to be crossed in love a little now and then. (Mr. Bennet in *Pride and Prejudice*)

(f) The wise want love; and those who love want wisdom. (Shelley)

(g) 'Tis better to have loved and lost than never to have loved at all. (Tennyson)

(h) Love is like the measles; we all have to go though it. (Jerome K. Jerome)

(i) It is a woman's business to get married as soon as possible, and a man's to keep unmarried as long as he can. (G. Bernard Shaw).

(j)   *A Decade*

> When you came, you were like red wine and honey,
> And the taste of you burnt in my mouth like sweetness.
> Now you are like morning bread.
> Smooth and pleasant.
> I hardly taste you at all, for I know your savour,
> But I am completely nourished.

AMY LOWELL

2. Prepare your favourite love-scene or love poem to read aloud. Alternatively prepare the passage from Corinthians mentioned above in 1.

3. Discuss the following propositions:

(a) That marriage is an obsolescent institution.

(b) That we should remove all stigma attaching to unmarried mothers or illegitimacy.

(c) That contraceptives and advice on birth control should be freely available to all adolescents.

(d) That we live in a decadent society whose permissiveness will be its downfall.

(e) That sexual promiscuity leads to a tragic inability to form deep or lasting relationships.

(f) That only religious people who care about the sanctity of marriage should be married in church.

(g) That in all sexual relationships, it is the responsibility of the girl to say "no" or to take the consequences.

(h) That a massive campaign to control the world's population, if necessary including compulsory sterilization, is now urgent.

(i) That abortions are not wrong.

(j) That sex is not as important as previous generations, most of them frustrated and guilt-ridden, thought it was.

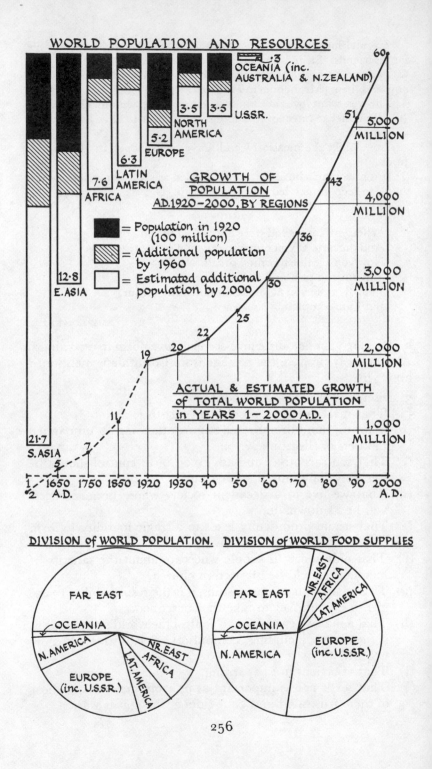

WORLD POPULATION AND RESOURCES

GROWTH OF
POPULATION
A.D. 1920 - 2000, BY REGIONS

■ = Population in 1920
    (100 million)
▨ = Additional population
    by 1960
□ = Estimated additional
    population by 2,000

OCEANIA (inc.
AUSTRALIA & N. ZEALAND) ·3

U.S.S.R. 3·5

NORTH
AMERICA 3·5

EUROPE 5·2

LATIN
AMERICA 6·3

AFRICA 7·6

E. ASIA 12·8

S. ASIA 21·7

ACTUAL & ESTIMATED GROWTH
of TOTAL WORLD POPULATION
in YEARS 1 - 2000 A.D.

5,000
MILLION

4,000
MILLION

3,000
MILLION

2,000
MILLION

1,000
MILLION

60
51
43
36
30
25
22
20
19
11
7
5

1/2   1650   1750   1850   1920   1930   '40   '50   '60   '70   '80   '90   2000
A.D.   A.D.

DIVISION of WORLD POPULATION.

FAR EAST
OCEANIA
N. AMERICA
EUROPE
(inc. U.S.S.R.)
LAT. AMERICA
AFRICA
NR. EAST

DIVISION of WORLD FOOD SUPPLIES

FAR EAST
OCEANIA
N. AMERICA
NR. EAST
AFRICA
LAT. AMERICA
EUROPE
(inc. U.S.S.R.)

256

Activities and Research

1. *Population*: Look again at the article quoted in Exercise 1 and the charts on page 256. Then write an account of the problems of overpopulation, birth control and food supply as we move towards the year 2000.

Find out who Malthus was and what his theory was. Find figures for declining infant mortality rates and lengthening expectation of life. What is the present position of the Catholic Church and other religious authorities on birth control? How much is being done by international organizations, such as specialized agencies of the United Nations? What hitherto untapped food resources could be exploited?

2. *Women and Marriage*: Make a study of the status of women in different societies (past and present) throughout the world. How far are women in general, and married women in particular, given full rights and protection in other cultures? What more can and should be done to ensure women equality of status (social, political and economic) and to protect them and their children under the law? Is there still a case to be made *against* equal rights, equal education, equal pay, or equal responsibility for women?

Further Reading

Far From the Madding Crowd by THOMAS HARDY (Macmillan)
This is one of Hardy's greatest love-stories, and concerns Bathsheba's relationship with three men, Sergeant Troy, the staunch Gabriel Oak, and her neighbour, Farmer Boldwood. The characters are all powerful people, and Bathsheba and Gabriel, particularly, have the courage to fight against their fate, and to out-face disillusionment and despair in the end.

The Trumpet Major by THOMAS HARDY (Macmillian)
Hardy classified this under the heading "Romances and Fantasies" and it is one of his most straightforward stories, concerned largely with the heroine's inability to decide between two brothers, one in the army and the other in the navy, at the time when all England feared the consequences of an invasion by Napoleon.

The Mayor of Casterbridge by THOMAS HARDY (Macmillan)
This novel, like *Far From the Madding Crowd*, was classified by Hardy as one of "Character and Environment". The story

begins when the future Mayor, in a fit of drunkenness, sells his wife and child to a sailor for five guineas. In later life, when he is reformed and respected and his wife returns, he is still wrongheaded and difficult, and his life ends in desolate loneliness.

The Sexual Behaviour of Young People by MICHAEL SCHOFIELD (Longmans; Penguin) (301.431)

One of the few comprehensive and reliable investigations into the sexual behaviour of British teenagers was carried out by the Central Council for Health Education. A representative selection of 1873 young people between the ages of 15 and 19 from seven areas in Great Britain was interviewed over a period of three years.

Supplementary Exercises

Revision Exercise 1

Idioms are those expressions, often figurative, that are peculiar to a language and defy translation because they cannot be taken literally. Write a clear and straightforward explanation of each of the following English idioms, including some idea of the origin if you know it. For instance:

To show one's true colours,

means to reveal one's real intentions and motives for something, and is based on the practice of pirates who flew false flags until they were close to their victims, and then hoisted their pirate flag.

- (a) To be within an ace of something.
- (b) To have no axe to grind.
- (c) To beat about the bush.
- (d) To kill two birds with one stone.
- (e) To know which side one's bread is buttered.
- (f) To burn the candle at both ends.
- (g) To give chapter and verse.
- (h) To play fast and loose.
- (i) To feather one's own nest.
- (j) To take French leave.
- (k) To be hand-in-glove with.
- (l) To keep one's countenance.
- (m) To kick over the traces.
- (n) To lay someone by the heels.
- (o) To pay through the nose.
- (p) To put someone's nose out of joint.
- (q) To out-Herod Herod.
- (r) To be caught between Scylla and Charybdis.
- (s) To be in the swim.
- (t) To be three sheets in the wind.

Revision Exercise 2

Write a clear explanation in straightforward language of the meaning (and origin, where you can) of each of the following proverbs. For example:

Use your wit as a buckler, not as a sword,

means that you should use your intelligence and sense of humour to defend yourself, not to attack other people (a "buckler" is a shield).

(a) A drowning man will clutch at a straw.
(b) A friend to all is a friend to none.
(c) Actions speak louder than words.
(d) Diamond cut diamond.
(e) Even a worm will turn.
(f) Everybody's business is nobody's business.
(g) God tempers the wind to the shorn lamb.
(h) Good wine needs no bush.
(i) Handsome is as handsome does.
(j) If the sky falls, we shall catch larks.
(k) Let the cobbler stick to his last.
(l) Many a mickle makes a muckle.
(m) No names, no pack drill.
(n) One man may steal a horse while another may not look over the hedge.
(o) Precepts may lead, but examples draw.
(p) That is a wise delay which makes the road safe.
(q) The game is not worth the candle.
(r) The road to hell is paved with good intentions.
(s) What is bred in the bone comes out in the flesh.
(t) You can't make an omelet without breaking eggs.

Revision Exercise 3

(a) Write short definitions of the following:
  (i) a slipper, a plimsoll, a football boot, a wellington boot, a flipper, a running shoe.
 (ii) an airship, a jet-plane, a space-rocket, a helicopter, a glider, a biplane.
(iii) a dinghy, a yacht, a rowing-boat, a barge, a tug, a coaster.
(iv) an anthology, a serial, an autobiography, a text-book, a periodical, an encyclopaedia.
 (v) a life-jacket, an anorak, a cape, a waistcoat, a dinner-jacket.

(b) Form adjectives from the following words. In each case, write down at least one more example of the same kind of adjective formation: e.g., power + ful = powerful; mournful.

rite, victory, panorama, Negro, infant, statue, Turk, quarrel, labyrinth, mathematics, province, ether, spectacle, money, possess.

(c) What prepositions normally follow these words?

e.g., different *from*, averse *to*.

absolve, accord, acquiesce, comply, comparable, consistent, correspond (2), deprive, dissent, indifferent, innocent, sympathetic

Revision Exercise 4

English has inherited a number of ways of forming verbs from root words: e.g.,

  (i) prefix be- (O.E. bi-), particularly used to make transitive verbs: befoul, behold, belittle.

 (ii) prefix en-, em- (O.F. en-, L. in-), particularly with the sense "put in, on": encrust, entrust, empower.

(iii) suffix -fy (L. facio = make), particularly with the sense "make something": liquefy, glorify, electrify.

(iv) suffix -ate (L. past participle ending), used to form adjectives and verbs in English: formulate, inoculate, prefabricate.

 (v) suffix -ize, -ise (Gk. -izo), again with the sense "make" or "become": energize, legalize, oxidize.

(a) Form verbs related to the following root words, using the prefix be-; give the meaning of each:

    calm, devil, grime, head, labour, lay, seek, speak, tide, witch.

(b) Form verbs related to the following root words, using the prefix en- (or em-); give the meaning of each:

    body, broil, chant, close, cumber, due, joy, merge, noble, visage.

(c) Form verbs related to the following root words, using the suffix -fy, giving the meaning in each case:

    clear, dignity, example, false, just, null, person, putrid, rare, vile.

(d) Find a suitable word ending in the suffix -ate to fit each of the following definitions:

  1. to succeed by turns, first one, then the other;
  2. to move in a circle, pass round;
  3. to dispose of the dead by burning;
  4. to explode, set off an explosion;
  5. to try to equal or excel; imitate;
  6. to involve in a crime or an accusation;
  7. to blow up, fill with air, etc.;
  8. to take delight in or abandon oneself to luxury;
  9. to calm down, conciliate, propitiate;
 10. to make as new, restore to good condition.

(e) Form a verb ending in the suffix -ize based upon each of the following root words:

    anaesthetic, circular, commerce, crystal, fossil, harmony, Pasteur, stigma, Tantalus, tranquil.

(f) Find a suitable word ending in the suffix -fy to fit each of the following definitions:

  1. to enlarge, add detail to, expand;
  2. to kill by nailing to a cross;
  3. to make a god of;
  4. to please or indulge (oneself);

5. to convert into stone;
6. to make valid, confirm (an agreement) formally;
7. to put right, make straight;
8. to make sacred, holy;
9. to bear witness (in court);
10. to confirm or prove something to be true.

Revision Exercise 5

(a) Give the meanings of the following foreign words or phrases that have been adopted and are used in English. If you can, give the original language and the literal meaning in each case:

e.g. A "fait accompli" is something already done without reference to other people and too late to be altered. It is from the French, literally meaning a completed act. Two young people eloping to be married secretly, for instance, might present their parents with a "fait accompli".

ad infinitum; ad lib. (ad libitum); à la carte; al fresco; alibi; a priori; au fait; badinage; bête noir; bona fide; carte blanche; coup d'état; de facto; élite; en masse; ex officio; faux pas; gratis; in camera; leit-motiv; mañana; non sequitur; nous; passé; passim; per se; prima facie; sang-froid; savoir faire; zeitgeist.

(b) Write sentences to illustrate the difference in meaning between the words in each of the following pairs. Usually, this will mean one sentence for each word, but occasionally you may be able to illustrate both words in one sentence, as in this example:

The referee was of course quite *disinterested*, since he had no reason to want either team to win, but he was far from *uninterested* in seeing how the game would go.

advance, advancement	orgy, obsequy
affinity, infinity	oscillate, osculate
alluminium, alluvium	recuperate, recriminate
auspicious, suspicious	reservation, preservation
collision, collusion	respectable, respectful
consternation, constellation	reversion, revision
corporal, corporate	rhyme, rhythm
emit, omit	severe, sever
enmity, amity	topical, typical
mitigate, mutilate	

(c) The following words are often wrongly used. *Either* write a short explanation of the correct use in each case, *or* compose a sentence for each showing clearly its correct use.

affect, aggravate, complementary, comprised, incredulous, individual, literally, momentary, principle, respectively.

Revision Exercise 6

Each of the following sentences illustrates one kind of common error of grammar, vocabulary or style. In each case, rewrite the sentence more correctly or more clearly, and then write a brief explanation of the fault and why it is wrong.

e.g. The old lady laid down on her bed for half an hour.

Corrected sentence: The old lady *lay* down on her bed for half an hour.

Explanation: Two verbs have been confused:
"to lie" (lay, was lying, has lain) is intransitive and means to put oneself in a lying position.
"to lay" (laid, was laying, has laid) is transitive, and means to put something down.

(a) The book he chose for you and I to work from looks rather difficult.

(b) We regard the work on this very unique project as completely essential.

(c) I like him as a person; but I cannot stand him wanting to help me all the time.

(d) He is expected to do better in the examinations than anyone in his class.

(e) If we build the wall this way, we shall require less gravel and less bags of cement.

(f) When one is finding things difficult, they can usually find someone to help with your problems.

(g) The reason for his success is because he had a very good education.

(h) As the flood-water rose to the upper floor of the wooden house, they jumped into the waiting boat and clung on as it swirled away with all their possessions in it

(i) This sort of people are difficult to tolerate; each of them must have their own way all the time.

(j) The trains in Britain are usually as good, if not better than, France.

(k) I want to meet the leading singer in that new radio programme, and whom, I believe, has just bought out a best-selling record.

(l) Like my friend said, he treated us like we were still children.

(m) Riding home late from a party, where he had had too much to drink, the squire's horse threw him into a muddy ditch, and he woke up cold and miserable.

(n) The British have never, are not now, and never will be a gay and reckless people.

263

Revision Exercise 7

(a) Rewrite the following passage including all the necessary punctuation, and setting it out in suitable paragraphs.

is that you george called mrs saxby as she heard the door slam there was no reply it was dark Mrs Saxby was alone in the house the telephone was in the hall george she called again in a voice shrill with fear stay where you are a mans voice commanded don't move until we tell you to mrs saxby was scarcely able to speak for terror who is it she asked what do you want dont be alarmed maam came the reply we are from passington zoo what on earth are you doing in my house said mrs saxby we have been chasing an escaped leopard since last night replied the voice and he was seen just now entering your house we think he is upstairs my goodness shrieked mrs saxby tearing open the door into the hall will he attack a cat my poor mitsys up there

(b) Rewrite the direct speech passage in (a) as reported speech.

Précis Exercise 1

The following passage, adapted from an article in the *New Statesman* (29th April, 1966), contains about 360 words. Summarize the argument in not more than 130 of your own words. Reduce the three paragraphs to one and state the exact number of words you use.

In Britain a man's employment-level is conditioned to a very large extent by his education, and it is becoming much harder to keep an intelligent man below his natural level for irrelevant reasons. Since there is no reason to suppose people with black faces are innately less intelligent than those with white, the first generation of coloured students born in Britain will shortly be passing out of our universities with degrees in no way inferior to their fellow-students of lighter hue. And if Birmingham Corporation thinks it is going to hire them as bus-conductors, Birmingham Corporation has got another think coming.

Every career that is open to the talented is about to be stormed, in large numbers, by British-born coloured people. I would guess that the biggest impact will be felt in the areas of the greatest "brain-drain": English Negro scientists and doctors, teachers and dons will be familiar figures. (Of course I know that they all exist already, that there is even a black J.P. or two; but they are still curiosities. Soon the curiosity will be the man who finds them curious.) The lawyers, whose closed shop is stronger than that of any manual-labour trades union, will no doubt resist longer. But even the legal professions must succumb in time. But then, so must all the other professions. Industry and the Civil

Service, the churches and the armed forces, the nationalized industries and TV, the press and retail trade, the City and MI6 —all will within my lifetime have their proportions of English Negro senior executives, recruited solely because their talents are deemed most suitable. . . .

The point is, our responses to our fellow-Britons with black faces are going to be very different from what they are to their parents, or grandparents. What is more—much more—we have an opportunity not given to any nation since the colour-question was first asked, an opportunity which sets us off very sharply from the United States, who never had the opportunity at all. We will, if we are sufficiently far-sighted and intelligent, be able to look on our coloured compatriots with eyes unclouded by guilt. For they will be, as the American Negroes are not, the descendents of men and women who came to Britain voluntarily, and who arrived with full equality under the law.

BERNARD LEVIN

Précis Exercise 2

The following description of "orienteering" contains about 375 words. Summarize it in not more than 125 words, avoiding the language of the passage as far as possible, except for the technical terms of the sport. Reduce the number of paragraphs.

Orienteering developed in Scandinavia, where it is now the main participant sport, with tens of thousands of competitors out each weekend. Introduced into Britain less than ten years ago it is making great strides, with a competition somewhere in Britain each weekend. It has been described as motor rallying on foot, with events usually staged over heavily forested terrain. Competitors, who start at minute intervals, are handed a copy of a $2\frac{1}{2}$ in. to the mile map, a list of controls to be visited, and a control card. After copying the exact location of the check-points on to their map from a master map they set off to find the controls, using map, compass, and a well-developed sense of direction. At each control hangs a red and white marker and a self-inking stamp. Contestants stamp their control card and carry on.

The route card carries a brief description of each control— "in the clearing," "junction of streams," "a cairn," "small ring-contour"—but finding these after travelling six or seven hundred metres through dense forest calls for great concentration and an ability to interpret the information provided by the map. Course planners try to present the orienteer with the difficult choice of route selection—detours to avoid a steep hill or to make use of a footpath, or straight bearings regardless of the terrain or the denseness of the forest. A wrong choice can waste several valuable minutes. An error in map reading can result in the competitor spending an hour or more searching for the elusive marker, or retiring and returning sadly to base. Speed is less important than skill in routefinding.

In Scandinavia family competitions are held, in which husband, wife, and at least one child must travel round as a group. In Britain a non-competitive "wayfinders" class is often included in an open competition. Families, complete with dog, have been known to go round, having a picnic lunch en route.

In orienteering there are two great consolations. Once you are swallowed up by the forest no one can see the mistakes you are making. And when you eventually arrive back there will be plenty of other contestants complaining that they couldn't find "the small depression" either. Orienteering thrives on hard luck stories.

(from a Guardian article by Bill Morris, 25 July, 1968)

Précis Exercise 3

(a) Read the passage carefully and then answer the questions. Each question has five suggested answers; select the best answer to each question.

In our family, as I have told, we lived an isolated life. No friend ever came to the house. Father always said he had no time for people. We had to ask permission to see our friends and that was rarely given; and if it was we had to dress up in our best
5 clothes. "Is your own family not good enough for you?" was the piercing question. My earliest pleasure was therefore in being alone; and to be alone in Paris, knowing nobody, was an intoxication; it was like being on the dizzy brink of knowing everybody. I felt I was drinking the lights of the city and the words I heard
10 spoken by passers-by. I walked to the Place de la Concorde and there by the bridge in the shade of the warm trees looked over the stone wall into the river. I was instantly under a spell. The water looked still yet it rustled like a dress. I had never seen water and stone in such pleasant conversation, the stone moonish,
15 shading to saffron like the cheese of Brie, and the water womanish and velvet. My solemn young eyes were seeing order and feeling united. I was so moved that I could feel myself grow into a new being. I repeated to myself my vow—for I was at the vowing age—never to leave France and I was so entranced that
20 tears came to my eyes. I walked from bridge to bridge along the Seine, past the acacias, the poplars and the planes that leaned with a graceful precision over the water, each tree like the stroke of a painter's brush. The orderliness of the trees, the gravely

spaced avenues, rearranged my mind. My English feeling was
25 for wild nature; here nature had been civilized. I was shocked
and converted in an hour and though, later in life I have often
lapsed, the conversion has remained.

1. Which one of the following
words is closest in meaning to
"solemn" as used in line 16?
    A Grave
    B Staid
    C Sombre
    D Sad
    E Pensive

2. "I was at the vowing age"
(line 18) means that the
writer was at that time of life
when young men
    A become deeply attached
       to certain places
    B are ready to plan their
       future lives
    C engage eagerly in great
       enterprises or undertak-
       ings
    D are legally entitled to
       decide their own futures
    E emotionally   dedicate
       themselves   to   various
       courses of action

3. Tears came into the writer's
eyes (line 20) because he
    A was deeply moved by the
       scene before him
    B found his loneliness had
       become too much to bear
    C knew that he would be
       unable to keep his vow
    D was sad at the thought of
       leaving France
    E was dazzled by the light
       reflected from the Seine

4. When the author says that
"nature had been civilized"
(line 25) he means that

    A trees had been taught to
       grow naturally in towns
    B the natural charm of wild
       country had been pre-
       served
    C human ideas of order had
       been   imposed   on   the
       natural elements of the
       scene
    D the wild trees of nature
       had been cut and lopped
       to suit men's tastes
    E nature had been reduced
       to being man's slave

5. When the writer says he was
"converted" (line 26) he
means that he had
    A learned to adapt to a
       new environment
    B changed his ideas about
       natural beauty
    C decided to live in France
       always
    D begun to love city life
    E found compensation for
       isolation

6. The passage shows the writer
learning to admire
    A harmony rather than dis-
       order
    B sound rather than silence
    C Parisians   rather   than
       Englishmen
    D buildings   rather   than
       countryside
    E company   rather   than
       isolation

7. In this passage the writer attributes to his upbringing the fact that he
A felt antagonistic to his father
B left England
C vowed never to return home
D enjoyed isolation
E longed for social acceptance

8. Which one of the following words best describes how the writer felt when walking on his own in Paris?
A Lonely
B Giddy
C Bewildered
D Exhilarated
E Sad

9. A summary of this passage should include all the following EXCEPT
A the pleasure the writer had in wandering alone round Paris
B the impact made on the writer by French art
C the father's treatment of his family
D the difference between French and English attitudes to nature
E the determination to live always in France

(b) Write a summary of this passage, beginning: "The writer explained that his father. . . .", and reducing it from 320 to about 105 words. Some of the answers in (a) may help you.

Précis Exercise 4

Study the following passage, and answer the questions printed below:

An intelligent sightseer who wishes to understand the mentality of ordinary people living in the Middle Ages will find a rich reward for even a superficial study of the carvings on Gothic choir stalls, particularly those of the misericords. The medieval
5 priests, finding the physical strain of standing through a succession of long services beyond their endurance, devised a hinged seat with a corbel projecting from its under-surface which, when the seat was tipped up, allowed them to combine the comfort of

268

sitting with the appearance of standing. In an age which was
10 lavish in the use of fine craftsmanship it was natural that these
corbels, although seldom seen, should be decorated with carvings,
and the work gave a rare opportunity for self-expression to the
carvers employed. There was no need for the carvings on misericords to conform to any logical scheme of decoration, or to con-
15 vey to an illiterate congregation some dogmatic significance;
on the contrary, sacred subjects are comparatively rare on
misericords, perhaps because it was felt that their humble purpose made them an unsuitable setting for such lofty themes. The
carvers were, therefore, free to draw their inspiration from the
20 world around them, or from the freakish flights of their own
fancy. Scenes of labour, of sport, or of domestic life, the romantic
tales which were the stock-in-trade of strolling minstrels, the tall
stories of returning travellers, the eerie but edifying monsters
illustrated in the Bestiary, all these are to be found in profusion
25 upon the misericords which are thus as revealing of the mentality
of the men who made them as is the sketch-book of a painter.

Who were the carvers of the misericords? The fabric rolls of
medieval buildings have preserved the names of many master
carpenters, chiefly those who served the King or the Chapter of
30 some cathedral. These were men of good position, who were
rewarded by grants of land and furred robes, and who often
influenced by their counsel more work than they directly controlled, thus contributing to the rapid spread of new styles
throughout the country. Some of the carvers, known to have
35 been the sons of master carpenters, probably received a general
education besides their professional training, but all of them
learned the practice of their craft as well as its theory. Unfortunately we cannot identify their early work for, by the time the
records tell us much about them, their duties had become largely
40 administrative. But in most places the carving of the misericords
was done, under the direction of the Master Carpenter, by men
whose names are merely entered on the fabric rolls as workers
in wood, who were paid so many pence for so many days' work.
The individuality of the carvings is their only memorial.
(About 460 words)

(Adapted from *Misericords*, by M. D. Anderson)

1. (a) A "misericord" was a small ledge projecting from the under-
side of a tip-up seat in church, so made that a monk could sit or
lean on it while apparently standing. Why were they found
necessary?
(b) Look up the word "misericord" and suggest why a word of
this meaning was used for this seat.

2. What two purposes for the *more easily seen* woodcarvings in medieval churches are mentioned?

3. Why then is the carving on the misericords often *more* interesting to us today than the more obvious wood-carving?

4. State clearly, in your own words, the contrast between the positions of the master carpenters and of the ordinary wood-carvers, and the contrast between the wages they received.

5. Explain why it is difficult to discover the authors of individual carvings.

6. Write out the simile in the first paragraph of this passage, and explain its effect.

7. Explain these words and phrases from this passage:
(a) Gothic (give the origin of this word) (line 3); (b) a corbel (line 7); (c) lavish (line 10); (d) some dogmatic significance (line 15); (e) stock-in-trade (line 22); (f) eerie but edifying (line 23); (g) the Bestiary (line 24); (h) fabric rolls (line 27) (this might have *two* distinct meanings; give them *both*).

8. Give this piece a title, and make a précis of it in 145–165 of your own words.

*Analysis Exercise 1

(a) The following sentences for analysis include various kinds of *adjective clauses* that have been discussed in Books Three and Four. What sentence has been analysed in columns here as an example?

	CLAUSE	KIND	FUNCTION	RELATIONSHIP
A	the book . . . was not the same one	Main clause		
a¹	you have been reading	Subordinate clause	Adjective	Qualifies noun "book" in main clause "A"
a²	as I recommended	Subordinate clause	Adjective	Qualifies pronouns "one" in main clause "A"

1. All that glitters is not gold.
2. The car I sold him was the kind of bargain you do not see every day.
3. He who rides a tiger may never dismount.
4. We were standing on the spot where the execution took place.
5. I cannot remember the time when I first learned to talk.

6. He had been growing such peaches as you might dream of.
7. That, that is, is.
8. On the occasions when he annoys me I say things for which I feel sorry afterwards.
9. The time and place when and where the explorer died will for ever remain a mystery.
10. Surely that is the same car as we saw leaving the shop where the burglary was committed?

(b) The following sentences for analysis include various kinds of *adverb clauses* that have been discussed in Books Three and Four. What sentence has been analysed in columns here as an example?

	CLAUSE	KIND	FUNCTION	RELATIONSHIP
A	he behaves	Main clause		
a¹	whenever he sees a pretty girl	Subordinate clause	Adverb of time	Modifies verb "behaves" in main clause "A"
a²	as (he would behave)	Subordinate clause	Adverb of manner	Modifies verb "behaves" in main clause "A"
a³	if he were struck dumb	Subordinate clause	Adverb of condition	Modifies verb "would behave" in subordinate clause "a²"

1. Since we left in such a hurry, we had no time to thank everybody.
2. Even if we had had more time, we would have found it difficult to express our gratitude adequately, as they had done so much for us.
3. Be it ne'er so humble, there's no place like home.
4. Unless you humour him, our dog behaves as though he hates you.
5. He attacks strangers as if his life depended upon it, so that it is quite dangerous to approach our house.
6. Were Mr. Williams to be elected, he would certainly make an excellent representative.
7. Even if I live until I am a hundred, I shall never meet such a man again.
8. Though she knew little about painting, her attempts were really good, so that the judges were able to commend her work.
9. We must take precautions lest the camp should be flooded, if the tide rises so high that it washes over the sea wall.
10. However difficult it may be, we must persevere to the end.

The following example illustrates how to analyse a sentence containing a *noun clause* in apposition to "it", using the column method:

	CLAUSE	KIND	FUNCTION	RELATIONSHIP
A	he said	Main clause		
a¹	it was unfortunate	Subordinate clause	Noun	Object of verb "said" in main clause "A"
a²	that we had been delayed	Subordinate clause	Noun	In apposition to "it", subject of "was" in subordinate clause "a¹"

Reconstruct the sentence analysed here.

Analyse the following sentences in columns: they include revision of the various kinds of *noun clauses* dealt with in Books Three and Four and in Chapter Four of this book.

1. You said you did not care anyway.
2. I do not know if you will like my idea.
3. Who was going to do it was our main problem.
4. His idea that we should all wear straw hats seemed very odd.
5. It was obvious that we would not reach home that night.
6. Just tell me where I should leave my case and when the train reaches Glasgow.
7. Do what I tell you, not what I do myself.
8. I was not certain about how I should do it, and his theory that I would learn by trying, did not work out.
9. As it was clear that he had had enough, we packed up what we had been working on.
10. He saw the things I had made and asked me which he could have.

In analysing sentences into clauses, it is important not to confuse *clauses* with *phrases*. In the following sentences, the phrases printed in italics can be replaced by clauses of approximately the same meaning. When you have rewritten each sentence replacing these phrases with clauses, analyse it into clauses, using the column method.

e.g. *Having no previous knowledge of the district*, I decided *to ask someone for help*.

As I had no previous knowledge of the district, I decided that I would ask someone for help.

	CLAUSE	KIND	FUNCTION	RELATIONSHIP
A	I decided	Main clause		
a¹	as I had no previous knowledge of the district	Subordinate clause	Adverb of cause	Modifies verb "decided" in main clause "A"
a²	that I would ask someone for help	Subordinate clause	Noun	Object of verb "decided" in main clause "A"

1. *In spite of having no breakfast*, he was still able to do without lunch.
2. *The sun having set*, the birds were silent.
3. The great "smog", *resulting from the mixture of factory smoke with fog*, killed many people.
4. The proposal *to work a ten-period day* was rejected by the Head.
5. I have not yet visited the site *of the new office block under construction*.
6. *Since leaving home*, he had not had so humiliating an experience.
7. He did not work so hard *as to strain himself unduly*.
8. He worked hard *to improve his chances*.
9. A mountain *with sheer rock faces* is very difficult to climb.
10. *Whilst agreeing with your analysis of the problem*, I disagree with your interpretation of *how to put things right*.

*Analysis Exercise 4

In Chapter Eleven we explained the function of the *adverb clause of degree*. Adverbs of degree differ from other adverbs in that they modify adjectives, other adverbs, or occasionally prepositions or conjunctions, but *not* verbs. The adverb clause of degree is therefore often used in comparisons:

1. He is taller than I am, but not as tall as my brother.
2. As fast as he earned the money, she spent it.

Study the column analysis of these examples:

	CLAUSE	KIND	FUNCTION	RELATIONSHIP
1.A	He is taller	Main clause		
a¹	than I am	Subordinate clause	Adverb of degree	Modifies adjective "taller" in main clause "A"
B	but (he is) not as tall	Main clause	Co-ordinate with main clause "A"	
b¹	as my brother (is)	Subordinate clause	Adverb of degree	Modifies adjective "tall" in main clause "B"
2.A	as fast . . . she spent it	Main clause		
a¹	as he earned the money	Subordinate clause	Adverb of degree	Modifies adverb "fast" in main clause "A"

Each of the following sentences for analysis contains at least one adverb clause of degree.

1. He is just as efficient as I am.
2. I had drawn out as much money as I wanted.
3. We had definitely done better than they in this race.
4. He left as soon as the bell went.
5. The selectors chose the team as impartially as if they had not known any of them personally.
6. She was as disappointed as a child who has been promised a new toy and has never received it.
7. The traffic problem becomes worse as more cars are produced than the roads can easily accommodate.
8. The water was so clear that they could study the sea-life as well as if they had had diving apparatus.
9. As soon as they heard the news they ran a great deal faster than they would have done otherwise.
10. Please leave the sink in cleaner condition than the previous tenants of the room.

*Analysis Exercise 5

Complex sentences can sometimes be *ambiguous*, according to the function and relationship of a particular subordinate clause. In these cases, the different possible meanings can be demonstrated by clause analysis. For example, this sentence:

The club committee agreed, since you arrived here, you should be given temporary membership.

can mean "after you arrived" or "because you arrived". The column analysis would be as follows in each case:

	CLAUSE	KIND	FUNCTION	RELATIONSHIP
1.A	The club committee agreed	Main clause		
a¹	since you arrived here	Subordinate clause	Adverb of time	Modifies verb "agreed" in main clause "A"
a²	(that) you should be given temporary membership	Subordinate clause	Noun	Object of verb "agreed" in main clause "A"
2.A	the club committee agreed	Main clause		
a¹	since you arrived here	Subordinate clause	Adverb of cause	Modifies verb "agreed" in main clause "A"
a²	(that) you should be given temporary membership	Subordinate clause	Noun	Object of verb "agreed" in main clause "A"

Analyse each of the following in *two* different ways:
1. Tell me tomorrow if you can come.
2. We did not know the time when we arrived.
3. When they reported their loss, the police enquired where they had called on the way.
4. As I worked with him he and I talked a lot.
5. He simply would not do it as I asked him to.
6. History teaches us the one lesson that we are unwilling to learn from our mistakes.
7. The ship was stuck on the mud and it was not clear when the tide was at its highest.
8. He must decide for himself whether his parents will pay for him or not.
9. Tell me where I should sit when you are ready to start the car.
10. Ask someone who will be there at the party.

*Analysis Exercise 6

In Chapter Thirteen we noted that the various *non-finite parts of verbs* (present and past participles, gerunds and infinitives) retain the verbal characteristic of being able to govern objects or to be modified by adverbs, although they are themselves acting as adjectives, nouns

275

or occasionally adverbs. This means that noun clauses and adverb clauses are quite often dependent upon non-finite parts of verbs instead of upon finite verbs.

Reconstruct the sentences analysed as examples below:

	CLAUSE	KIND	FUNCTION	RELATIONSHIP
1.A	They discovered the lost child swimming	Main clause		
a¹	where the current was most dangerous	Subordinate clause	Adverb of place	Modifies present participle "swimming" in main clause "A"
2.A	I enjoy working	Main clause		
a¹	when I feel like it	Subordinate clause	Adverb of time	Modifies gerund "working" in main clause "A"
3.A	I asked him to say frankly	Main clause		
a¹	that he disagreed	Subordinate clause	Noun	Object of infinitive "to say" in main clause "A"
4.A	He won the cup by fencing	Main clause		
a¹	as he had been taught by the professor	Subordinate clause	Adverb of manner	Modifies the gerund "fencing" in main clause "A"

Each of the following sentences contains at least one subordinate clause dependent upon a non-finite part of a verb.

1. It is no use believing what he says.
2. Liking what you have to do makes a job much easier.
3. I saw the officials discussing where the royal party should sit.
4. Most people wish to live where they can have the ordinary comforts that they are used to.
5. My ambitions are to make as much money as my father did and to work when I choose.
6. He has been away all summer running what you might call a holiday camp.

276

7. We found the old house ruined because some teenage hooligans had wrecked it.
8. After we got home we spent some time comparing what we had collected.
9. I suggested that we should take a holiday without considering where the money would come from.
10. As I crossed the quadrangle, I heard someone singing while he repaired the roof of the dining hall.

*Analysis Exercise 7

The following sentences for analysis include many of the different kinds of subordinate clauses dealt with in these books. There are also some sentences containing coordinate main or coordinate subordinate clauses. In analysing longer sentences, it is useful to begin by noting all the finite verbs and all the introductory words, in order to see how many clauses one has to deal with.

1. What he said was quite different from what he did when he was faced with the need for action.
2. When I asked him, he told me whom I should approach about what had been worrying the men who were to do the job.
3. He said I had said that I would never come if they did not invite me more politely than they had done.
4. Although he felt lost at first, he enjoyed working in the factory where he felt more grown-up than he had done at school.
5. As I had nothing better to do, I wandered down where the path follows the bank of the stream, and I was just in time to see something that otherwise I should have very much have regretted not seeing when I was in the vicinity.
6. Unless I am feeling very stupid, I can usually manage to understand when I listen to my parents saying things in French that they do not want me to know about.
7. Although he was quite sure of his facts and although he suspected that his opponent was less sure than he was, he gave in because he felt that this was not an issue on which to force a decision.
8. Whenever I consider the annual problem of where I should take my holiday, I begin to wonder whether I really enjoy holidays so much that they are worth all the trouble I have in arranging them.
9. It is a matter of constant surprise to me that, whenever one goes on the Continent, if one has the money, one can always get a hot, nourishing meal, even if it is very late in the evening.
10. Even though I know that I often buy goods because I have been influenced by advertisements, I still believe I have a free choice and that I buy things which really are worth buying.

277

Books Recommended

An alphabetical author index of the books recommended in the Further Reading sections of this volume.

ALLPORT, GORDON W.	*The Nature of Prejudice* ..	Addison-Wesley
BALDWIN, MICHAEL (ed.)	*Billy the Kid*	Hutchinson
BLISHEN, EDWARD	*Roaring Boys*	C. Chivers
BRADDON, RUSSELL	*The Proud American Boy* ..	Hutchinson
BRAITHWAITE, E. R.	*To Sir, With Love* ..	Blackie, Bodley Head; Heinemann
CAMPTON, DAVID	*Incident, Funeral Dance* and *Soldiers from the Wars Returning*	Garnet Miller
CARY, JOYCE	*The Horse's Mouth* ..	Michael Joseph; Penguin
	To Be a Pilgrim, Aissa Saved, Charlie is my Darling and *Herself Surprised*	Michael Joseph
CARSON, RACHEL	*Silent Spring*	Hamish Hamilton; Penguin
	The Edge of the Sea and *The Sea Around Us* ..	Panther
	The Sea	MacGibbon & Kee
CONRAD, JOSEPH	*Typhoon*	Longmans; Heinemann
DEBRIX, J. R. (see under STEPHENSON)		
DICKENS, CHARLES	*Nicholas Nickleby*	Various
ELIOT, GEORGE	*Adam Bede* and *The Mill on the Floss*	Various
EYSENCK, H. J.	*Uses and Abuses of Psychology*	Penguin
FLEMING, IAN	*Dr No* and other "James Bond" books	Cape; Pan
GOLDING, WILLIAM	*Free Fall* and *Lord of the Flies*	Faber; Penguin
	The Inheritors	Faber
GRAVES, ROBERT	*Goodbye to All That* ..	Cassell; Penguin
	Proceed, Sergeant Lamb ..	Methuen
	Sergeant Lamb of the Ninth	Methuen; Penguin
GREENE, GRAHAM	*Brighton Rock, Our Man In Havana* and *Twenty-one Stories*	Heinemann; Penguin
GRIMBLE, SIR ARTHUR	*A Pattern of Islands* and *Return to the Islands* ..	Murray
HARDY, THOMAS	*Far From the Madding Crowd, The Mayor of Casterbridge* and *The Trumpet Major*	Macmillan
HOGGART, RICHARD	*The Uses of Literacy* ..	Chatto & Windus; Penguin

HOUSTON, PENELOPE	*The Contemporary Cinema* ..	Penguin
HUGHES, RICHARD	*A High Wind in Jamaica*	
	and *In Hazard*	Chatto & Windus;
		Penguin
HUNTER, EVAN	*The Blackboard Jungle* ..	Constable
ISHERWOOD,	*Goodbye to Berlin*	Penguin
CHRISTOPHER	*Mr Norris Changes Trains,*	Hogarth; Penguin
	Prater Violet	Methuen; Penguin
JACOBSON, DAN	*Trap and Dance in the Sun*	Penguin
JOYCE, JAMES	*Dubliners*	Chatto; Cape;
		Penguin
JUNGK, ROBERT	*Brighter Than a Thousand*	
	Suns	Penguin
	Children of the Ashes ..	Heinemann;
		Penguin
LAWRENCE, D. H.	*The Rainbow*	Heinemann; Penguin
LE CARRÉ, JOHN	*The Spy Who Came in from*	
	the Cold	Gollancz
LEE, HARPER	*To Kill a Mockingbird* ..	Heinemann; Pan
MACINNES, COLIN	*Absolute Beginners* and *June*	
	in Her Spring	Panther
MARLAND, MICHAEL	*Conflicting Generations* and	
(ed.)	*Z Cars*	Longmans
MEAD, MARGARET	*Coming of Age in Samoa* and	
	Growing Up in New Guinea	Penguin
MILLER, ARTHUR	*The Crucible*	Heinemann; Penguin;
		Secker & Warburg
MITCHELL, L. M. M. (ed.)	*Pacific Picture*	Angus & Robertson
MORRIS, DESMOND	*The Naked Ape*	Cape; Corgi
ORWELL, GEORGE	*Homage to Catalonia* ..	Secker & Warburg;
		Penguin
OSBORNE, JOHN	*The Entertainer* and *Look*	
	Back in Anger	Evans; Faber
QUENNELL, PETER (ed.)	*Mayhew's Characters* ..	Spring Books
SCHOFIELD, MICHAEL	*The Sexual Behaviour of*	
	Young People	Longmans; Penguin
SHAW, GEORGE BERNARD	*Androcles and the Lion, Arms and the Man,*	
	Caesar and Cleopatra, Pygmalion	
	and *Saint Joan*	Longmans; Penguin
SHUTE, NEVIL	*On the Beach*	Heinemann;
		Longmans; Pan
SLOCUM, J.	*Sailing Alone Around the*	
	World	Adlard Coles; Dover
STEPHENSON, RALPH	*The Cinema as Art* ..	Penguin
and DEBRIX, J. R.		
WESKER, ARNOLD	*Chicken Soup with Barley, I'm Talking About*	
	Jerusalem and *Roots* ..	Longmans; Penguin
	Chips With Everything and	
	The Kitchen	Cape
WISEMAN, THOMAS	*Cinema*	Cassell

Index

An alphabetical list of the main comprehension, techniques and composition work only, in Book Five. References are to page numbers.